ANGEL

The Curse

IDW PUBLISHING
SAN DIEGO, CA

IDW Publishing is:
Ted Adams, President
Robbie Robbins, EVP/Sr. Graphic Artist
Clifford Meth, EVP of Strategies/Editorial
Chris Ryall, Publisher/Editor-in-Chief
Alan Payne, VP of Sales
Neil Uyetake, Art Director
Justin Eisinger, Editor
Tom Waltz, Editor
Andrew Steven Harris, Editor
Chris Mowry, Graphic Artist
Amauri Osorio, Graphic Artist
Matthew Ruzicka, CPA, Controller
Alonzo Simon, Shipping Manager
Kris Oprisko, Editor/Foreign Lic. Rep.

ISBN: 978-1-933239-79-8
10 09 08 07   2 3 4 5

www.idwpublishing.com

ANGEL created by Joss Whedon and David Greenwalt • Thanks to Debbie Olshan at Fox Worldwide Publishing for her invaluable assistance.

ANGEL
The Curse

jeff mariott
written b

DAVID MESSIN
art b

andrea fattor
ink assistar

DAVIDE AMIC
color assistar

neil uyetak
designed b

tom b. Lon,
lettered b

CHRIS RyaL
edited b

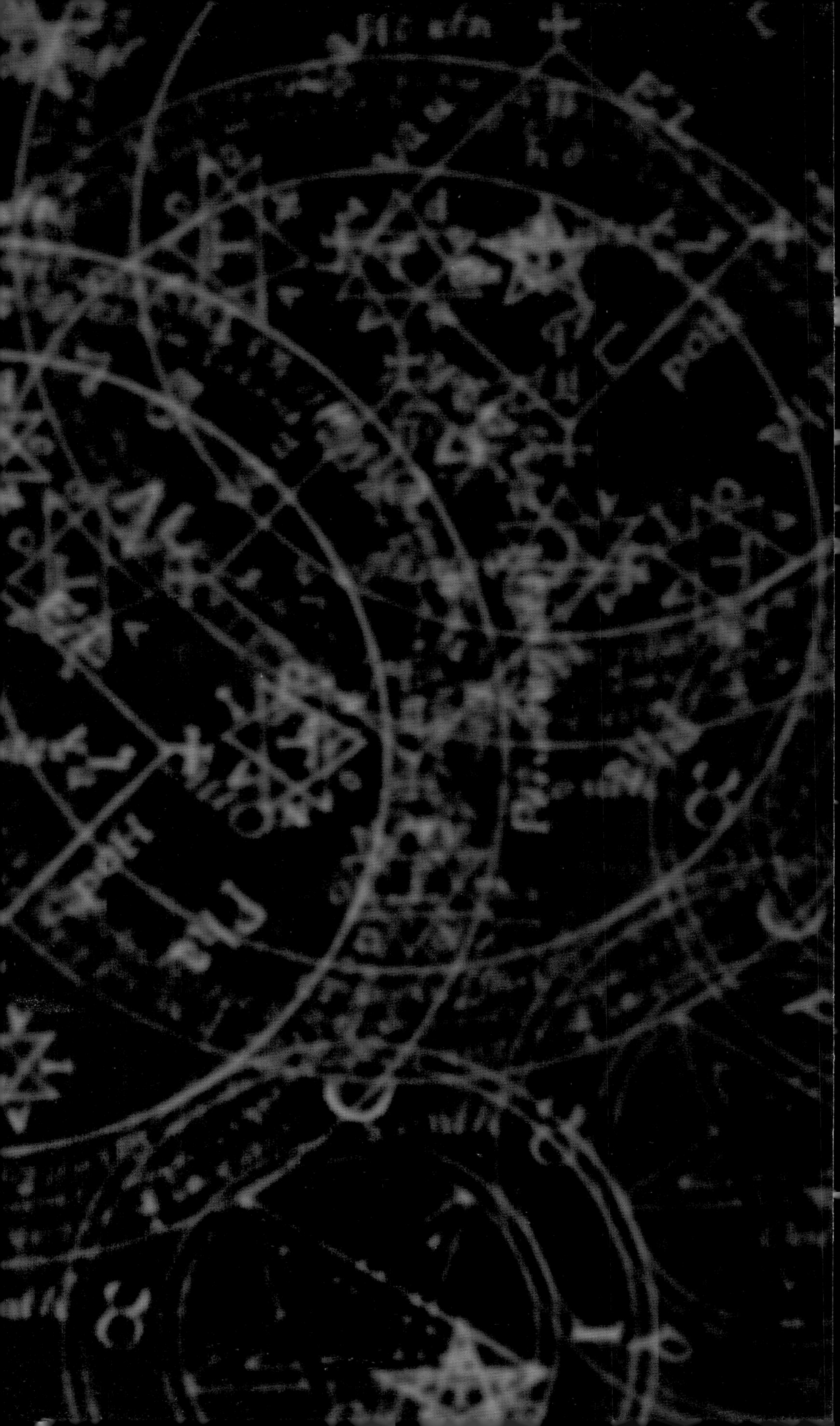

chapter one

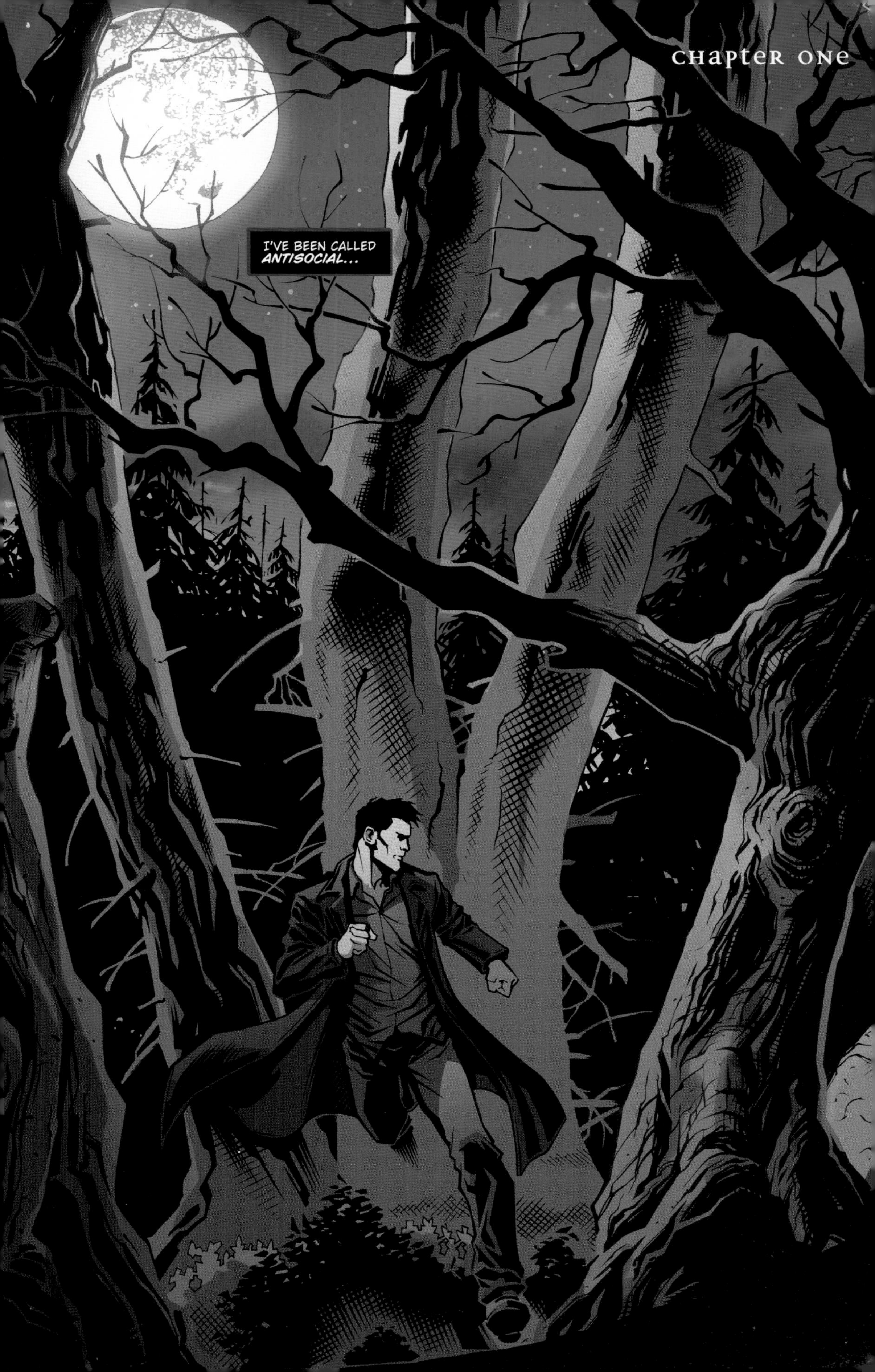
I'VE BEEN CALLED ANTISOCIAL...

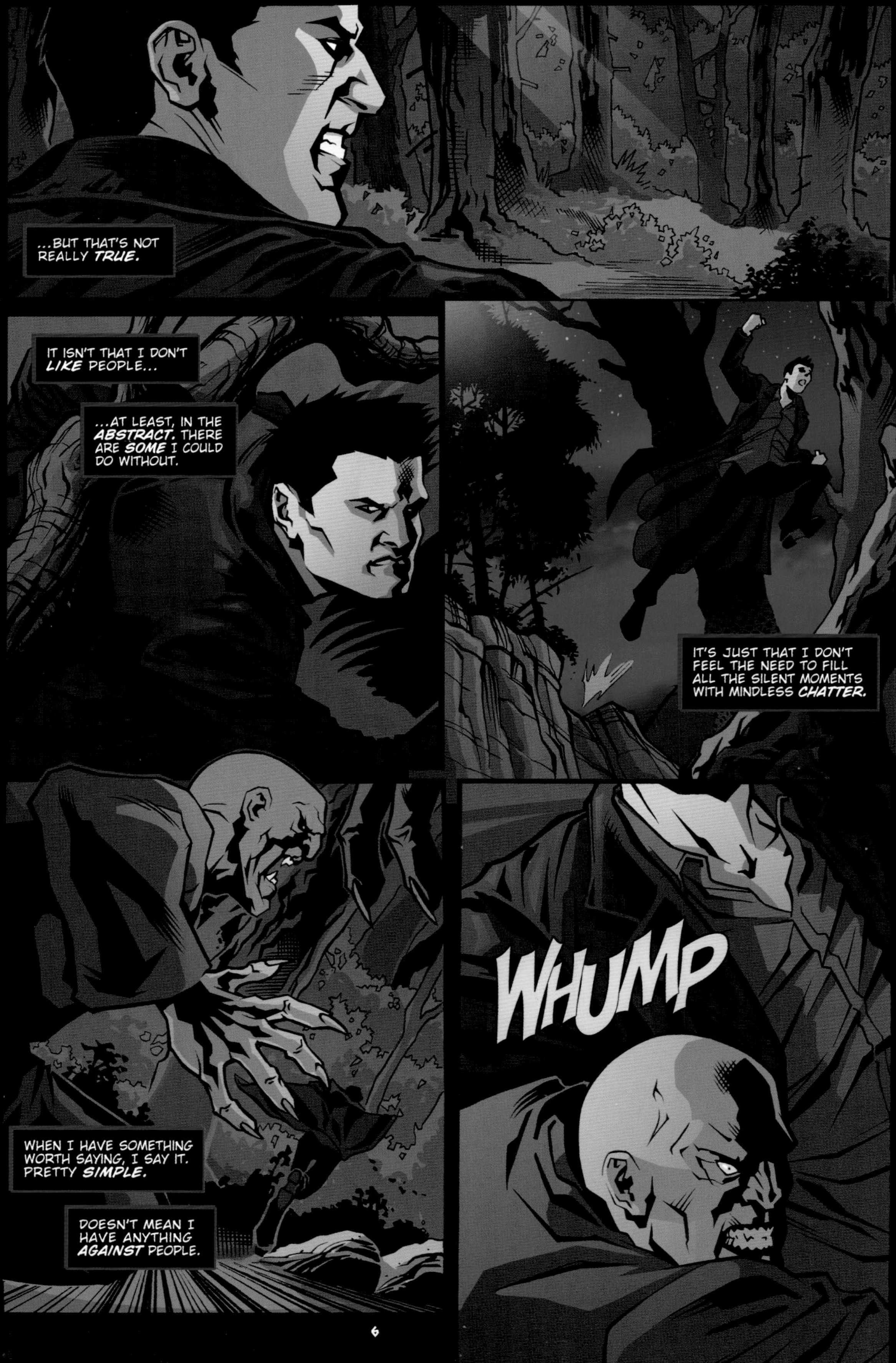
...BUT THAT'S NOT REALLY TRUE.
IT ISN'T THAT I DON'T LIKE PEOPLE...
...AT LEAST, IN THE ABSTRACT. THERE ARE SOME I COULD DO WITHOUT.
IT'S JUST THAT I DON'T FEEL THE NEED TO FILL ALL THE SILENT MOMENTS WITH MINDLESS CHATTER.
WHEN I HAVE SOMETHING WORTH SAYING, I SAY IT. PRETTY SIMPLE.
DOESN'T MEAN I HAVE ANYTHING AGAINST PEOPLE.
WHUMP

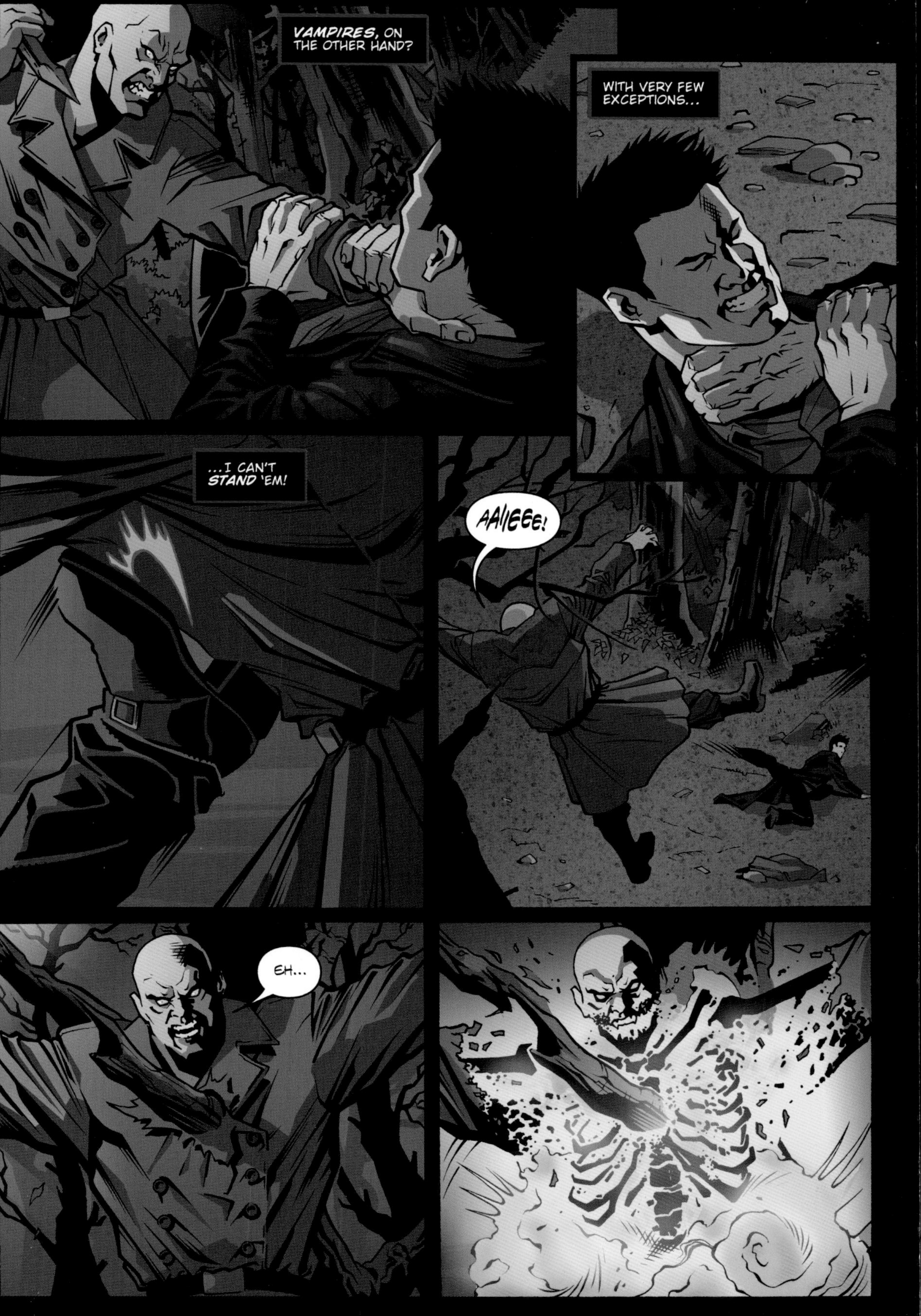
VAMPIRES, ON THE OTHER HAND?
WITH VERY FEW EXCEPTIONS...
...I CAN'T STAND 'EM!
AAIIEEE!
EH...

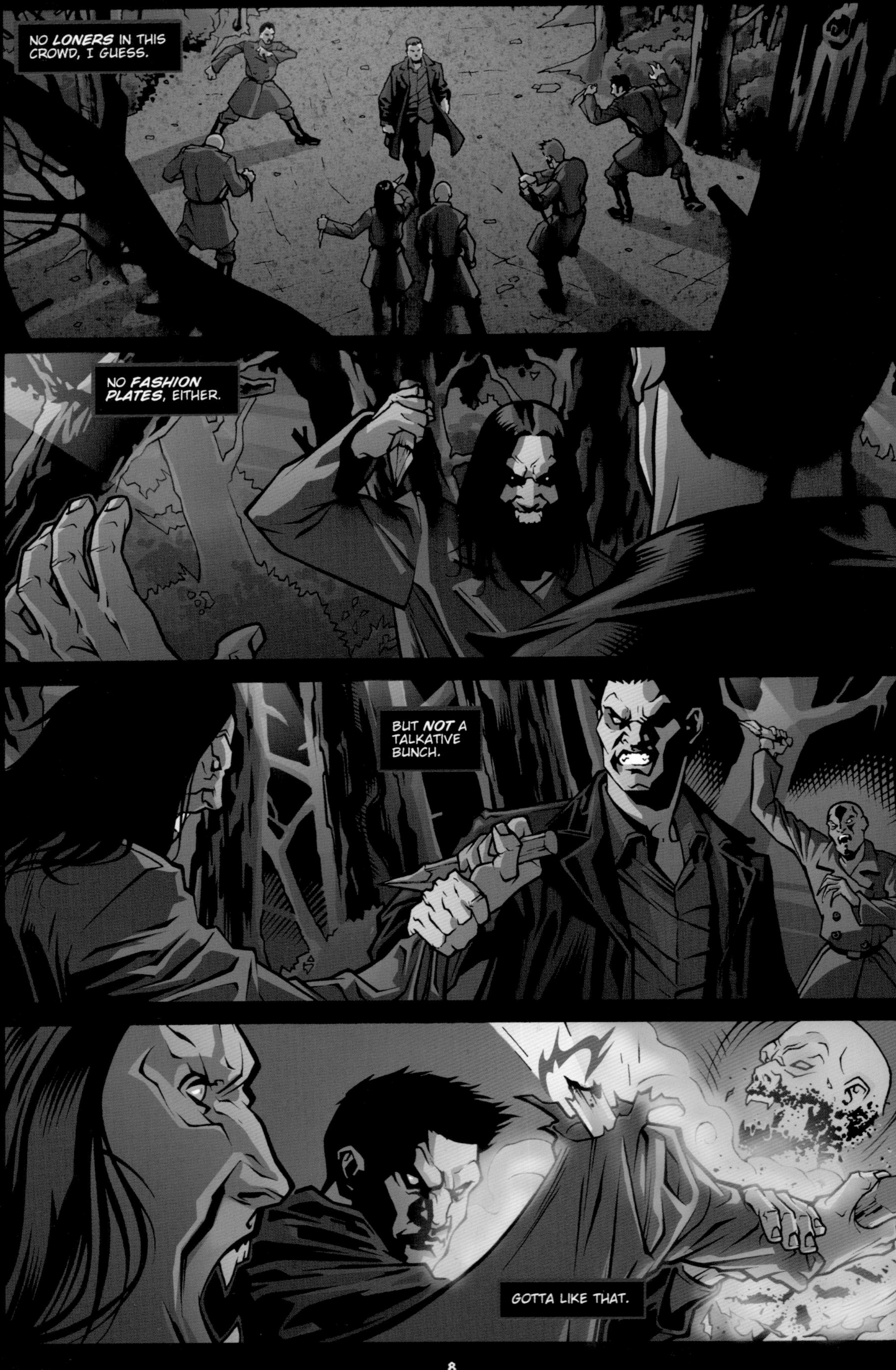
NO LONERS IN THIS CROWD, I GUESS.
NO FASHION PLATES, EITHER.
BUT NOT A TALKATIVE BUNCH.
GOTTA LIKE THAT.

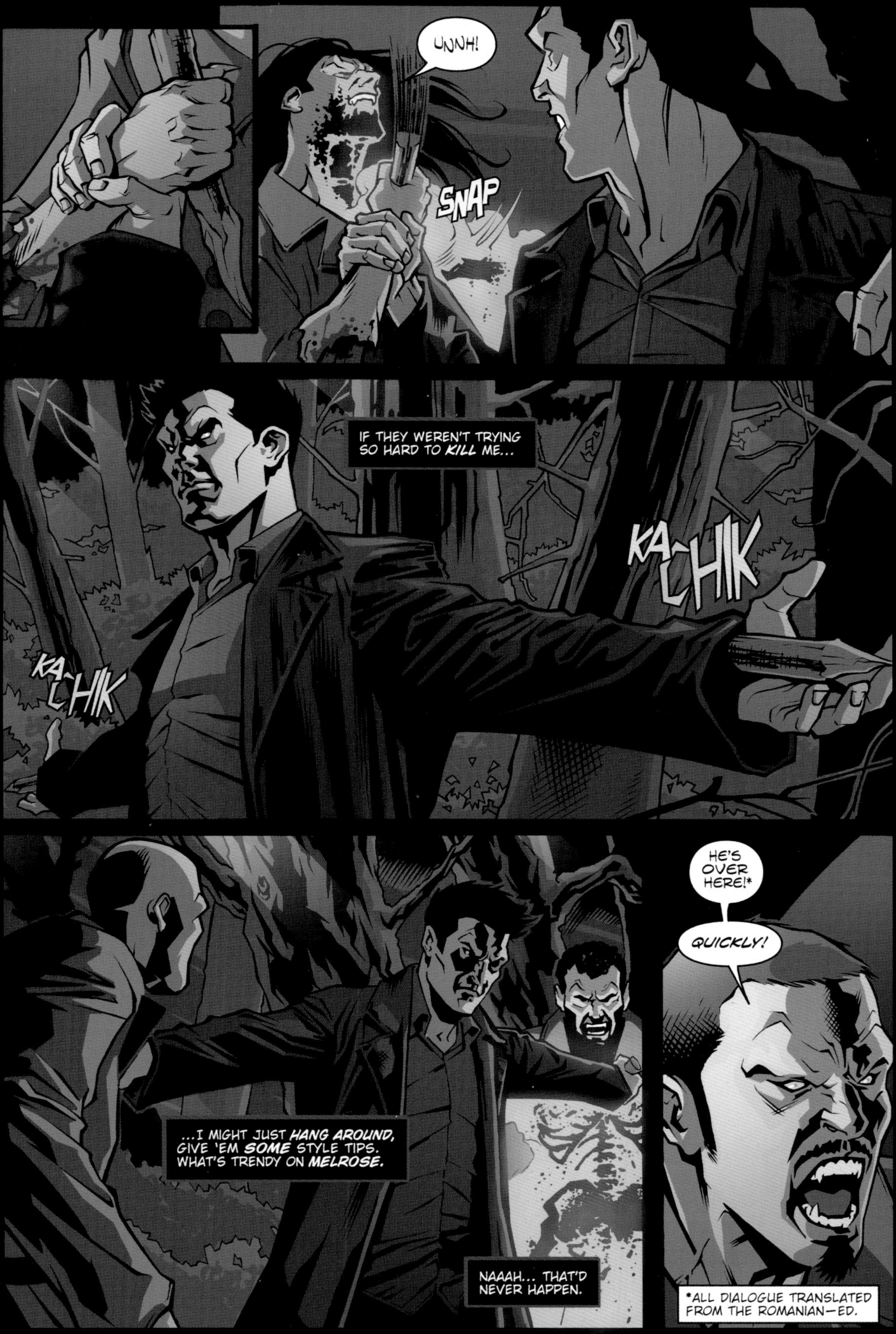
UNNH!
SNAP
IF THEY WEREN'T TRYING SO HARD TO KILL ME...
KA-CHIK
KA-CHIK
HE'S OVER HERE!*
QUICKLY!
...I MIGHT JUST HANG AROUND, GIVE 'EM SOME STYLE TIPS. WHAT'S TRENDY ON MELROSE.
NAAAH... THAT'D NEVER HAPPEN.
*ALL DIALOGUE TRANSLATED FROM THE ROMANIAN—ED.

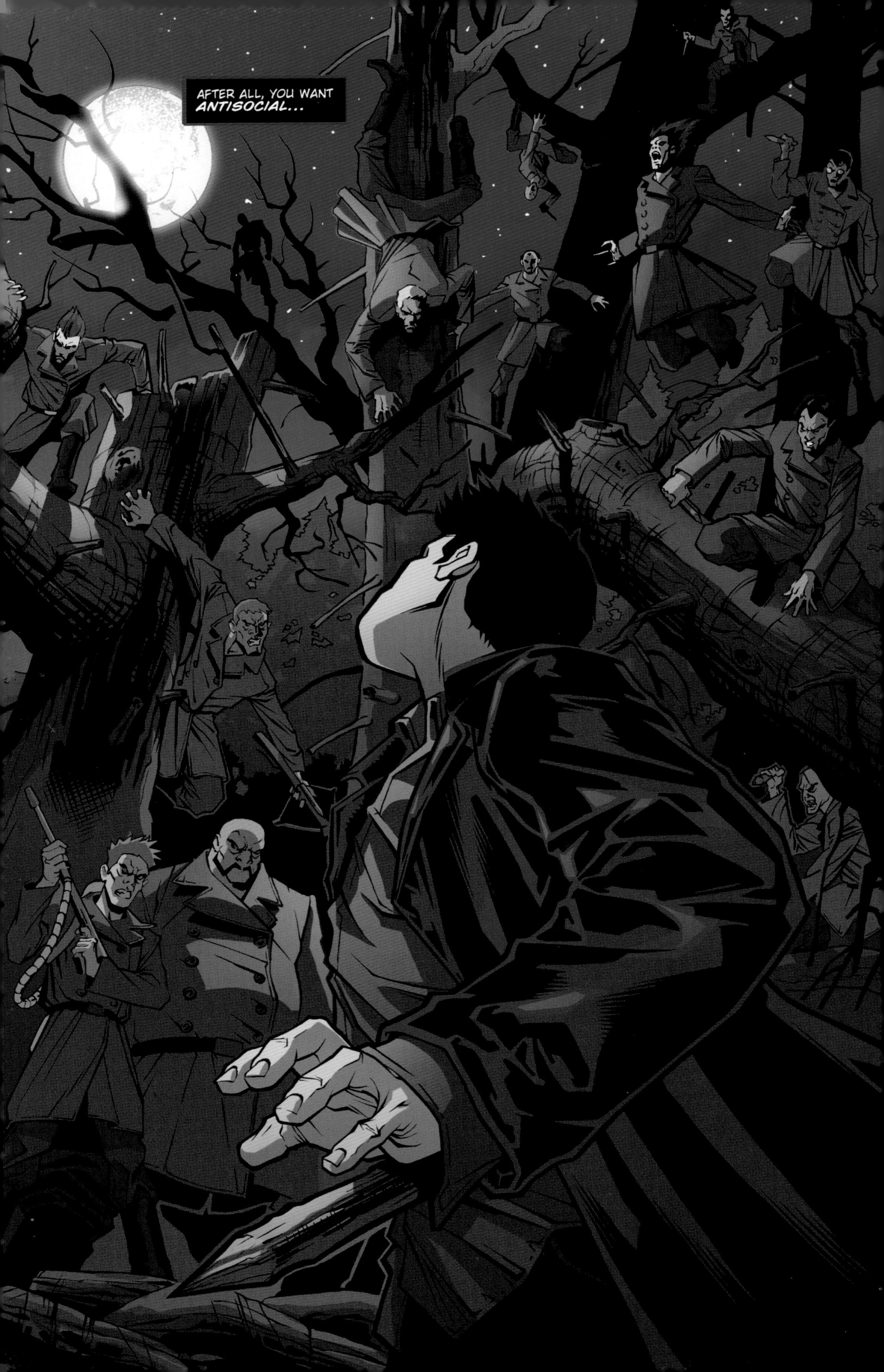
AFTER ALL, YOU WANT
ANTISOCIAL...

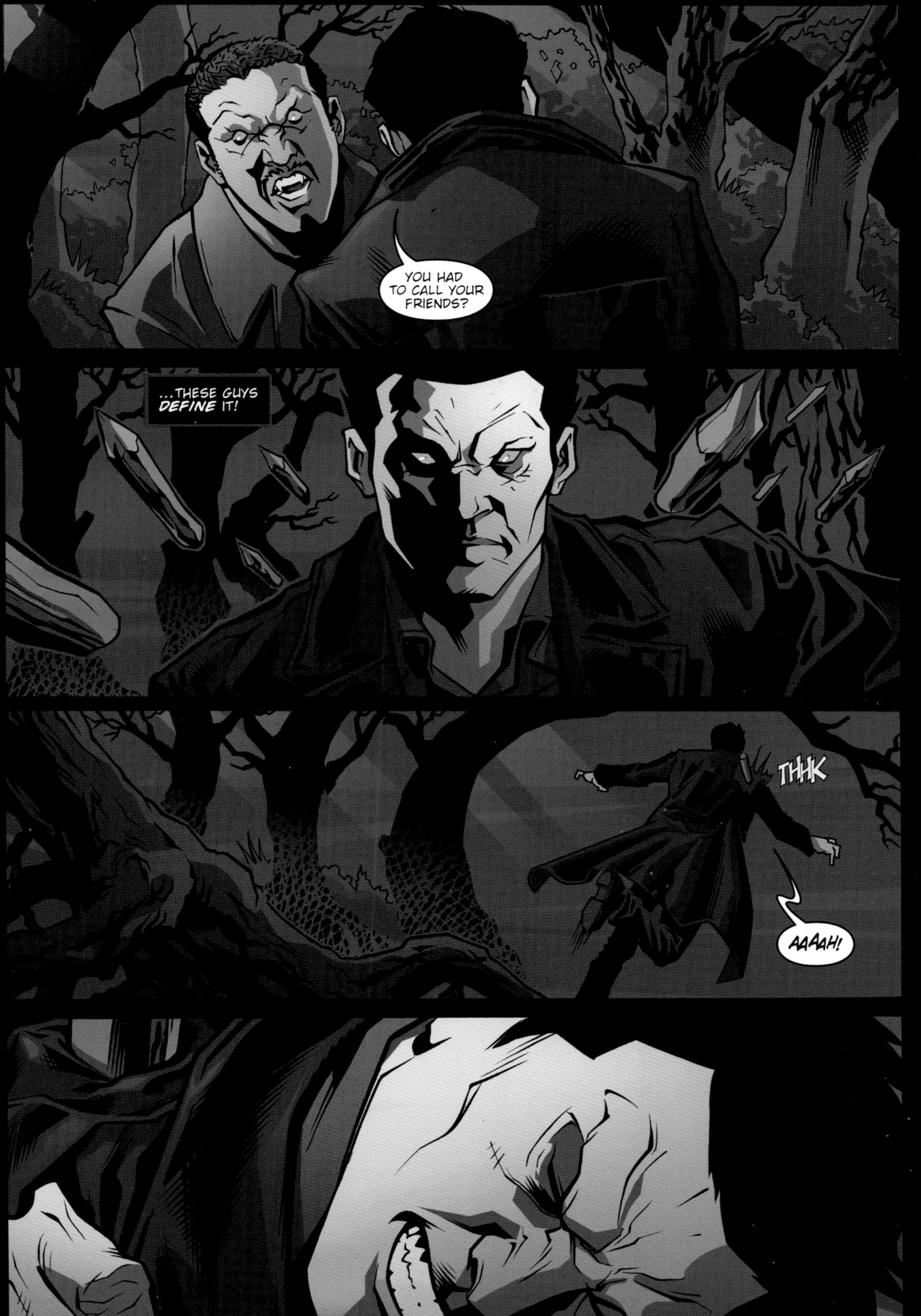
YOU HAD TO CALL YOUR FRIENDS?
...THESE GUYS DEFINE IT!
THHK
AAAAH!

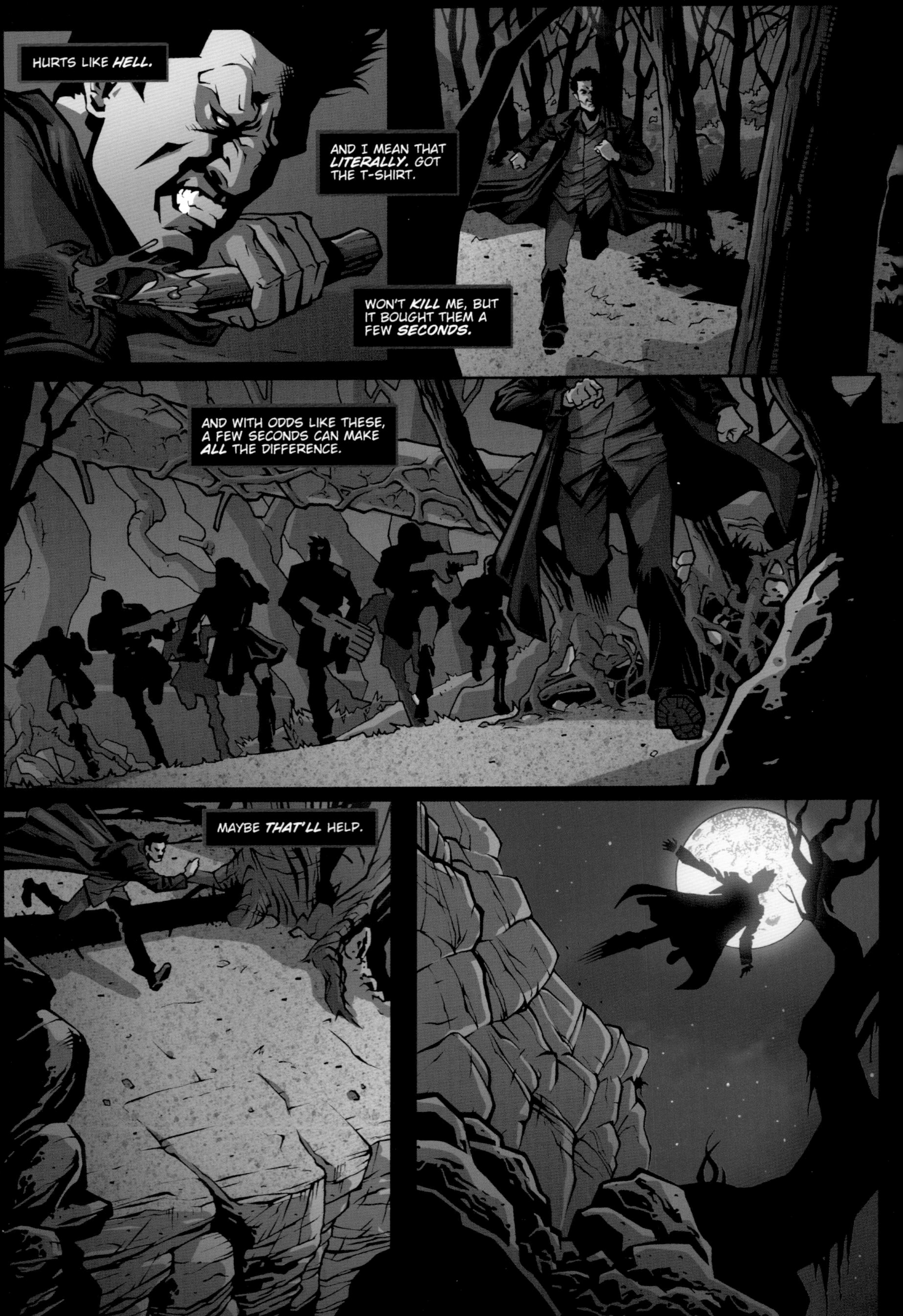
HURTS LIKE HELL.
AND I MEAN THAT LITERALLY. GOT THE T-SHIRT.
WON'T KILL ME, BUT IT BOUGHT THEM A FEW SECONDS.
AND WITH ODDS LIKE THESE, A FEW SECONDS CAN MAKE ALL THE DIFFERENCE.
MAYBE THAT'LL HELP.

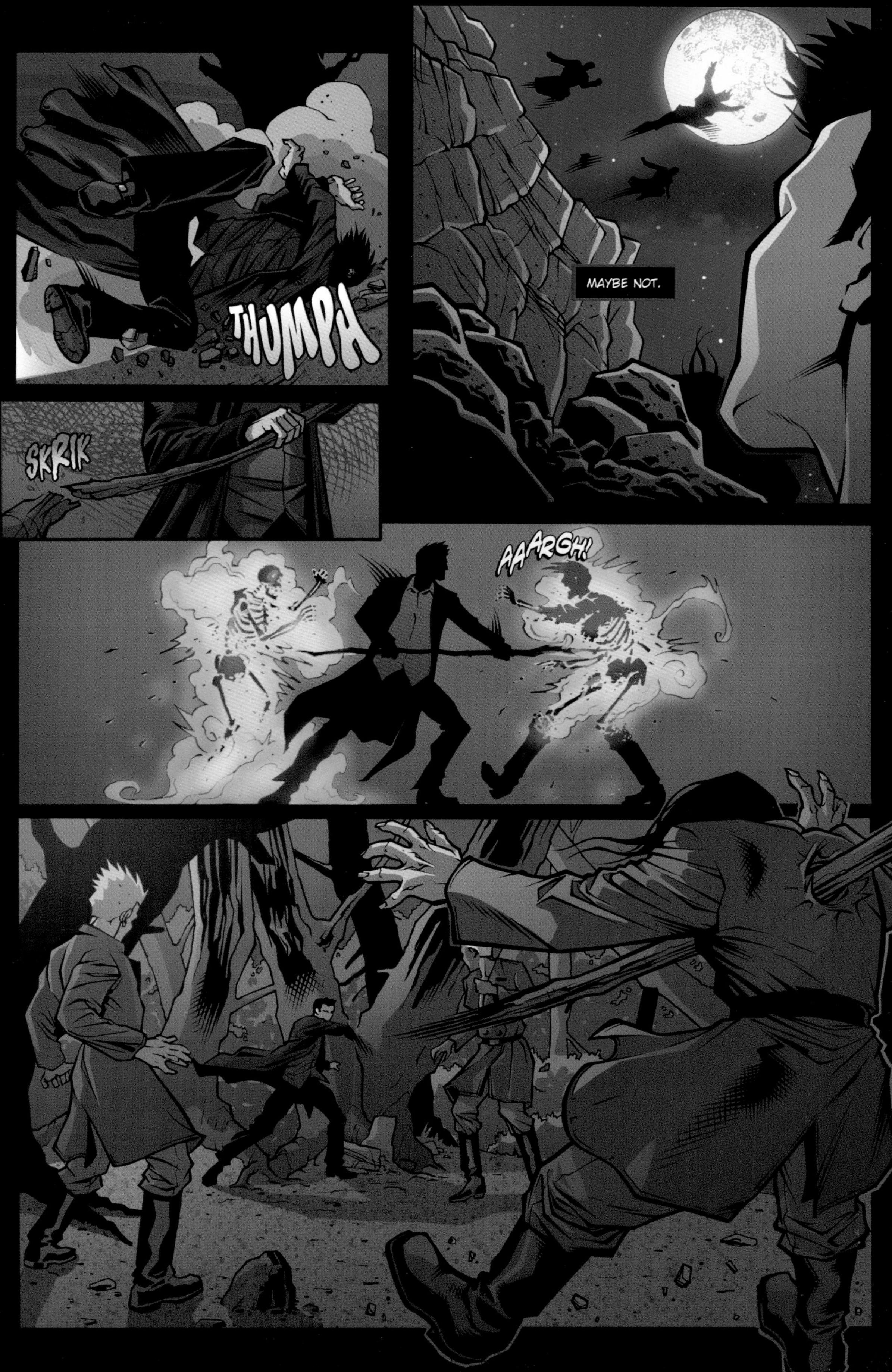

THUMPA
MAYBE NOT.
SKRIK
AAARGH!

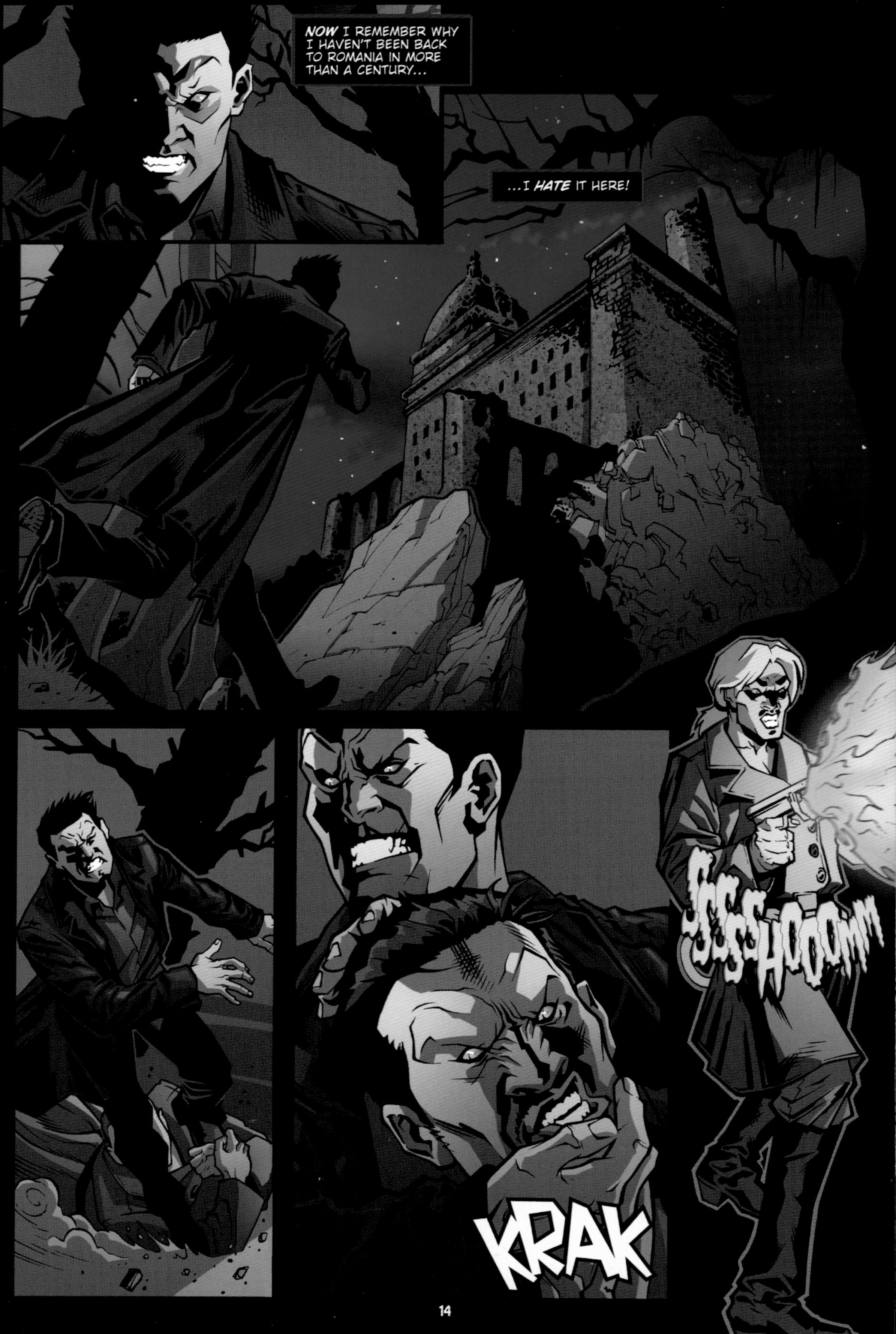
NOW I REMEMBER WHY I HAVEN'T BEEN BACK TO ROMANIA IN MORE THAN A CENTURY...
...I HATE IT HERE!
SSSSHOOOMM
KRAK

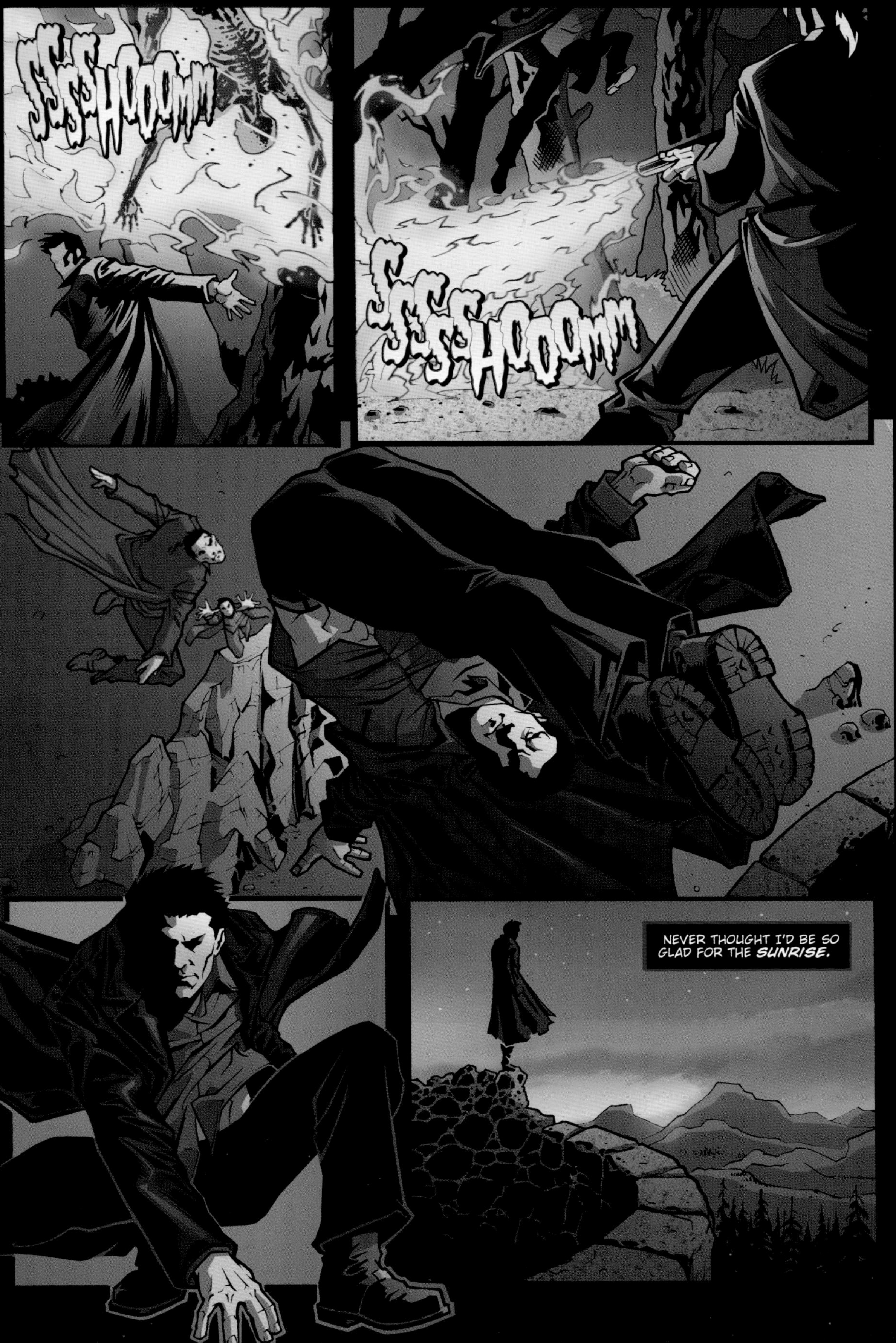
SSSSHOOOMM
SSSSHOOOMM
NEVER THOUGHT I'D BE SO GLAD FOR THE *SUNRISE.*

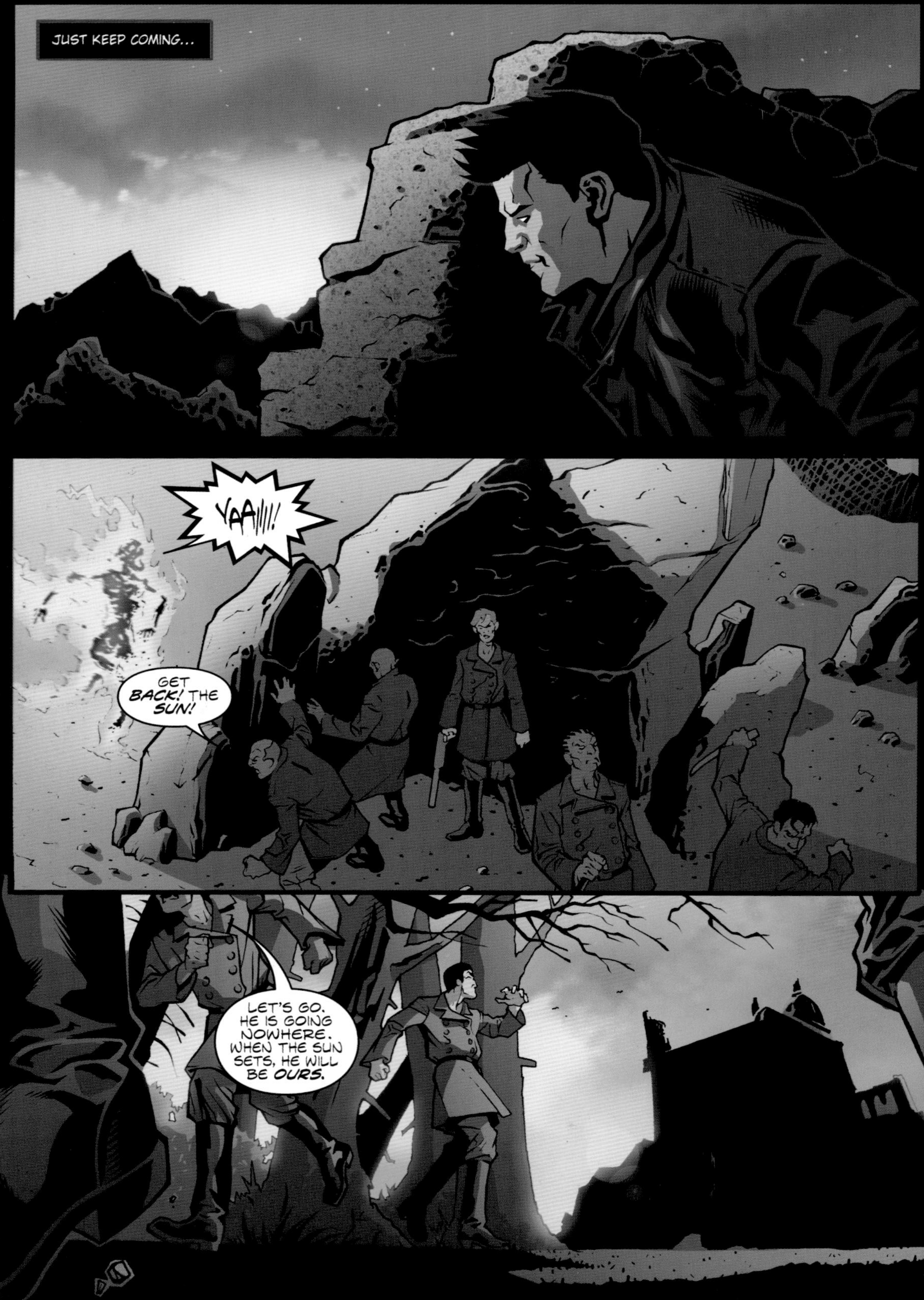
JUST KEEP COMING...
YAAIII!
GET BACK! THE SUN!
LET'S GO. HE IS GOING NOWHERE. WHEN THE SUN SETS, HE WILL BE OURS.

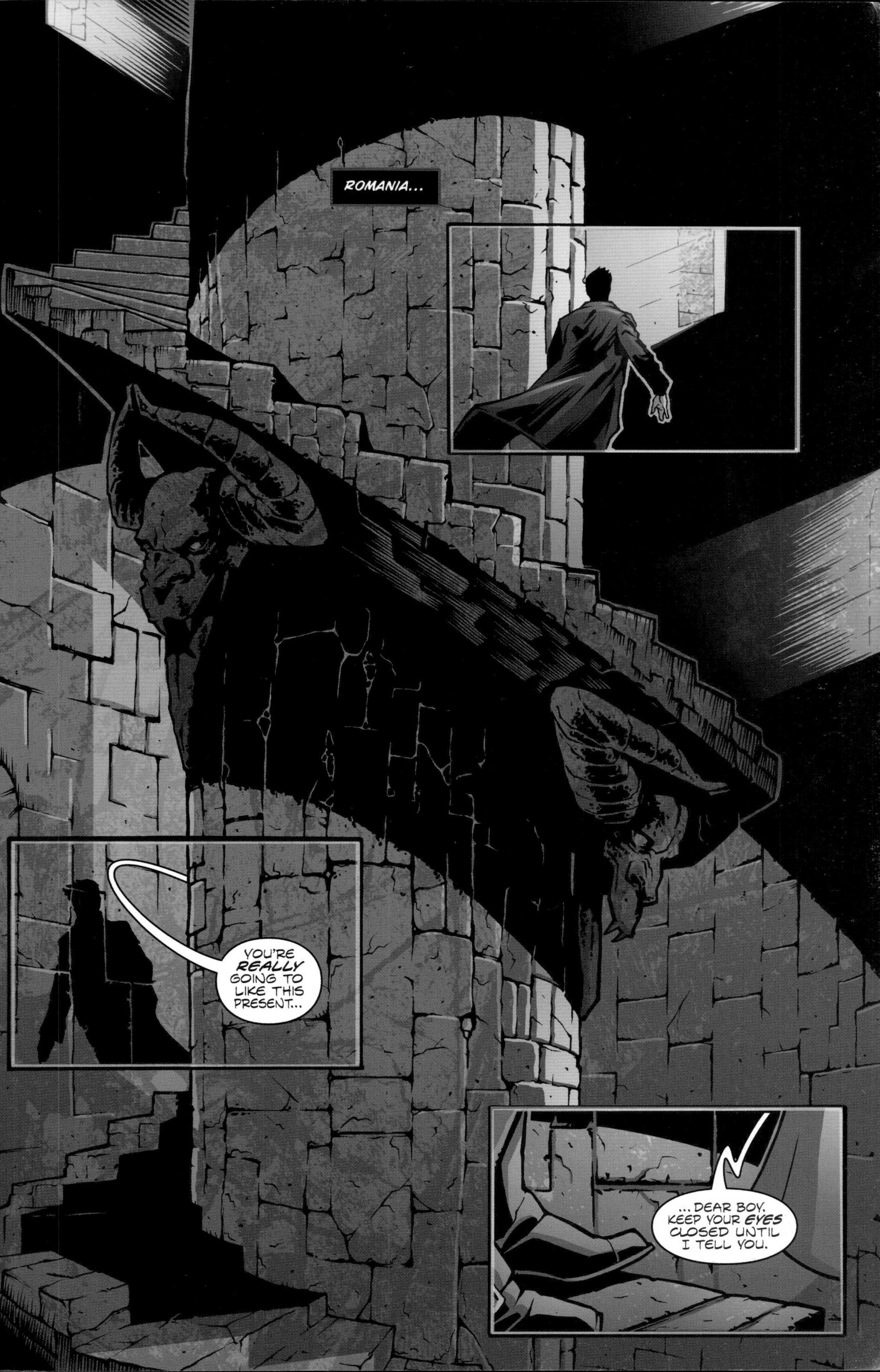
ROMANIA...
YOU'RE REALLY GOING TO LIKE THIS PRESENT...
...DEAR BOY. KEEP YOUR EYES CLOSED UNTIL I TELL YOU.

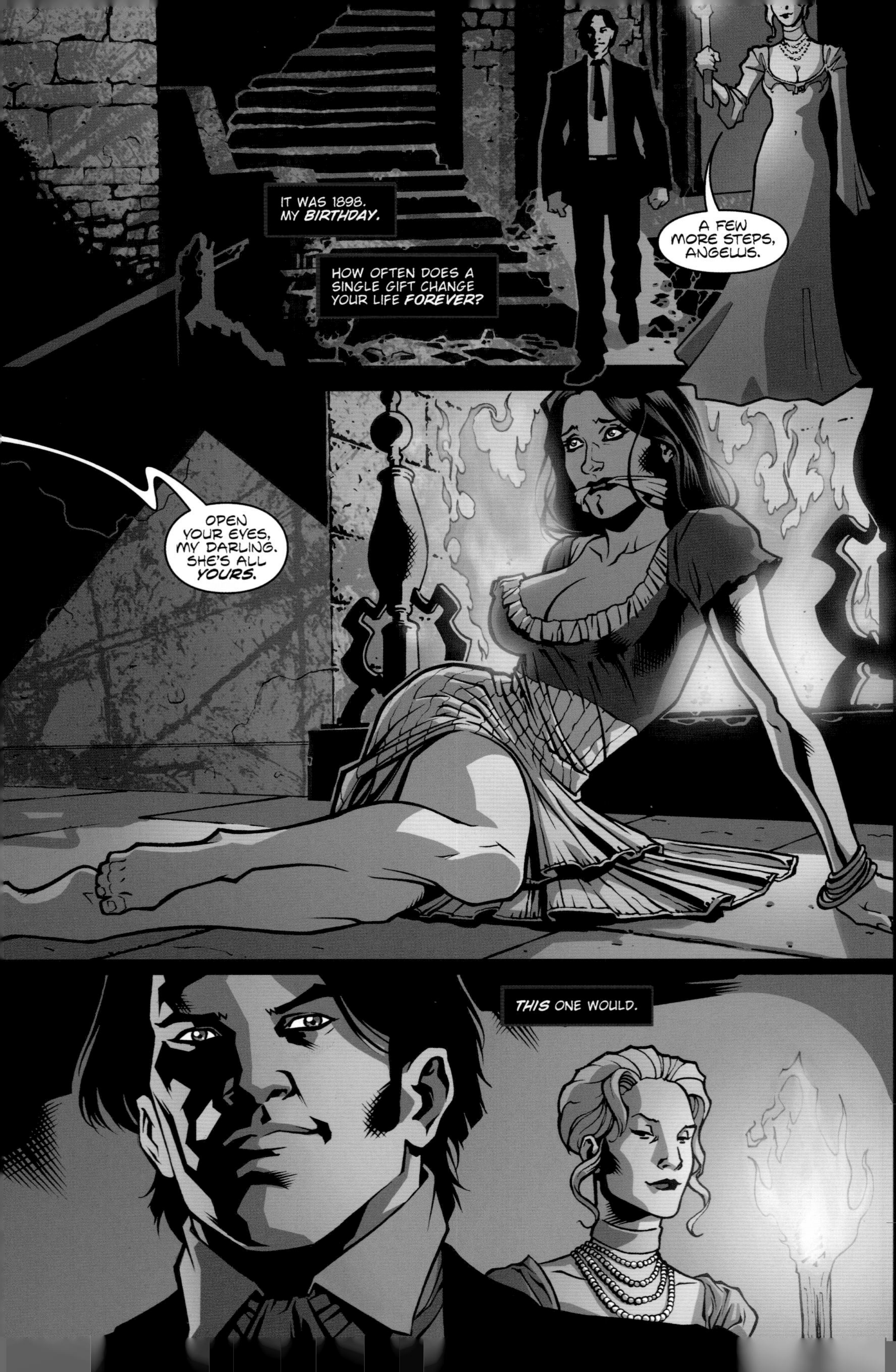
IT WAS 1898. MY BIRTHDAY.
HOW OFTEN DOES A SINGLE GIFT CHANGE YOUR LIFE FOREVER?
A FEW MORE STEPS, ANGELUS.
OPEN YOUR EYES, MY DARLING. SHE'S ALL YOURS.
THIS ONE WOULD.

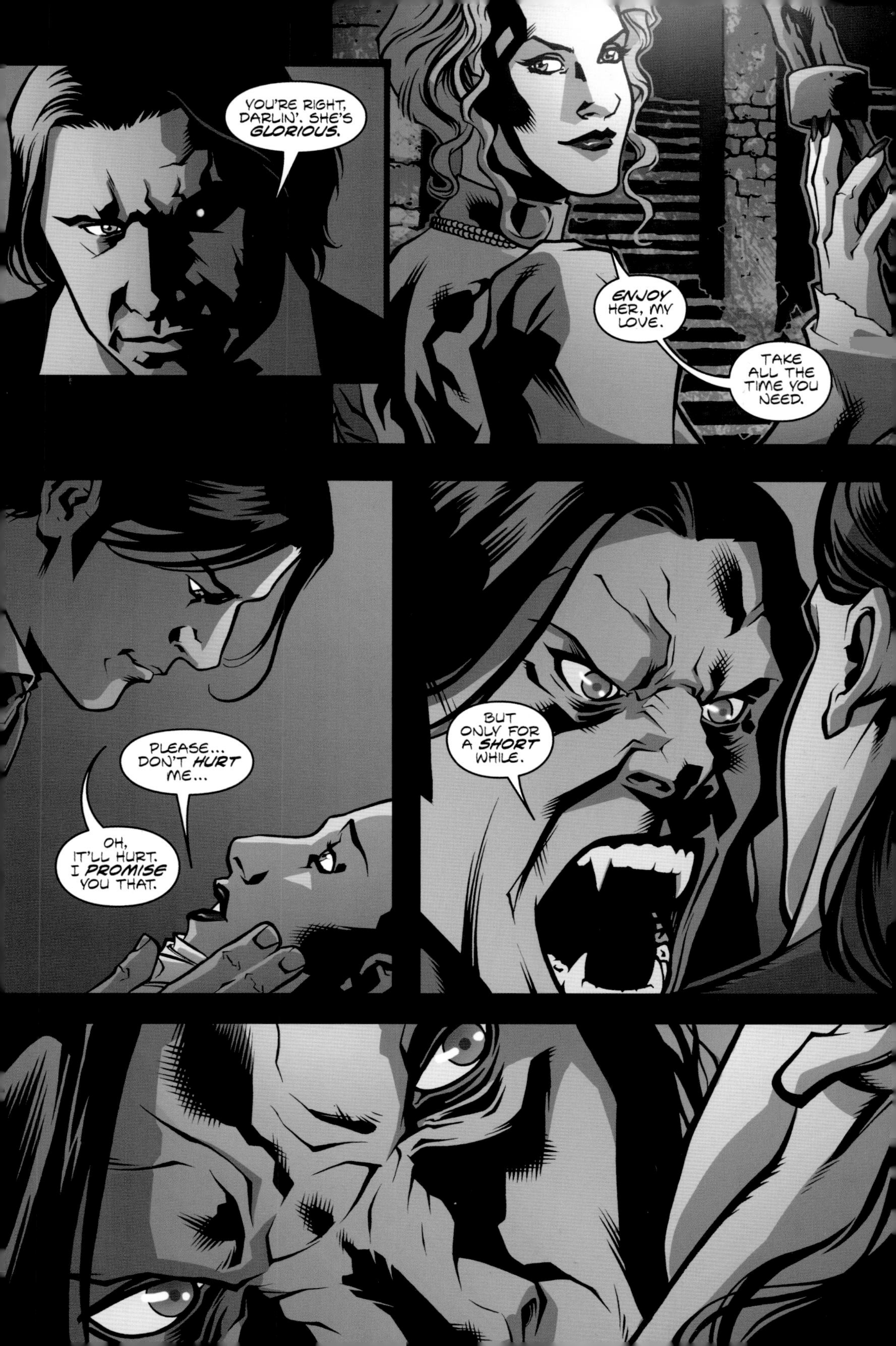

YOU'RE RIGHT, DARLIN'. SHE'S *GLORIOUS.*
ENJOY HER, MY LOVE.
TAKE ALL THE TIME YOU NEED.
PLEASE... DON'T *HURT* ME...
OH, IT'LL HURT. I *PROMISE* YOU THAT.
BUT ONLY FOR A *SHORT* WHILE.

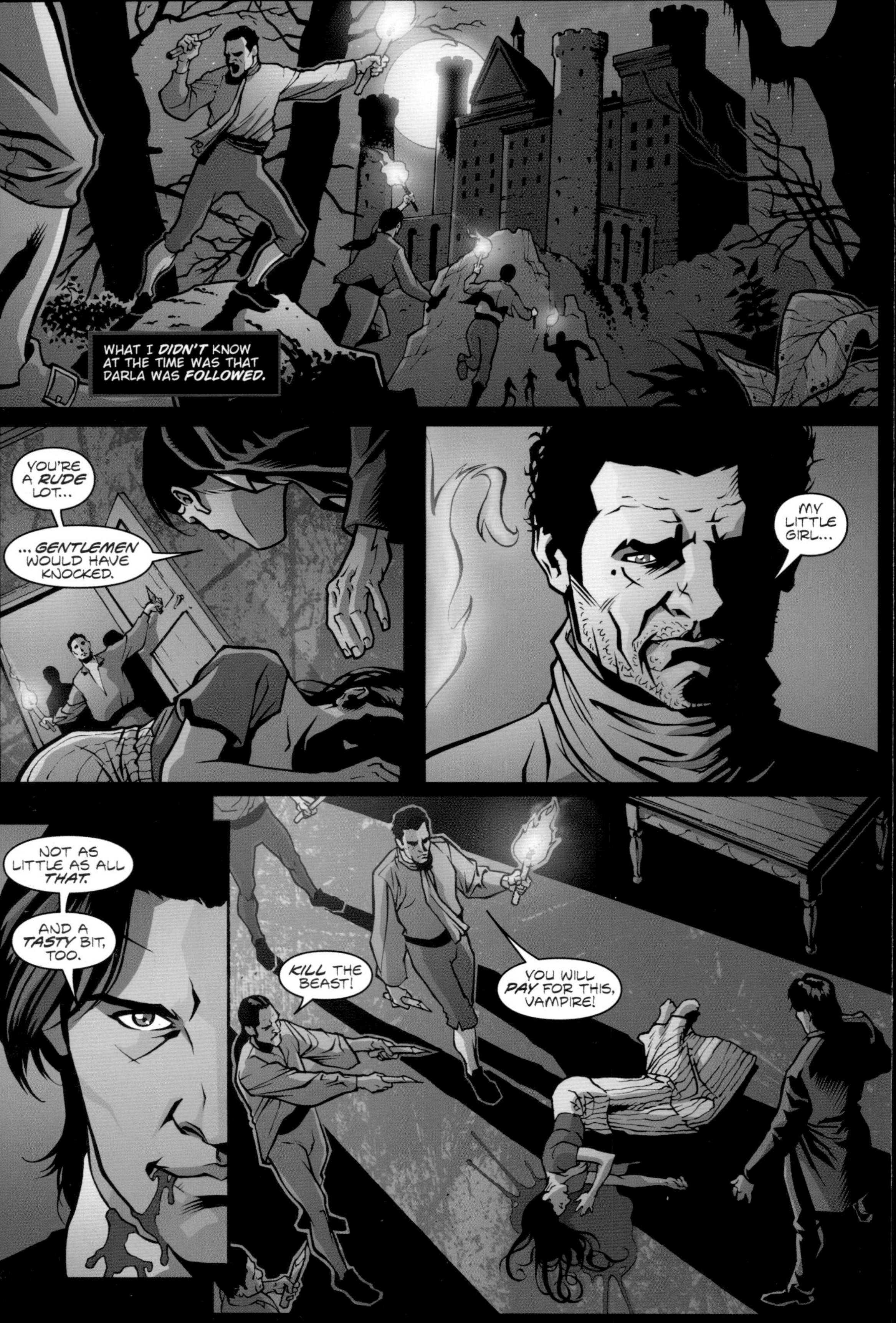
WHAT I DIDN'T KNOW AT THE TIME WAS THAT DARLA WAS FOLLOWED.
YOU'RE A RUDE LOT...
...GENTLEMEN WOULD HAVE KNOCKED.
MY LITTLE GIRL...
NOT AS LITTLE AS ALL THAT.
AND A TASTY BIT, TOO.
KILL THE BEAST!
YOU WILL PAY FOR THIS, VAMPIRE!

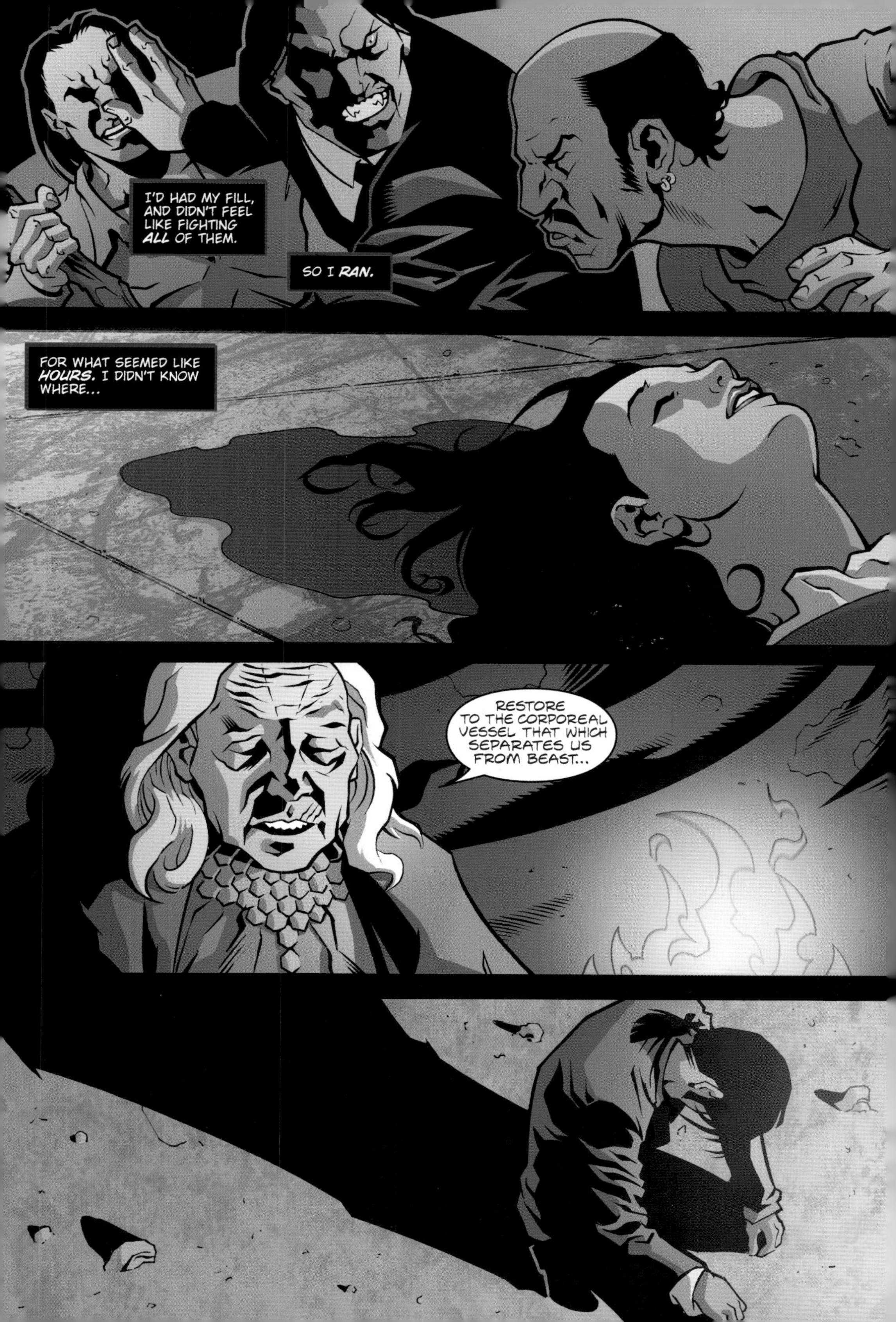

I'D HAD MY FILL, AND DIDN'T FEEL LIKE FIGHTING ALL OF THEM.
SO I RAN.
FOR WHAT SEEMED LIKE HOURS. I DIDN'T KNOW WHERE...
RESTORE TO THE CORPOREAL VESSEL THAT WHICH SEPARATES US FROM BEAST...

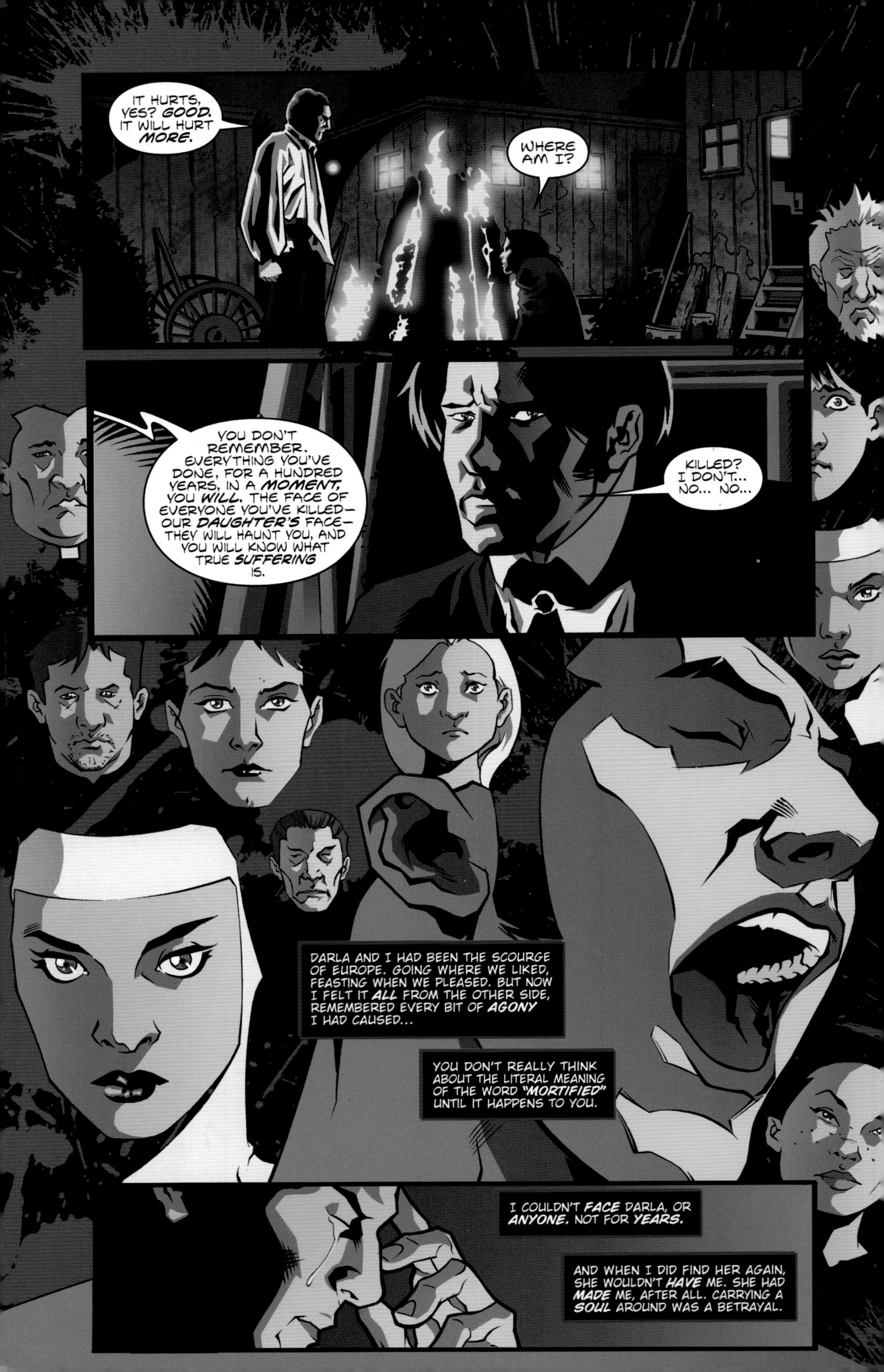
IT HURTS, YES? GOOD. IT WILL HURT MORE.
WHERE AM I?
YOU DON'T REMEMBER. EVERYTHING YOU'VE DONE, FOR A HUNDRED YEARS, IN A MOMENT, YOU WILL. THE FACE OF EVERYONE YOU'VE KILLED—OUR DAUGHTER'S FACE—THEY WILL HAUNT YOU, AND YOU WILL KNOW WHAT TRUE SUFFERING IS.
KILLED? I DON'T... NO... NO...
DARLA AND I HAD BEEN THE SCOURGE OF EUROPE. GOING WHERE WE LIKED, FEASTING WHEN WE PLEASED. BUT NOW I FELT IT ALL FROM THE OTHER SIDE, REMEMBERED EVERY BIT OF AGONY I HAD CAUSED...
YOU DON'T REALLY THINK ABOUT THE LITERAL MEANING OF THE WORD "MORTIFIED" UNTIL IT HAPPENS TO YOU.
I COULDN'T FACE DARLA, OR ANYONE. NOT FOR YEARS.
AND WHEN I DID FIND HER AGAIN, SHE WOULDN'T HAVE ME. SHE HAD MADE ME, AFTER ALL. CARRYING A SOUL AROUND WAS A BETRAYAL.

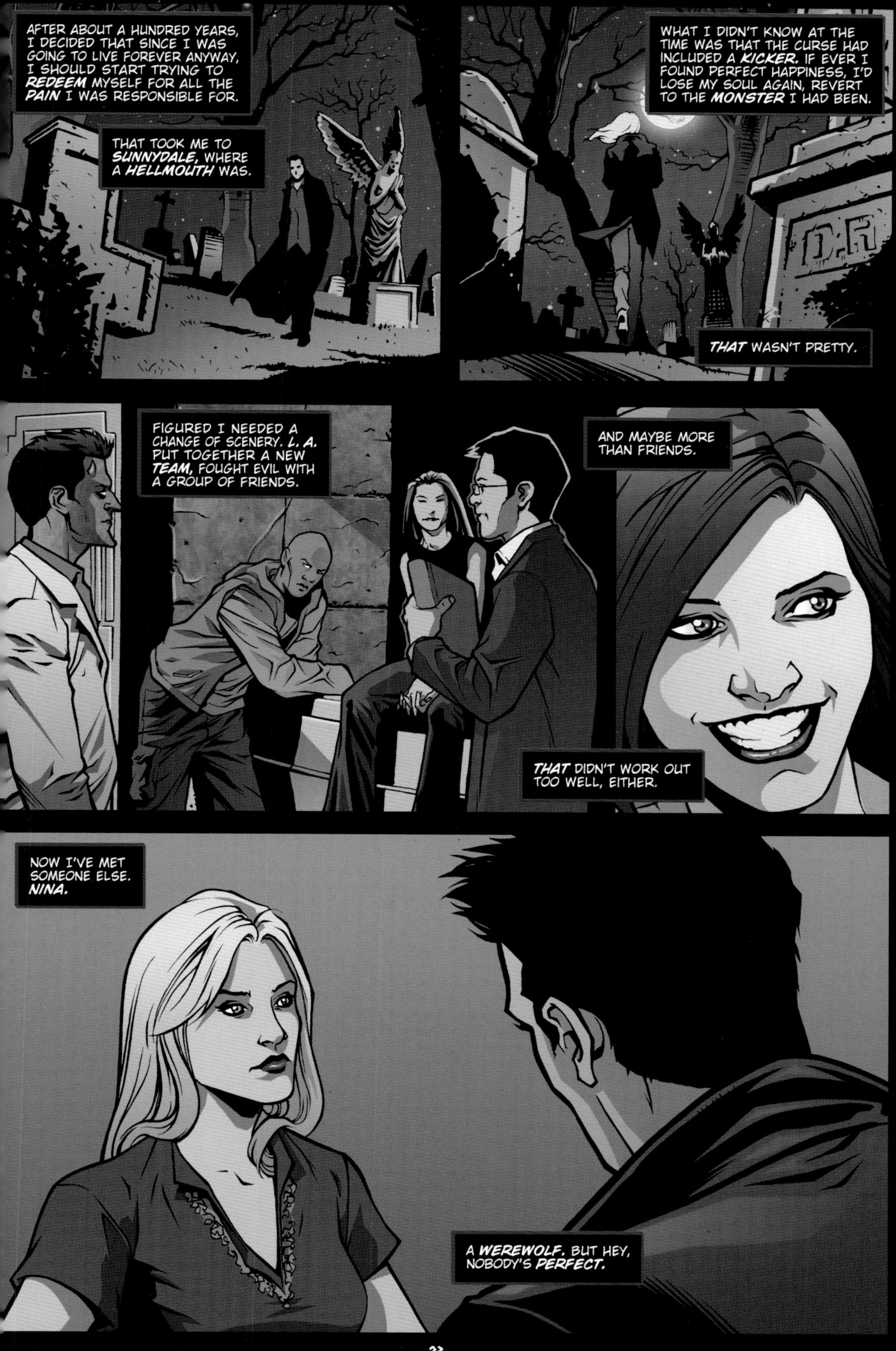
AFTER ABOUT A HUNDRED YEARS, I DECIDED THAT SINCE I WAS GOING TO LIVE FOREVER ANYWAY, I SHOULD START TRYING TO REDEEM MYSELF FOR ALL THE PAIN I WAS RESPONSIBLE FOR.
THAT TOOK ME TO SUNNYDALE, WHERE A HELLMOUTH WAS.
WHAT I DIDN'T KNOW AT THE TIME WAS THAT THE CURSE HAD INCLUDED A KICKER. IF EVER I FOUND PERFECT HAPPINESS, I'D LOSE MY SOUL AGAIN, REVERT TO THE MONSTER I HAD BEEN.
THAT WASN'T PRETTY.
FIGURED I NEEDED A CHANGE OF SCENERY. L. A. PUT TOGETHER A NEW TEAM, FOUGHT EVIL WITH A GROUP OF FRIENDS.
AND MAYBE MORE THAN FRIENDS.
THAT DIDN'T WORK OUT TOO WELL, EITHER.
NOW I'VE MET SOMEONE ELSE. NINA.
A WEREWOLF. BUT HEY, NOBODY'S PERFECT.

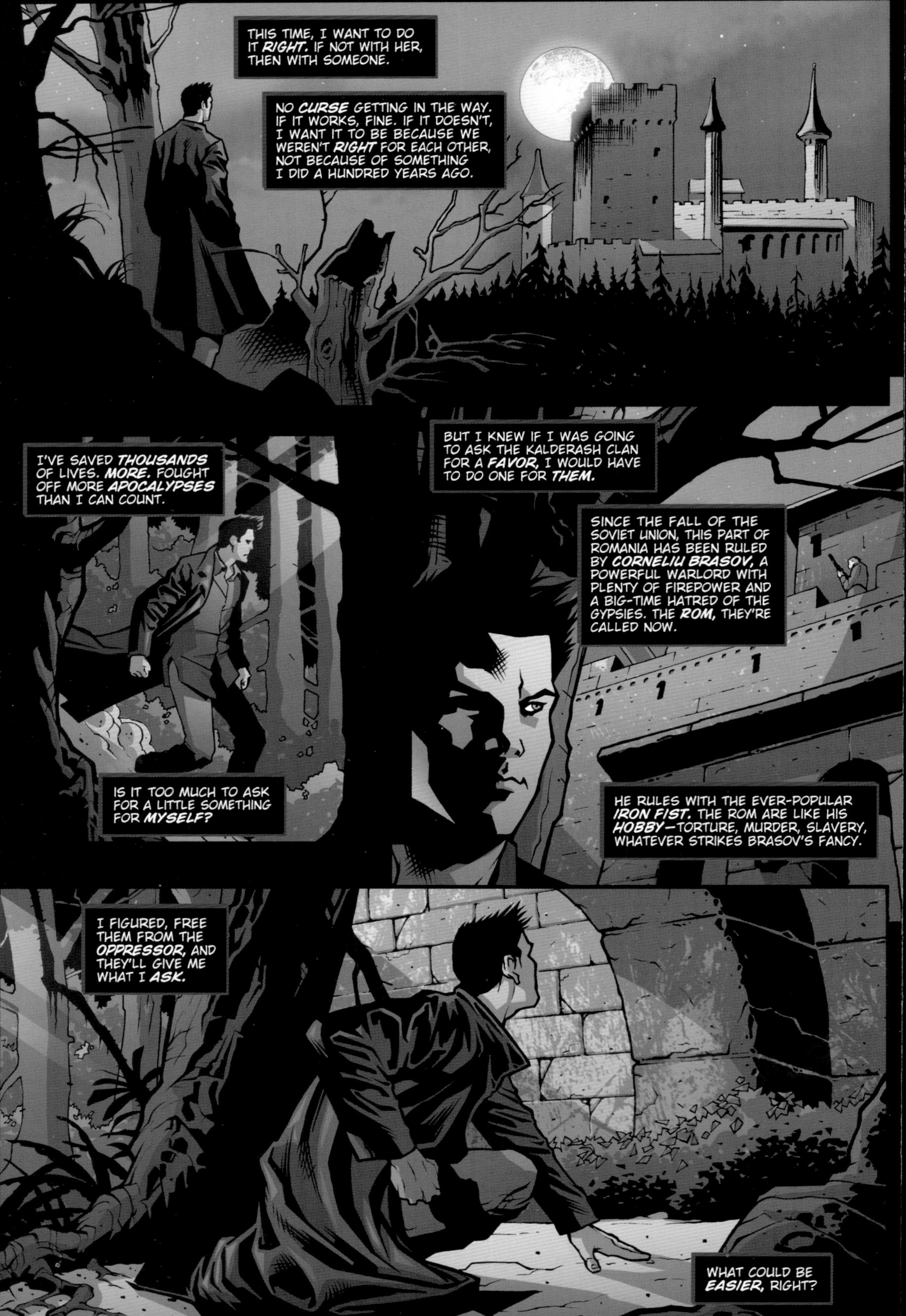
THIS TIME, I WANT TO DO IT RIGHT. IF NOT WITH HER, THEN WITH SOMEONE.
NO CURSE GETTING IN THE WAY. IF IT WORKS, FINE. IF IT DOESN'T, I WANT IT TO BE BECAUSE WE WEREN'T RIGHT FOR EACH OTHER, NOT BECAUSE OF SOMETHING I DID A HUNDRED YEARS AGO.
I'VE SAVED THOUSANDS OF LIVES. MORE. FOUGHT OFF MORE APOCALYPSES THAN I CAN COUNT.
IS IT TOO MUCH TO ASK FOR A LITTLE SOMETHING FOR MYSELF?
BUT I KNEW IF I WAS GOING TO ASK THE KALDERASH CLAN FOR A FAVOR, I WOULD HAVE TO DO ONE FOR THEM.
SINCE THE FALL OF THE SOVIET UNION, THIS PART OF ROMANIA HAS BEEN RULED BY CORNELIU BRASOV, A POWERFUL WARLORD WITH PLENTY OF FIREPOWER AND A BIG-TIME HATRED OF THE GYPSIES. THE ROM, THEY'RE CALLED NOW.
HE RULES WITH THE EVER-POPULAR IRON FIST. THE ROM ARE LIKE HIS HOBBY—TORTURE, MURDER, SLAVERY, WHATEVER STRIKES BRASOV'S FANCY.
I FIGURED, FREE THEM FROM THE OPPRESSOR, AND THEY'LL GIVE ME WHAT I ASK.
WHAT COULD BE EASIER, RIGHT?

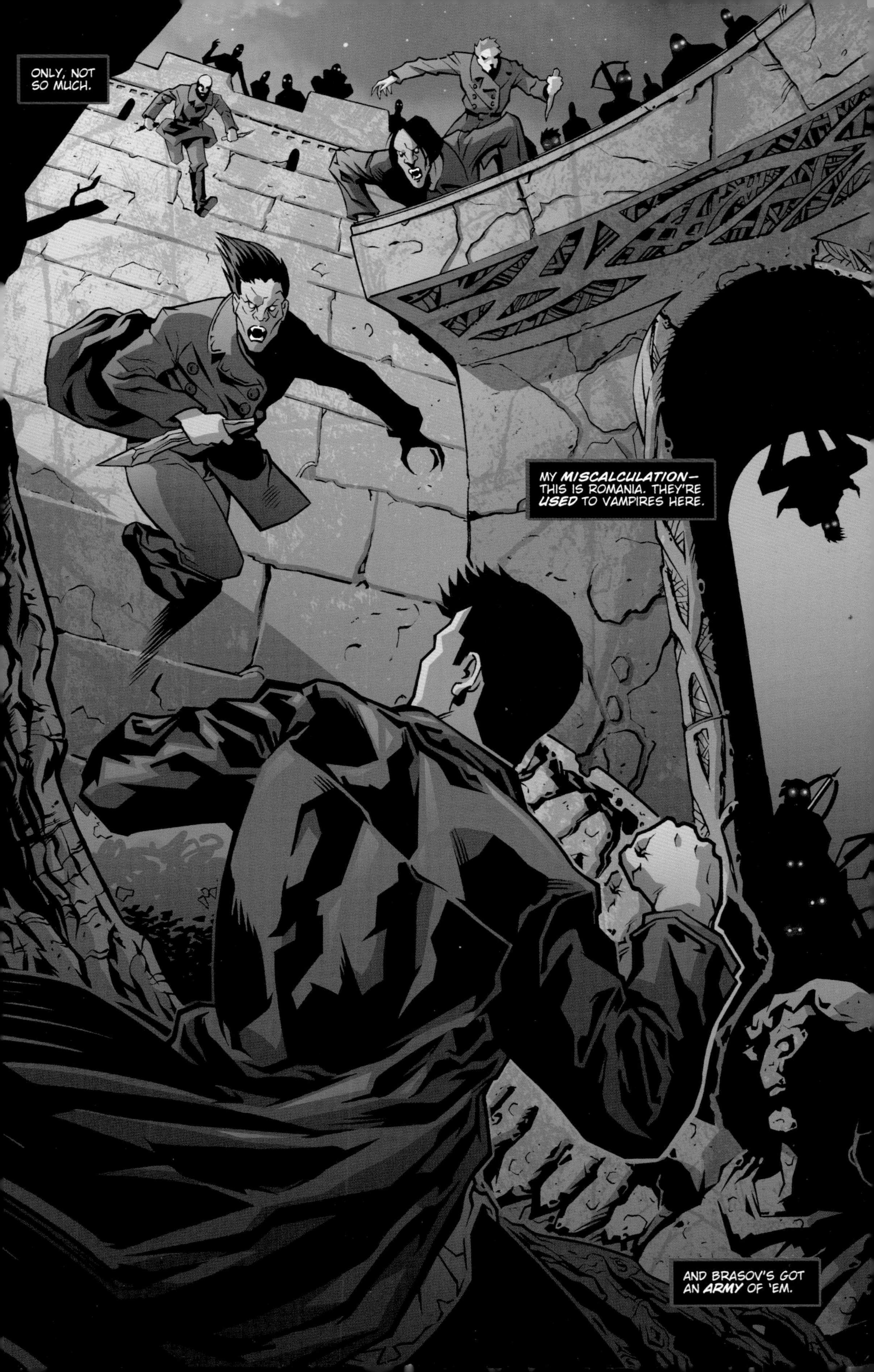
ONLY, NOT SO MUCH.
MY MISCALCULATION— THIS IS ROMANIA. THEY'RE USED TO VAMPIRES HERE.
AND BRASOV'S GOT AN ARMY OF 'EM.

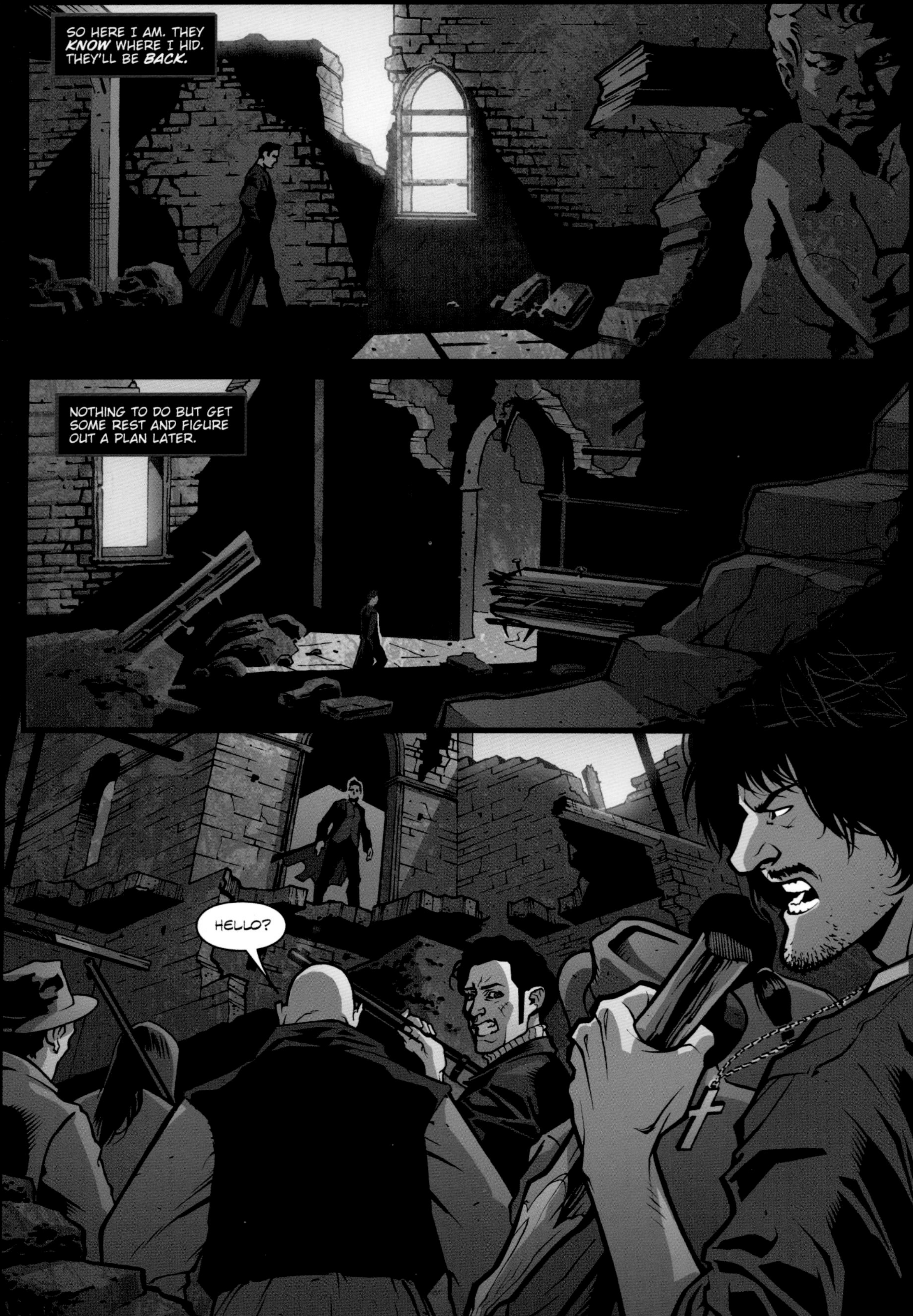

SO HERE I AM. THEY KNOW WHERE I HID. THEY'LL BE BACK.
NOTHING TO DO BUT GET SOME REST AND FIGURE OUT A PLAN LATER.
HELLO?

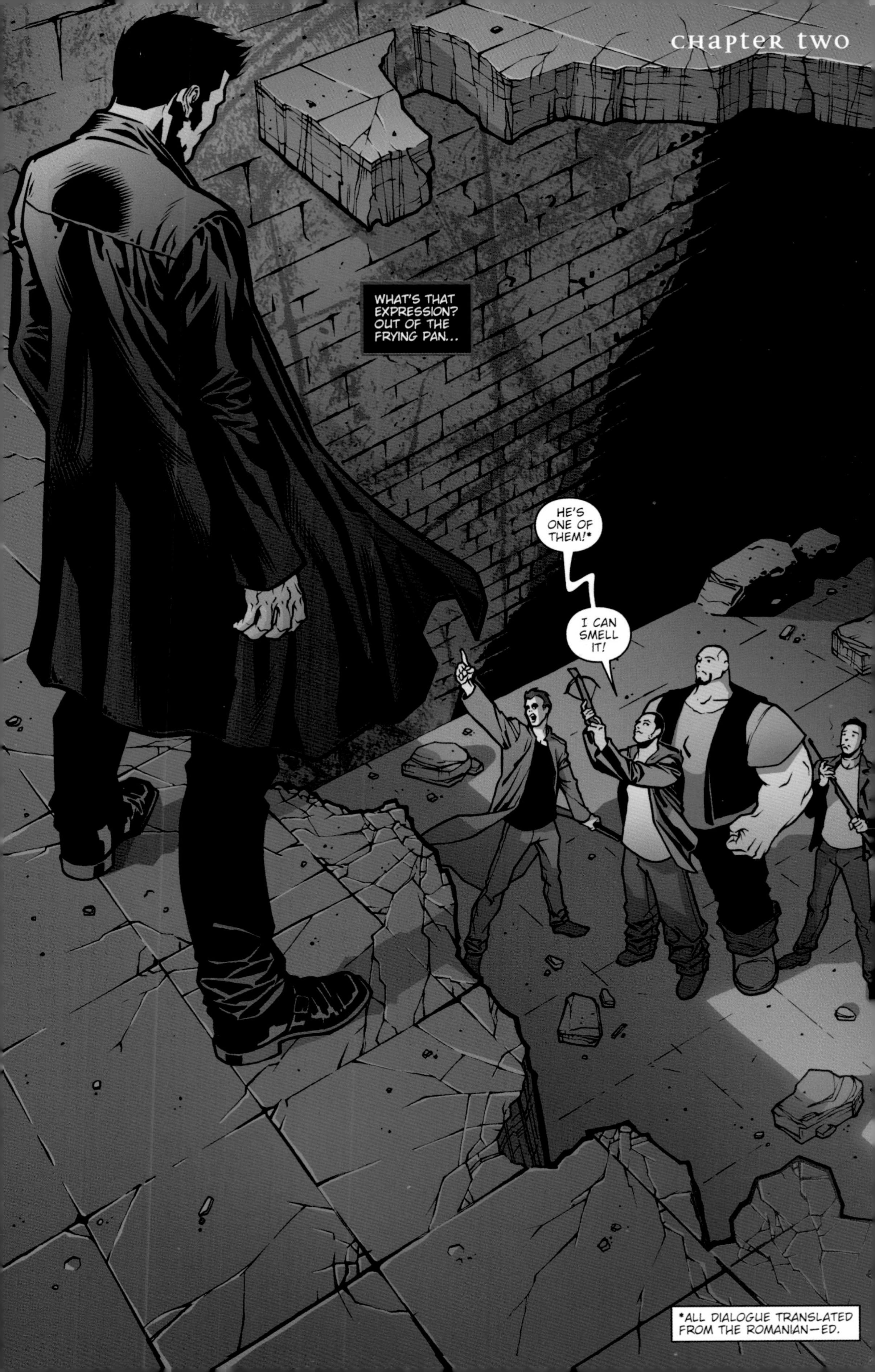
chapter two
WHAT'S THAT EXPRESSION? OUT OF THE FRYING PAN...
HE'S ONE OF THEM!*
I CAN SMELL IT!
*ALL DIALOGUE TRANSLATED FROM THE ROMANIAN—ED.

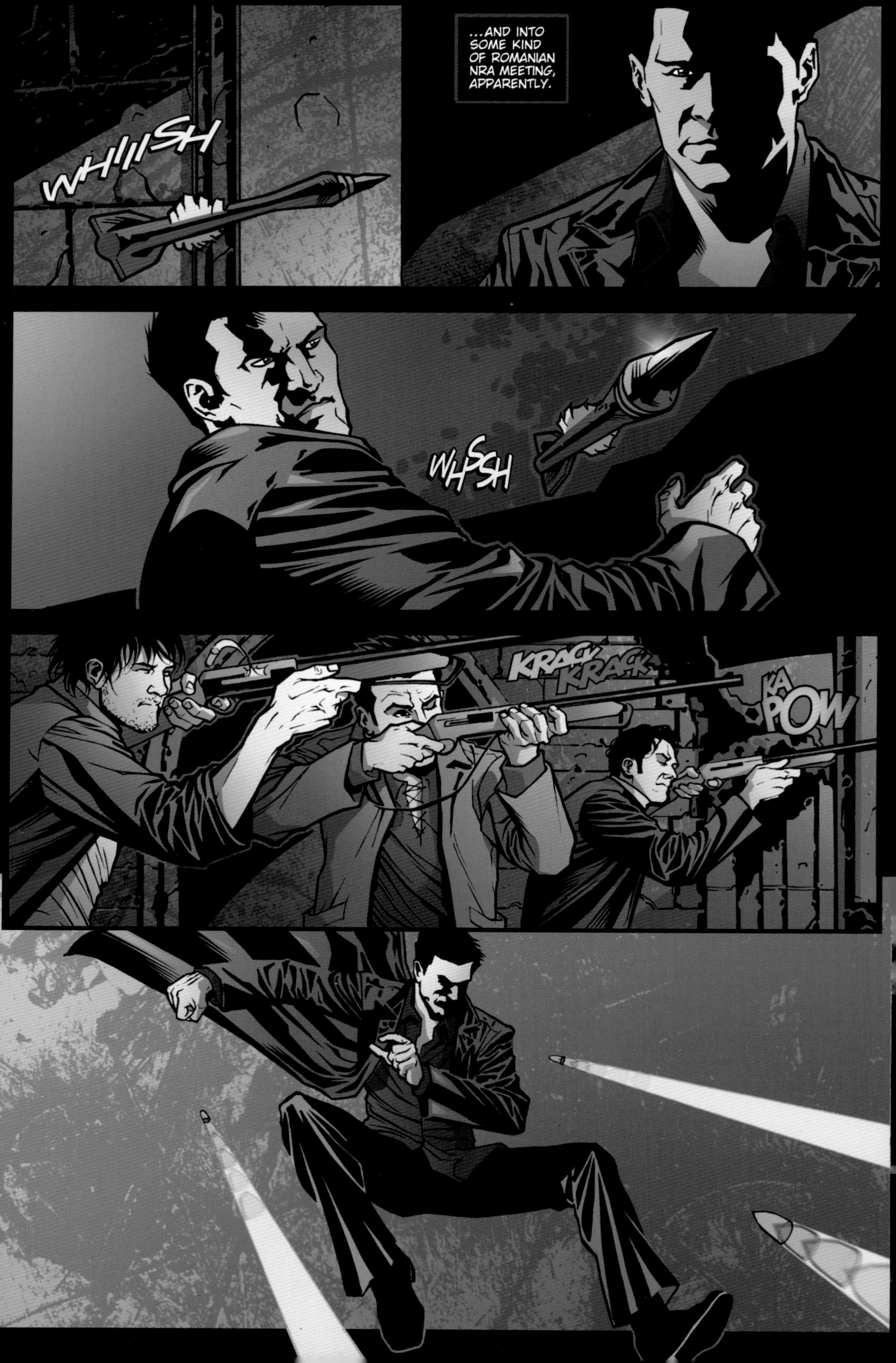

WHIIIISH
...AND INTO SOME KIND OF ROMANIAN NRA MEETING, APPARENTLY.
WHSSH
KRACK KRACK
KA POW

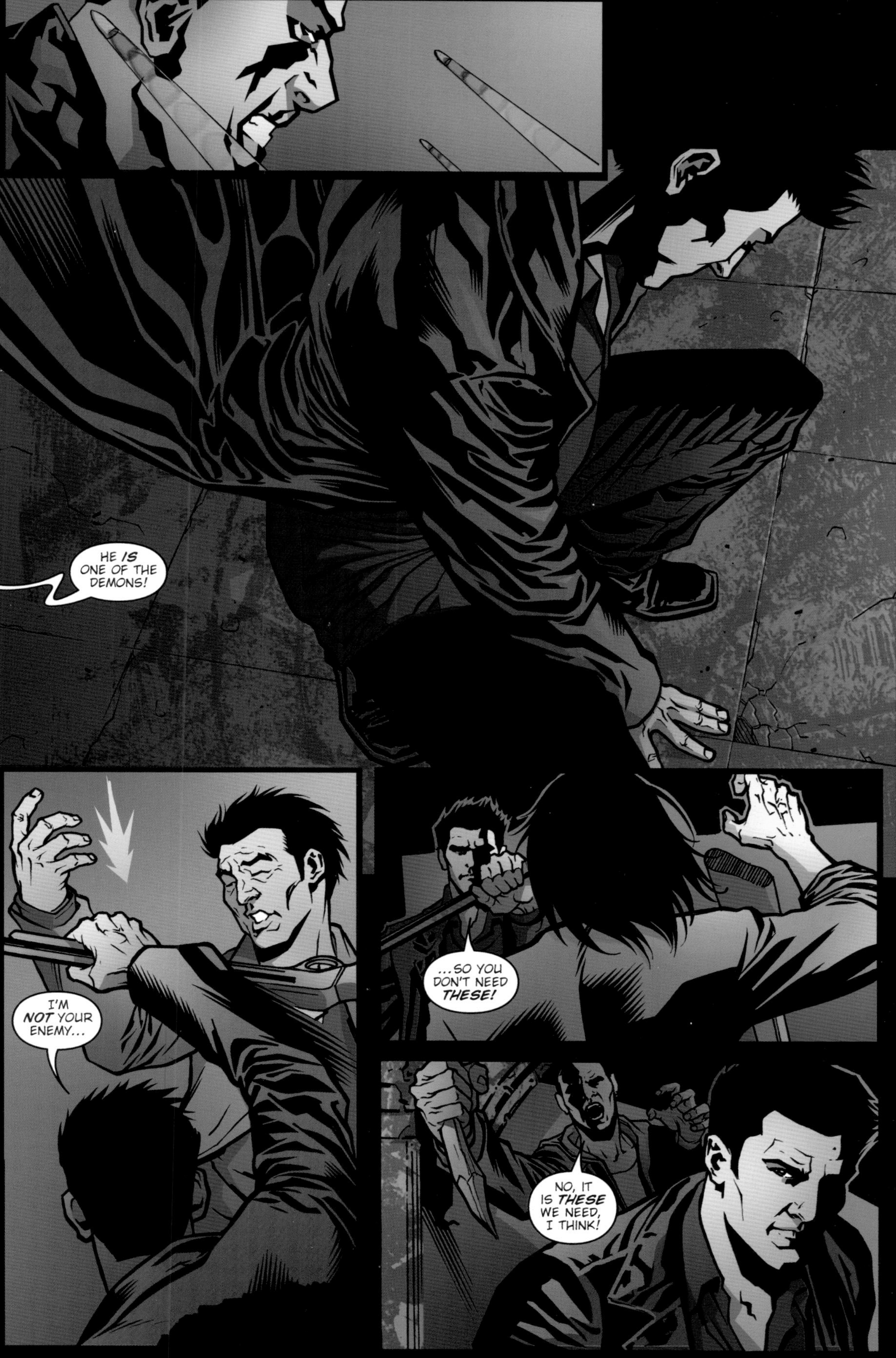
HE IS ONE OF THE DEMONS!
I'M NOT YOUR ENEMY...
...SO YOU DON'T NEED THESE!
NO, IT IS THESE WE NEED, I THINK!

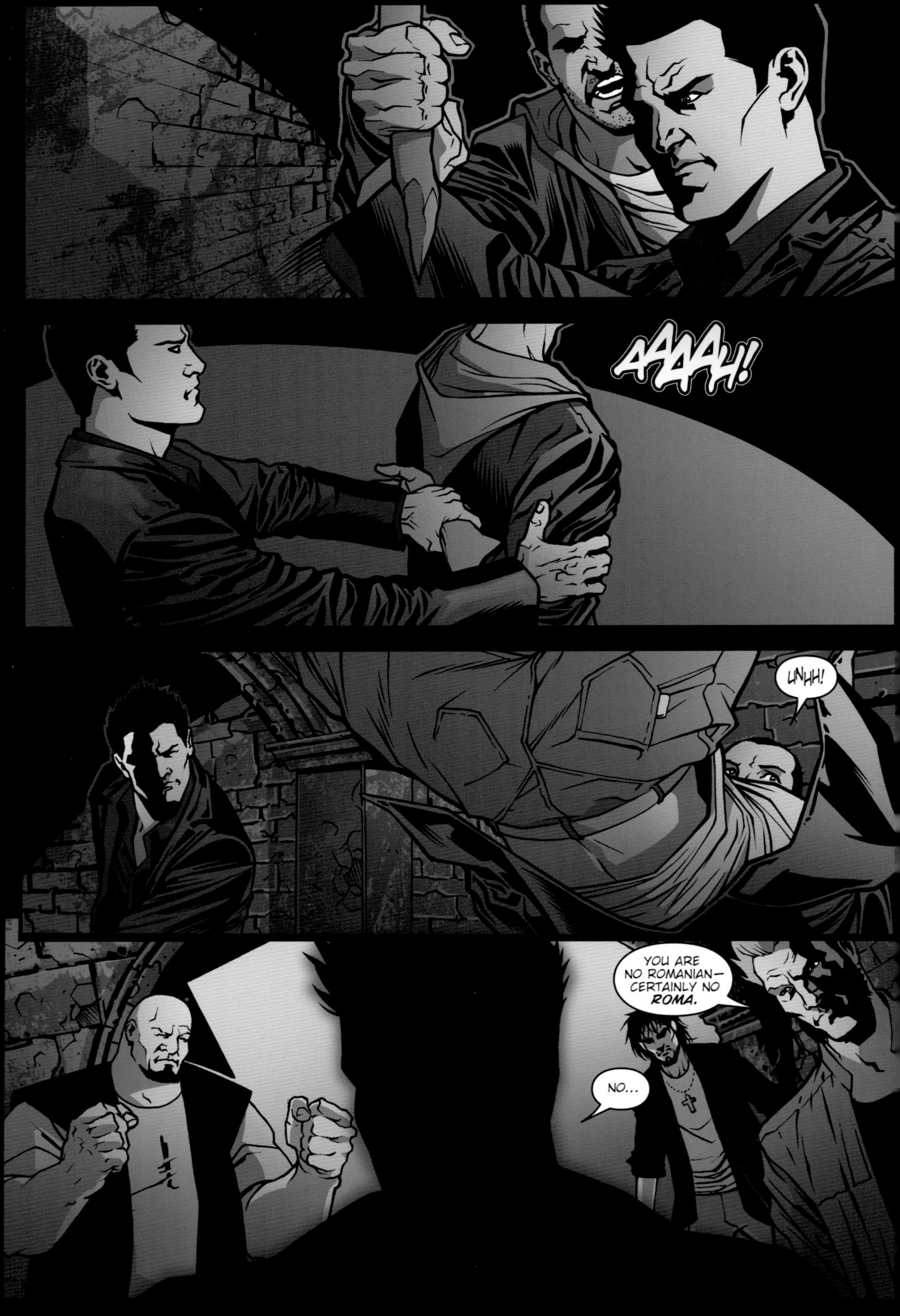
AAAAH!
UNHH!
YOU ARE NO ROMANIAN— CERTAINLY NO ROMA.
NO...

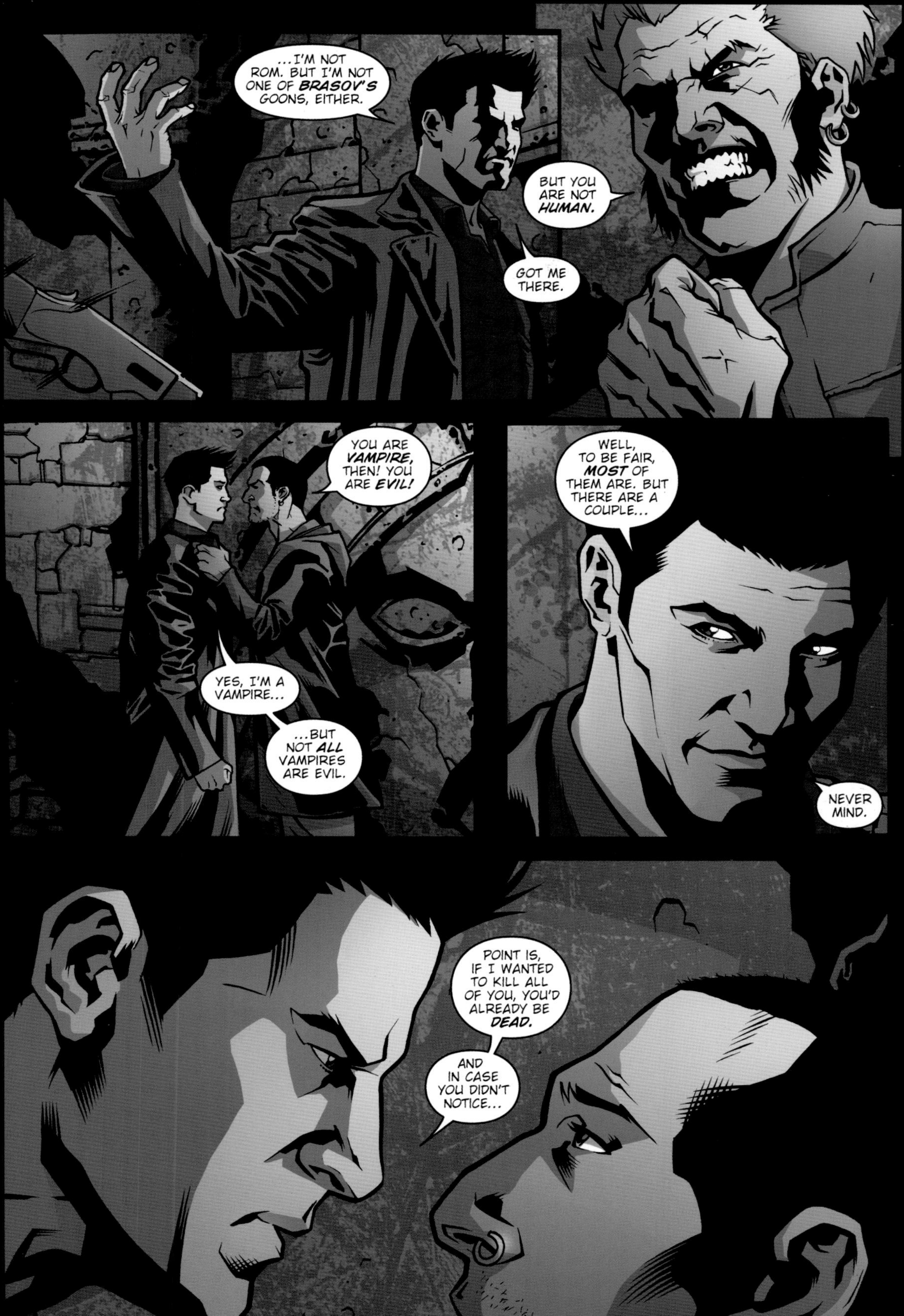
...I'M NOT ROM. BUT I'M NOT ONE OF BRASOV'S GOONS, EITHER.
BUT YOU ARE NOT HUMAN.
GOT ME THERE.
YOU ARE VAMPIRE, THEN! YOU ARE EVIL!
YES, I'M A VAMPIRE...
...BUT NOT ALL VAMPIRES ARE EVIL.
WELL, TO BE FAIR, MOST OF THEM ARE. BUT THERE ARE A COUPLE...
NEVER MIND.
POINT IS, IF I WANTED TO KILL ALL OF YOU, YOU'D ALREADY BE DEAD.
AND IN CASE YOU DIDN'T NOTICE...

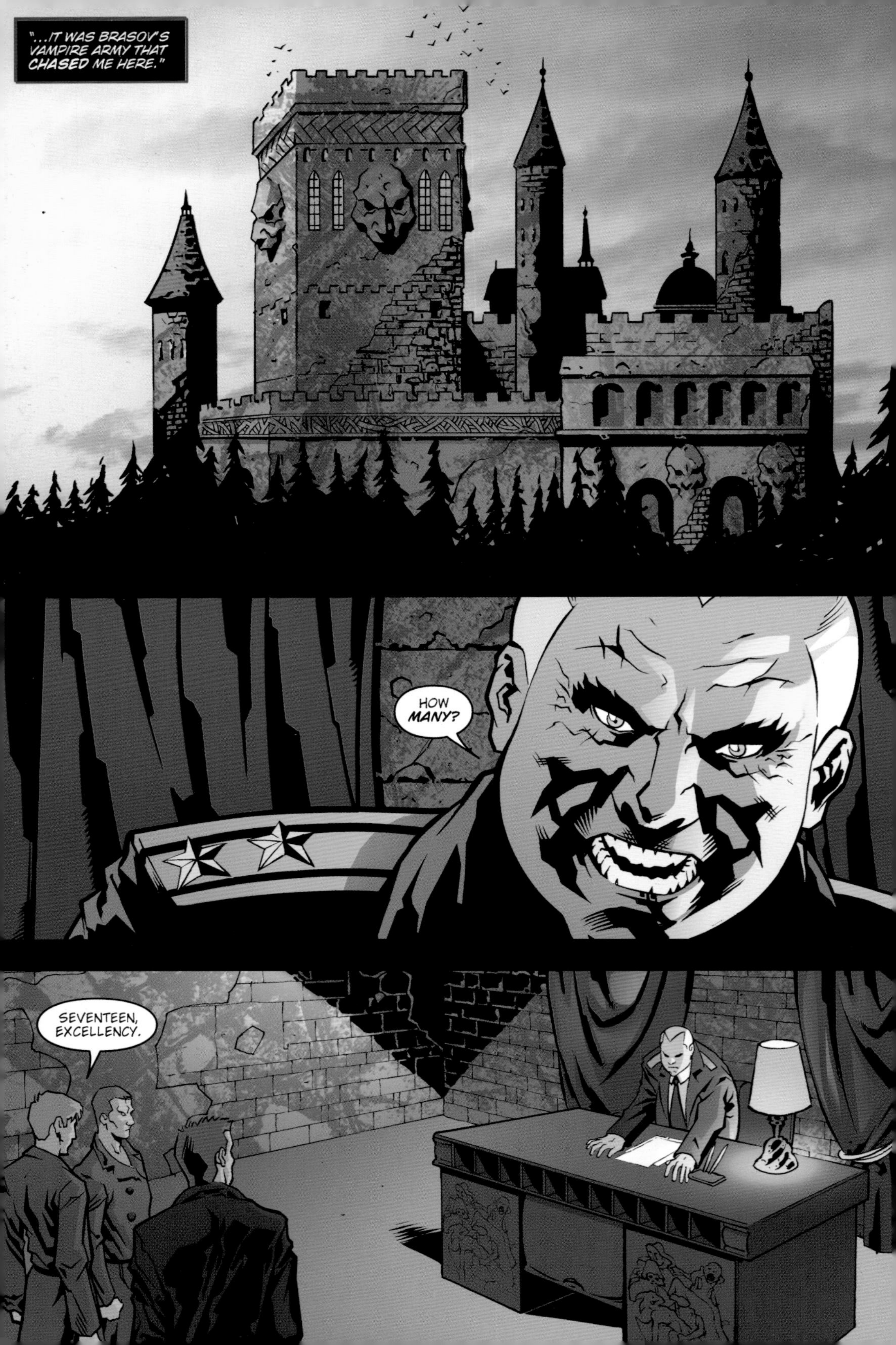
"...IT WAS BRASOV'S VAMPIRE ARMY THAT CHASED ME HERE."
HOW MANY?
SEVENTEEN, EXCELLENCY.

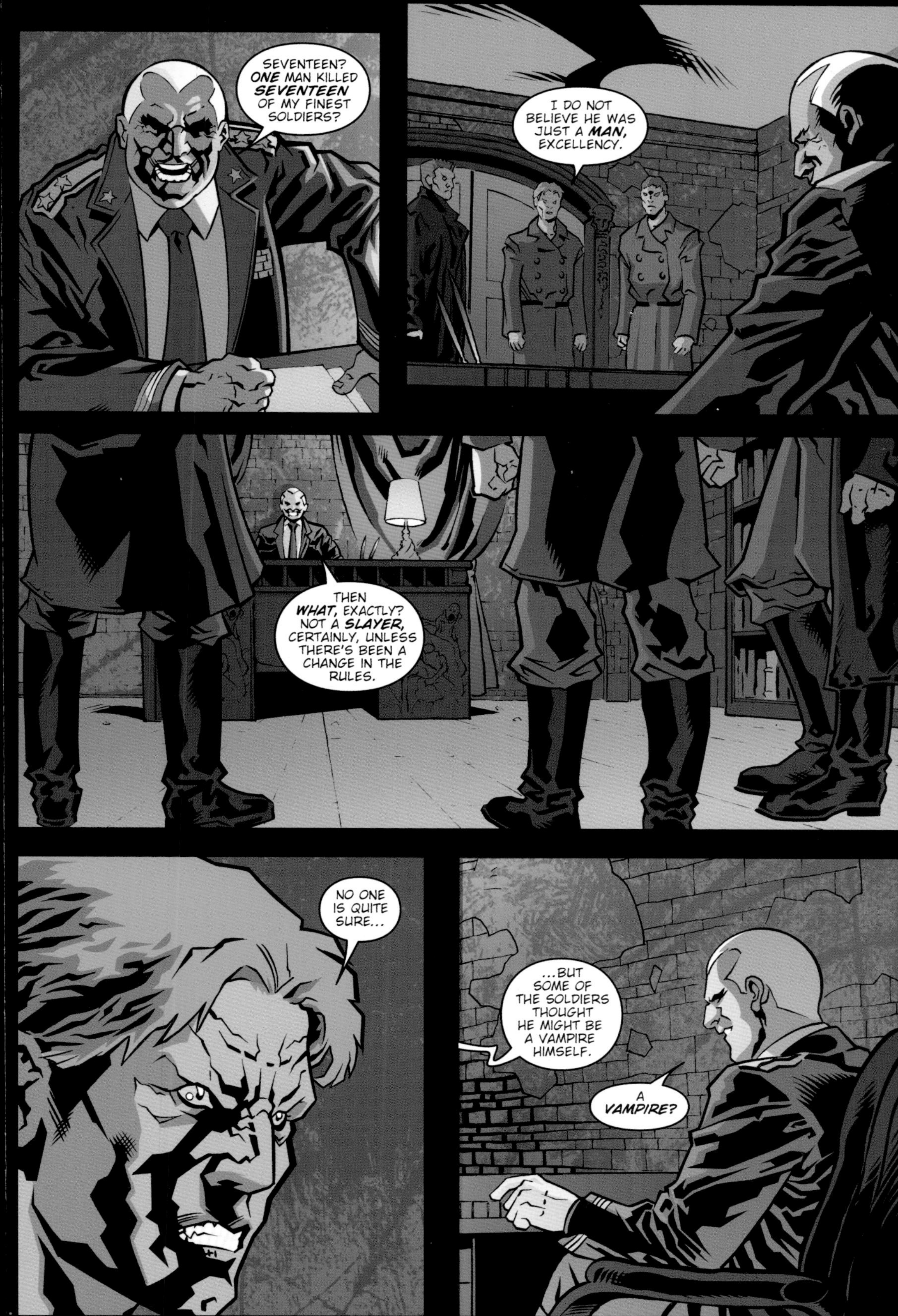
SEVENTEEN? ONE MAN KILLED SEVENTEEN OF MY FINEST SOLDIERS?
I DO NOT BELIEVE HE WAS JUST A MAN, EXCELLENCY.
THEN WHAT, EXACTLY? NOT A SLAYER, CERTAINLY, UNLESS THERE'S BEEN A CHANGE IN THE RULES.
NO ONE IS QUITE SURE...
...BUT SOME OF THE SOLDIERS THOUGHT HE MIGHT BE A VAMPIRE HIMSELF.
A VAMPIRE?

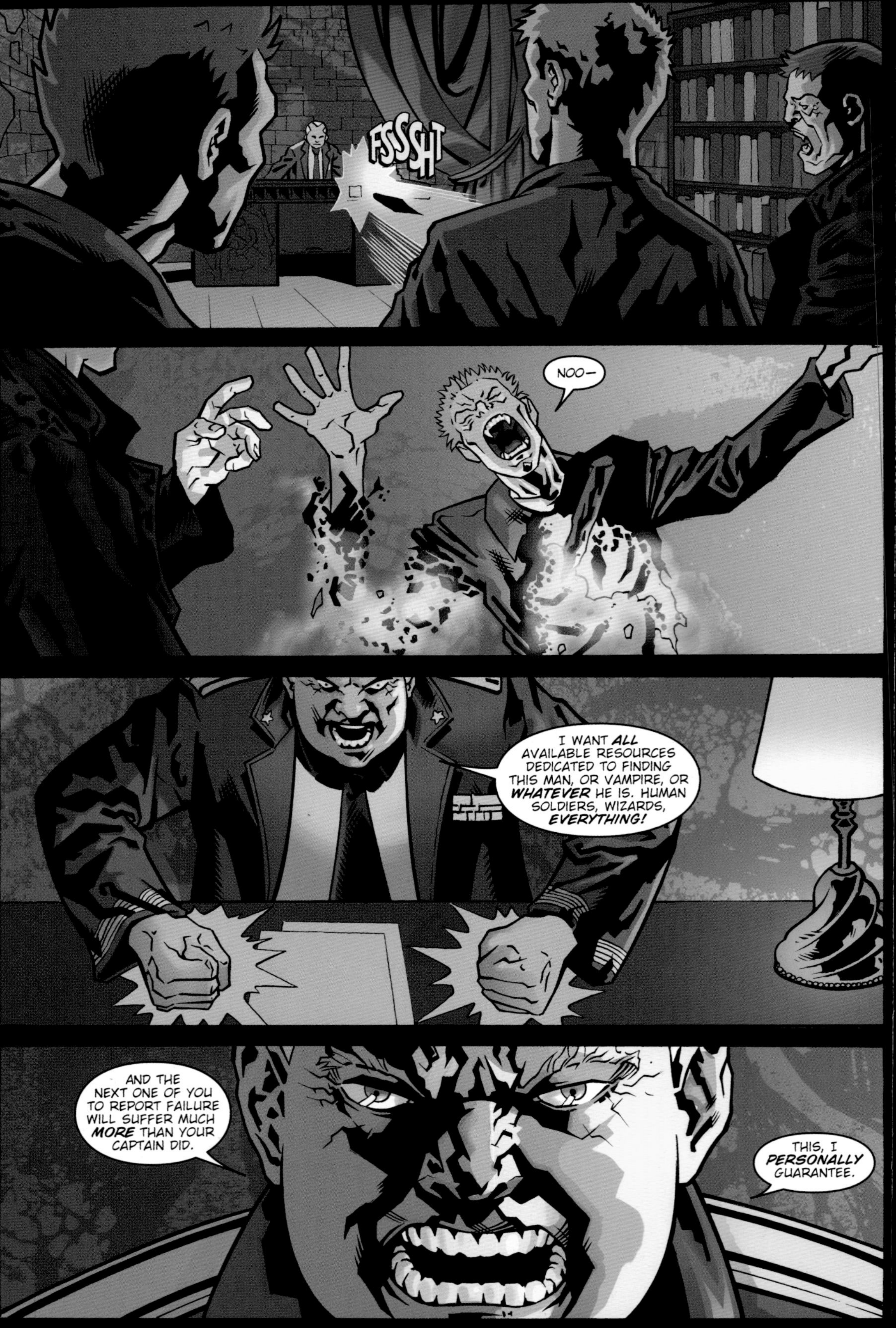
FSSSHT
NOO—
I WANT ALL AVAILABLE RESOURCES DEDICATED TO FINDING THIS MAN, OR VAMPIRE, OR WHATEVER HE IS. HUMAN SOLDIERS, WIZARDS, EVERYTHING!
AND THE NEXT ONE OF YOU TO REPORT FAILURE WILL SUFFER MUCH MORE THAN YOUR CAPTAIN DID.
THIS, I PERSONALLY GUARANTEE.

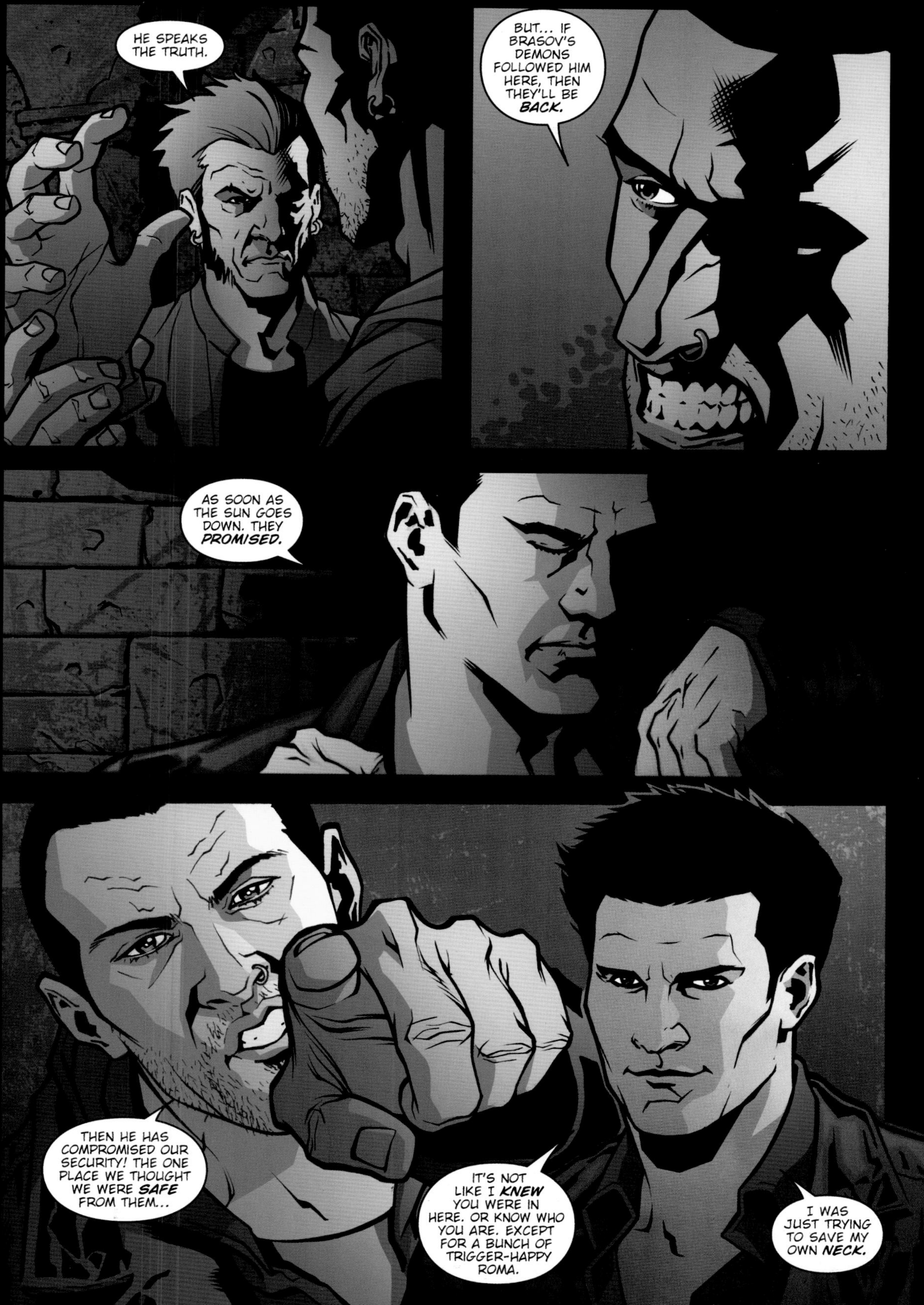
HE SPEAKS THE TRUTH.
BUT... IF BRASOV'S DEMONS FOLLOWED HIM HERE, THEN THEY'LL BE *BACK.*
AS SOON AS THE SUN GOES DOWN. THEY *PROMISED.*
THEN HE HAS COMPROMISED OUR SECURITY! THE ONE PLACE WE THOUGHT WE WERE *SAFE* FROM THEM...
IT'S NOT LIKE I *KNEW* YOU WERE IN HERE. OR KNOW WHO YOU ARE. EXCEPT FOR A BUNCH OF TRIGGER-HAPPY ROMA.
I WAS JUST TRYING TO SAVE MY OWN *NECK.*

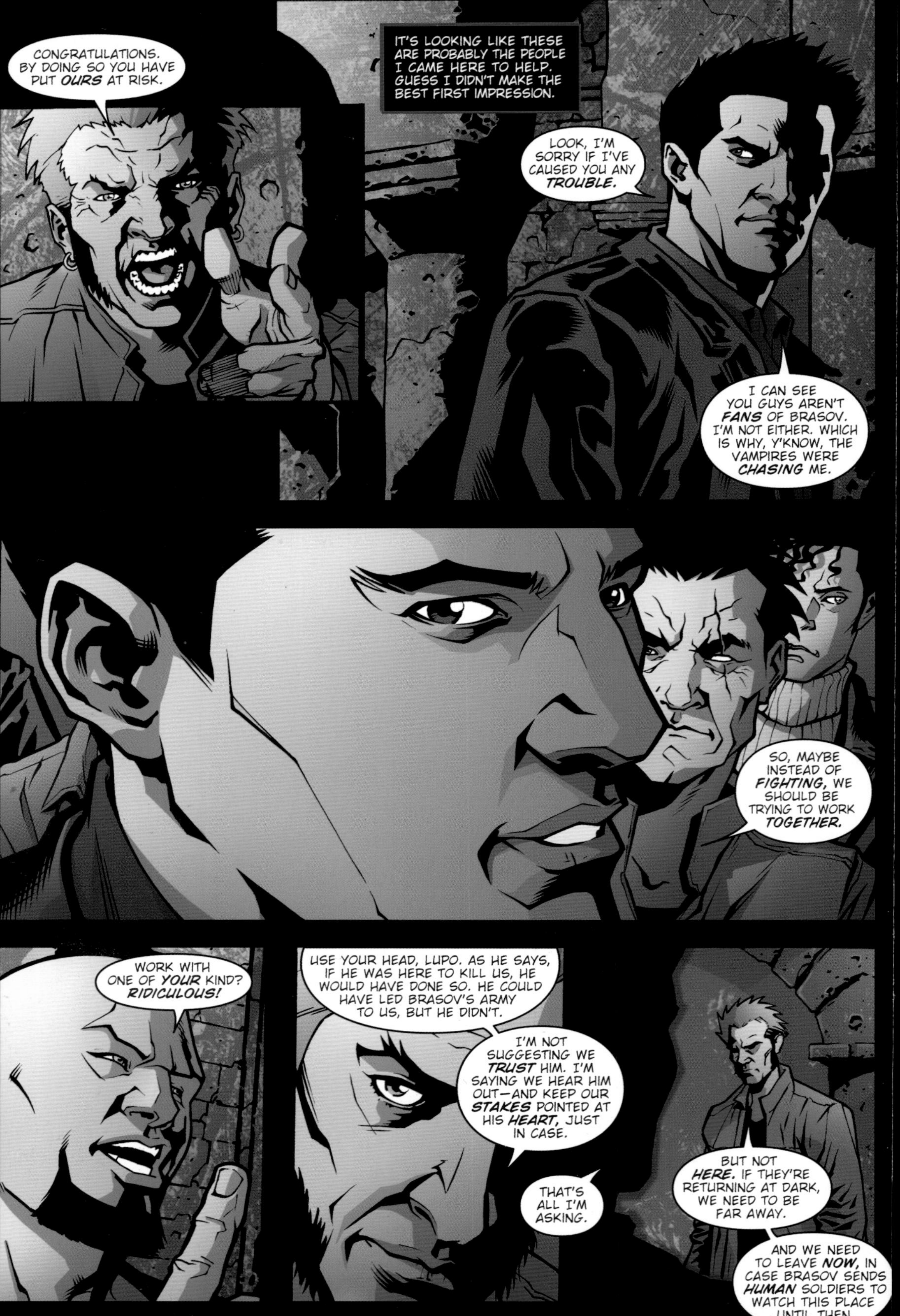
CONGRATULATIONS. BY DOING SO YOU HAVE PUT OURS AT RISK.
IT'S LOOKING LIKE THESE ARE PROBABLY THE PEOPLE I CAME HERE TO HELP. GUESS I DIDN'T MAKE THE BEST FIRST IMPRESSION.
LOOK, I'M SORRY IF I'VE CAUSED YOU ANY TROUBLE.
I CAN SEE YOU GUYS AREN'T FANS OF BRASOV. I'M NOT EITHER. WHICH IS WHY, Y'KNOW, THE VAMPIRES WERE CHASING ME.
SO, MAYBE INSTEAD OF FIGHTING, WE SHOULD BE TRYING TO WORK TOGETHER.
WORK WITH ONE OF YOUR KIND? RIDICULOUS!
USE YOUR HEAD, LUPO. AS HE SAYS, IF HE WAS HERE TO KILL US, HE WOULD HAVE DONE SO. HE COULD HAVE LED BRASOV'S ARMY TO US, BUT HE DIDN'T.
I'M NOT SUGGESTING WE TRUST HIM. I'M SAYING WE HEAR HIM OUT—AND KEEP OUR STAKES POINTED AT HIS HEART, JUST IN CASE.
THAT'S ALL I'M ASKING.
BUT NOT HERE. IF THEY'RE RETURNING AT DARK, WE NEED TO BE FAR AWAY.
AND WE NEED TO LEAVE NOW, IN CASE BRASOV SENDS HUMAN SOLDIERS TO WATCH THIS PLACE UNTIL THEN.

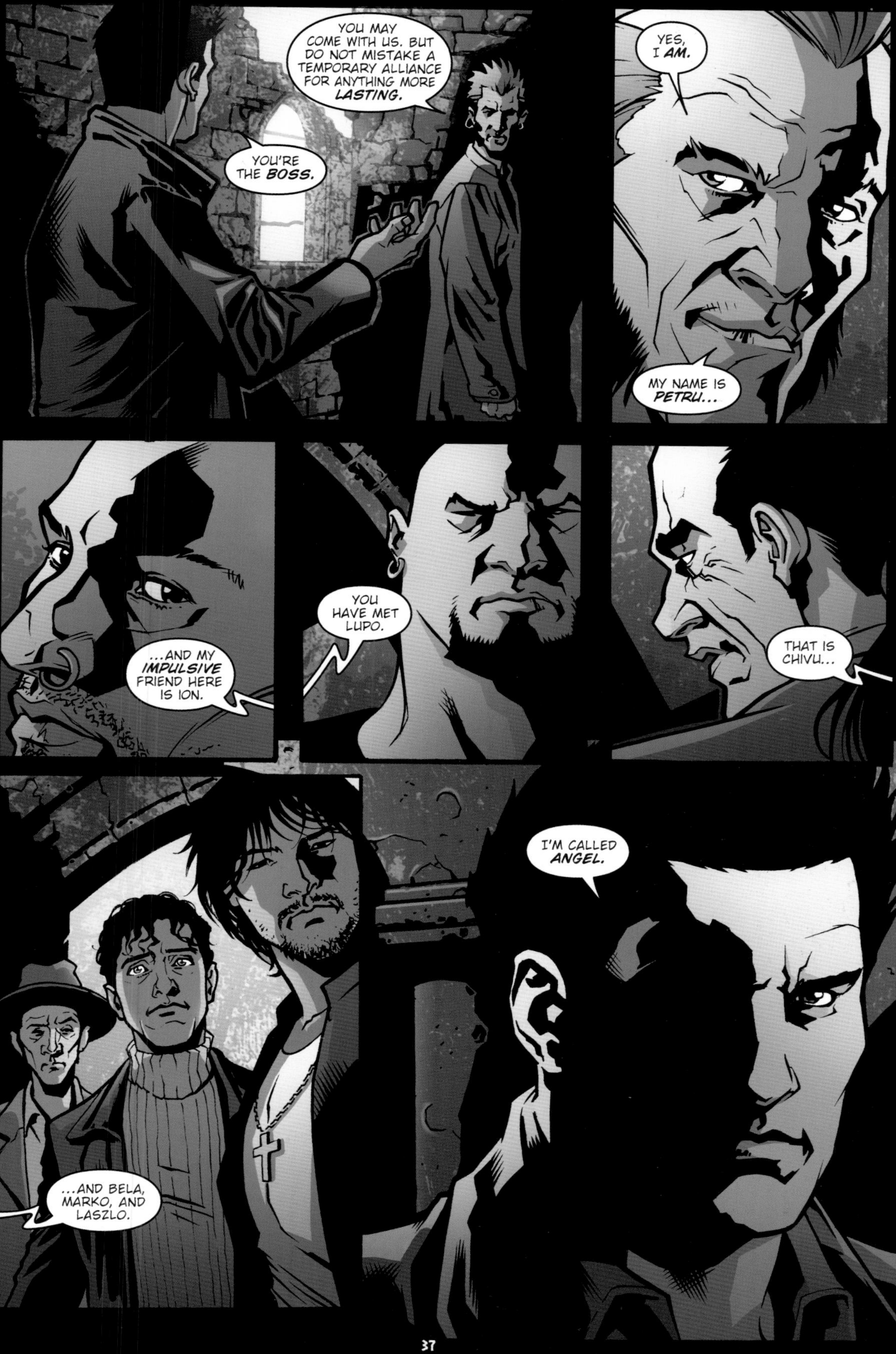
YOU MAY COME WITH US. BUT DO NOT MISTAKE A TEMPORARY ALLIANCE FOR ANYTHING MORE LASTING.
YOU'RE THE BOSS.
YES, I AM.
MY NAME IS PETRU...
...AND MY IMPULSIVE FRIEND HERE IS ION.
YOU HAVE MET LUPO.
THAT IS CHIVU...
...AND BELA, MARKO, AND LASZLO.
I'M CALLED ANGEL.

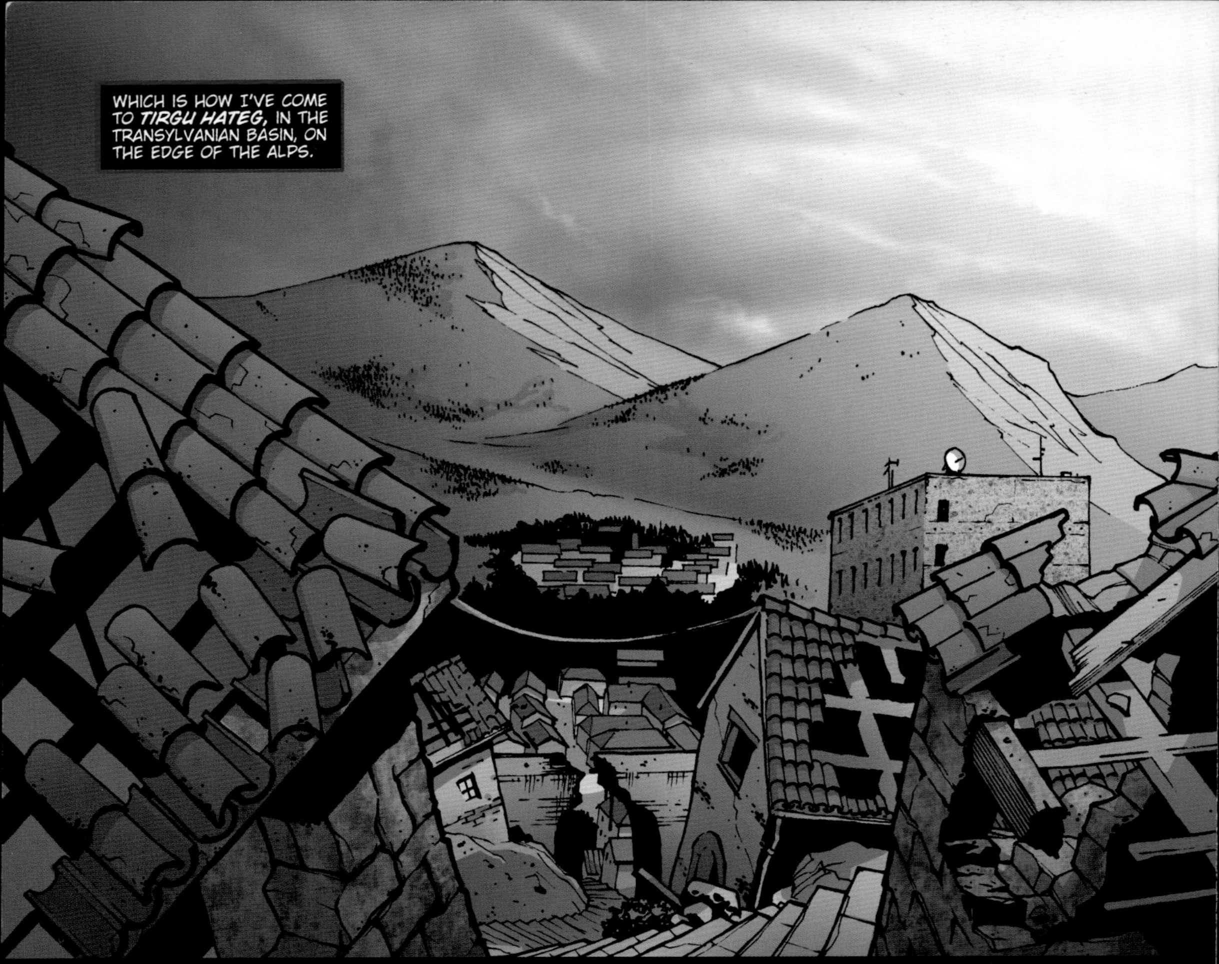
WHICH IS HOW I'VE COME TO ***TIRGU HATEG,*** IN THE TRANSYLVANIAN BASIN, ON THE EDGE OF THE ALPS.

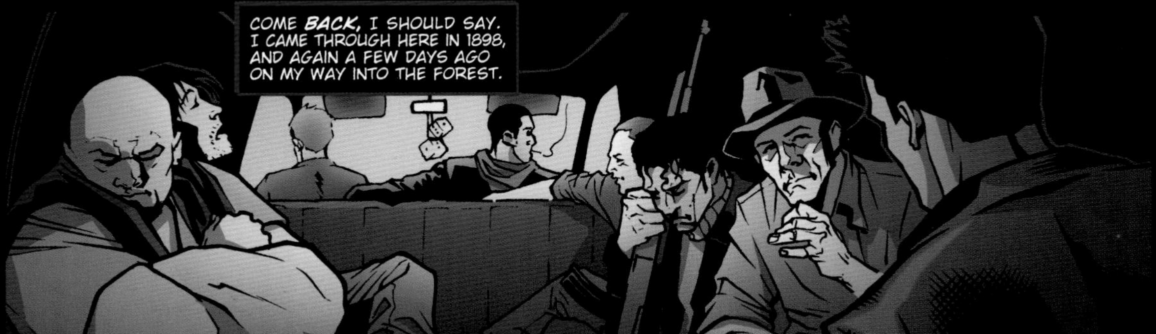
COME ***BACK,*** I SHOULD SAY. I CAME THROUGH HERE IN 1898, AND AGAIN A FEW DAYS AGO ON MY WAY INTO THE FOREST.

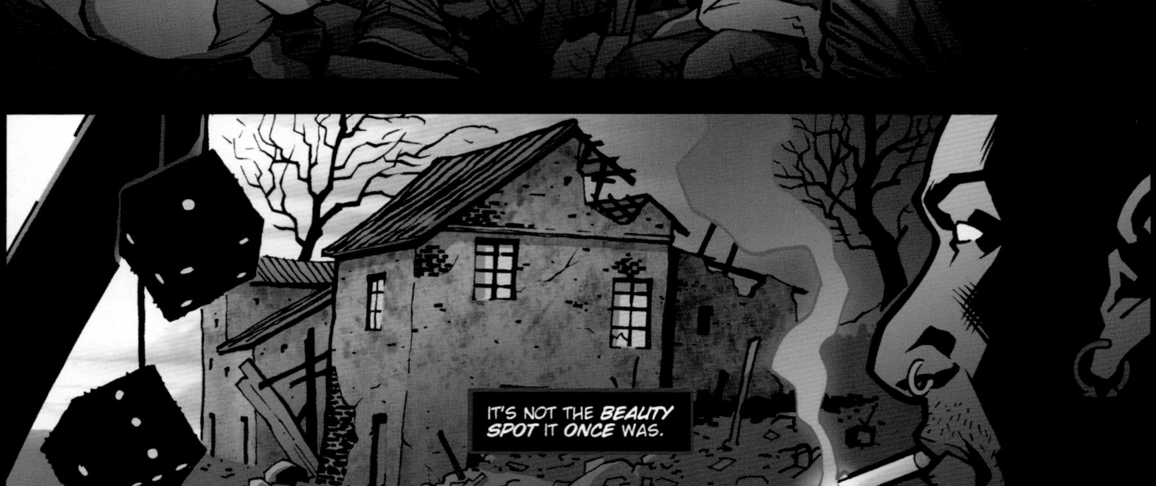
IT'S NOT THE ***BEAUTY SPOT*** IT ***ONCE*** WAS.

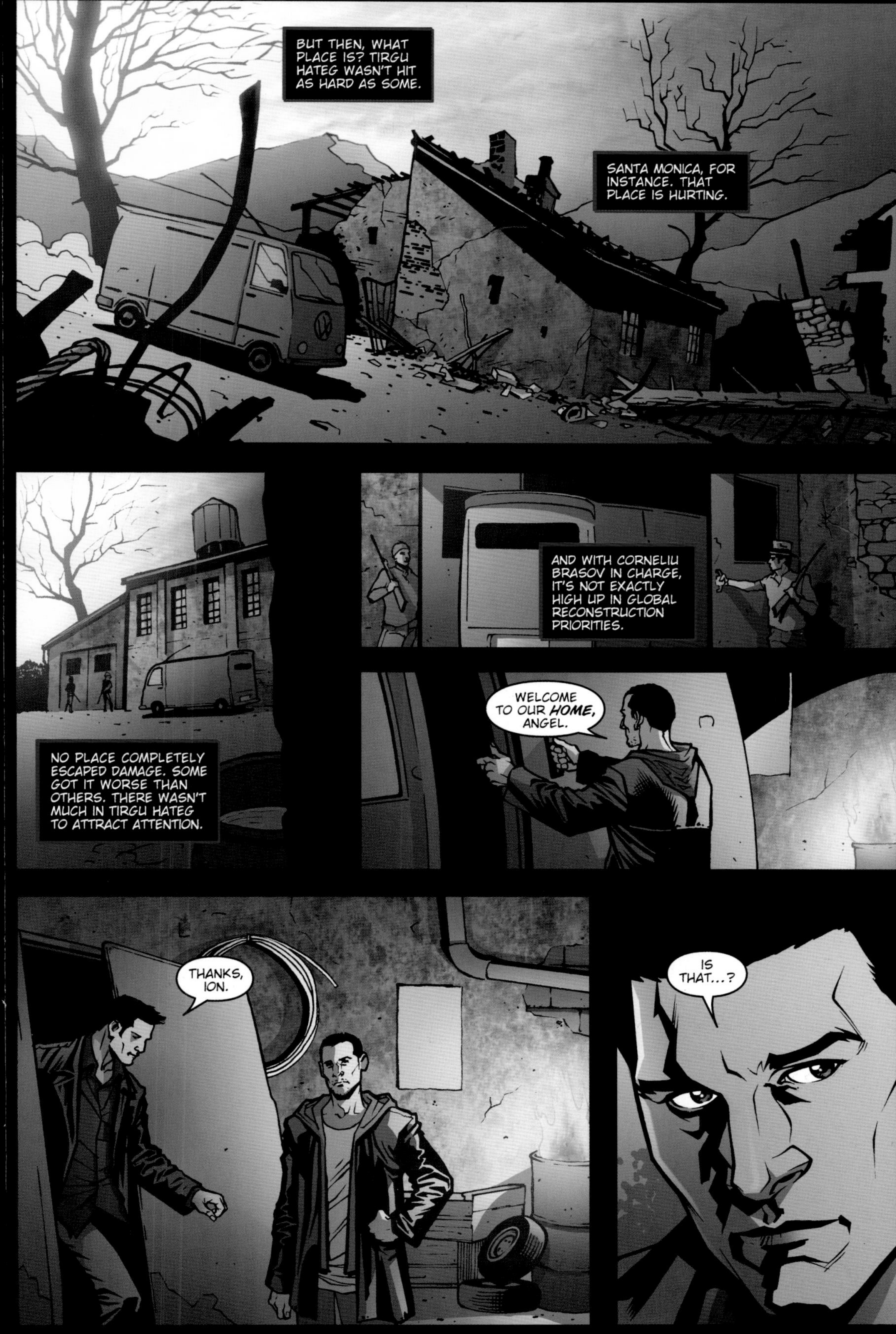

BUT THEN, WHAT PLACE IS? TIRGU HATEG WASN'T HIT AS HARD AS SOME.
SANTA MONICA, FOR INSTANCE. THAT PLACE IS HURTING.
NO PLACE COMPLETELY ESCAPED DAMAGE. SOME GOT IT WORSE THAN OTHERS. THERE WASN'T MUCH IN TIRGU HATEG TO ATTRACT ATTENTION.
AND WITH CORNELIU BRASOV IN CHARGE, IT'S NOT EXACTLY HIGH UP IN GLOBAL RECONSTRUCTION PRIORITIES.
WELCOME TO OUR *HOME,* ANGEL.
THANKS, ION.
IS THAT...?

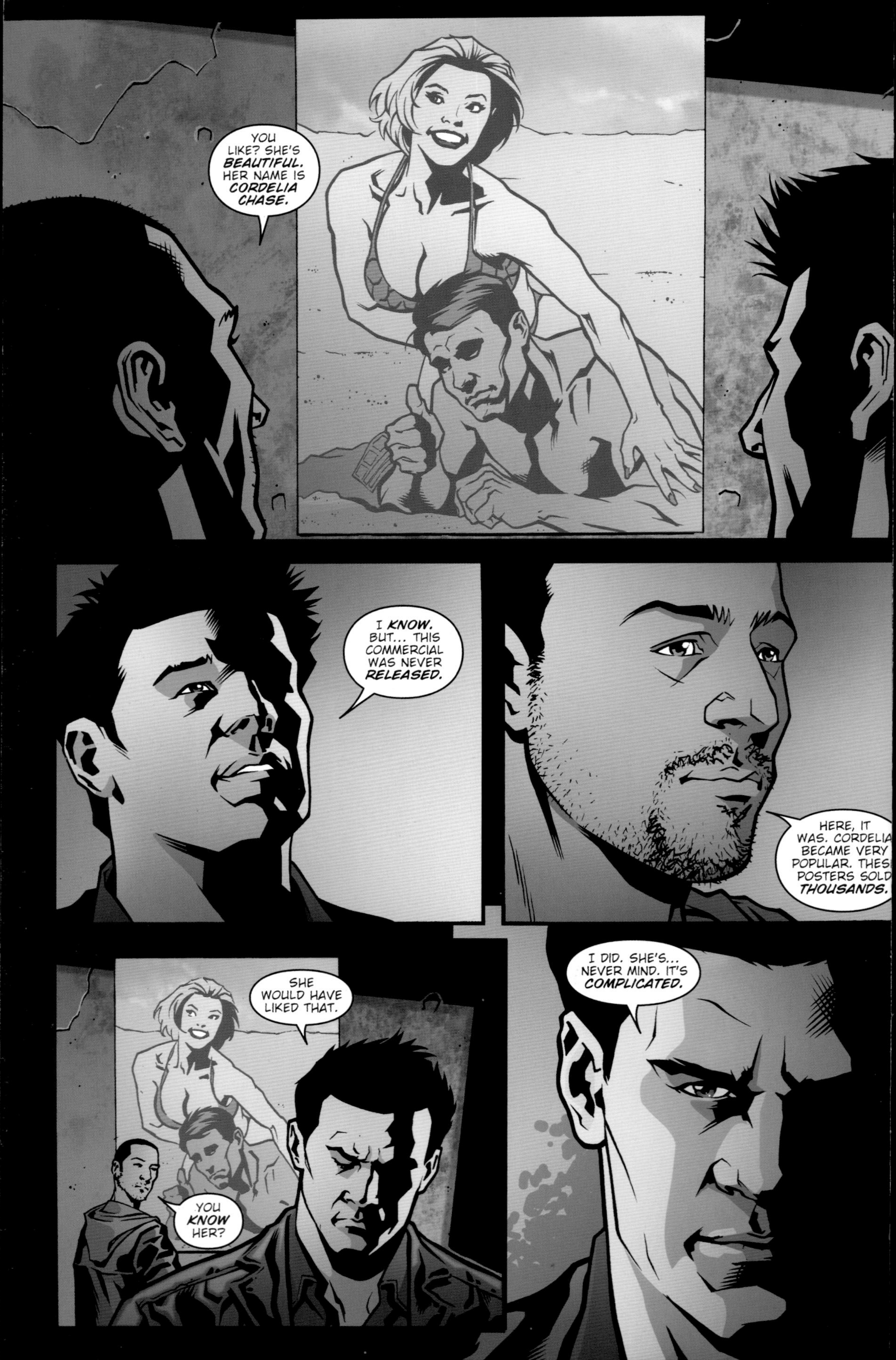

YOU LIKE? SHE'S BEAUTIFUL. HER NAME IS CORDELIA CHASE.
I KNOW. BUT... THIS COMMERCIAL WAS NEVER RELEASED.
HERE, IT WAS. CORDELIA BECAME VERY POPULAR. THESE POSTERS SOLD THOUSANDS.
SHE WOULD HAVE LIKED THAT.
YOU KNOW HER?
I DID. SHE'S... NEVER MIND. IT'S COMPLICATED.

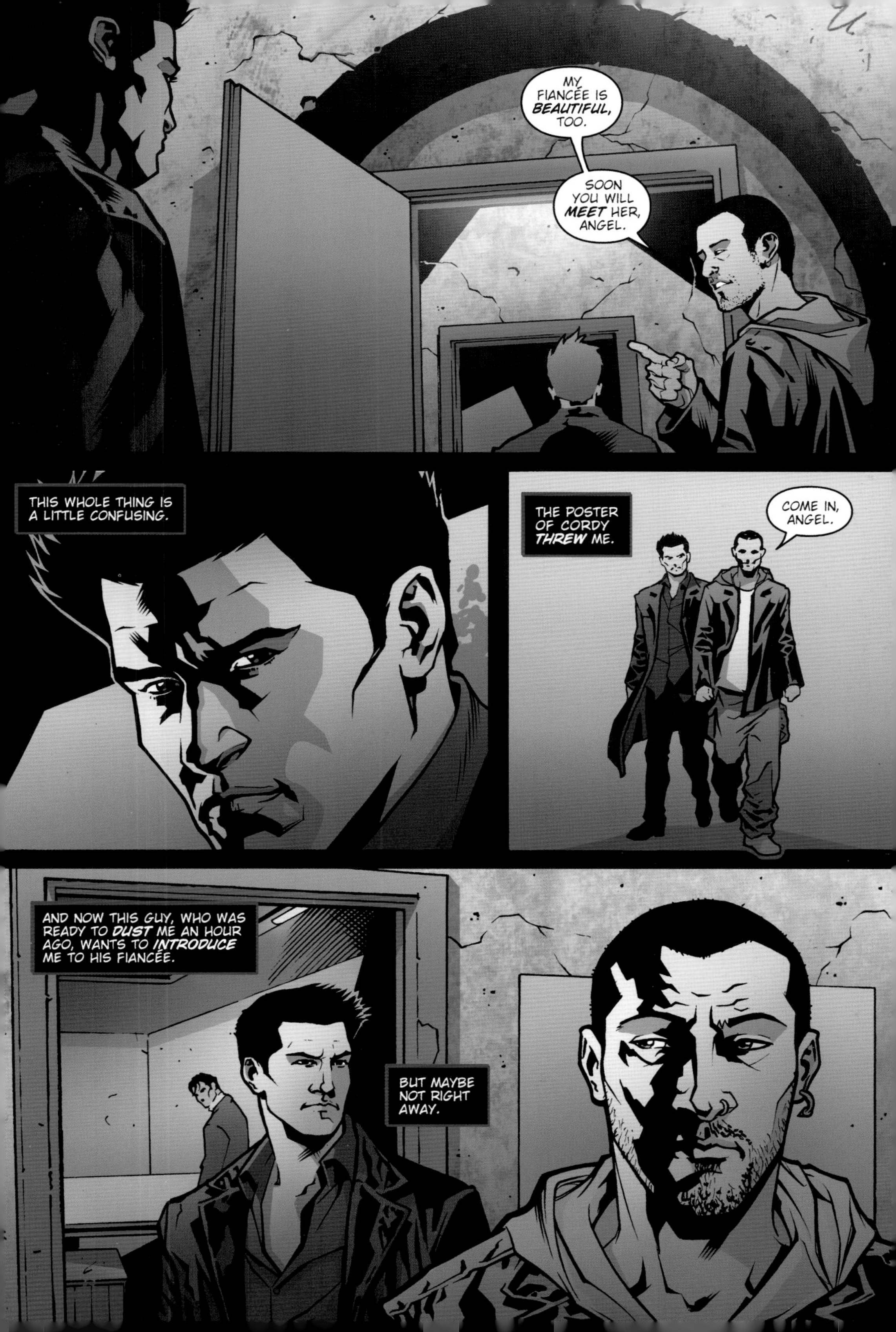
MY FIANCÉE IS BEAUTIFUL, TOO.
SOON YOU WILL MEET HER, ANGEL.
THIS WHOLE THING IS A LITTLE CONFUSING.
THE POSTER OF CORDY THREW ME.
COME IN, ANGEL.
AND NOW THIS GUY, WHO WAS READY TO DUST ME AN HOUR AGO, WANTS TO INTRODUCE ME TO HIS FIANCÉE.
BUT MAYBE NOT RIGHT AWAY.

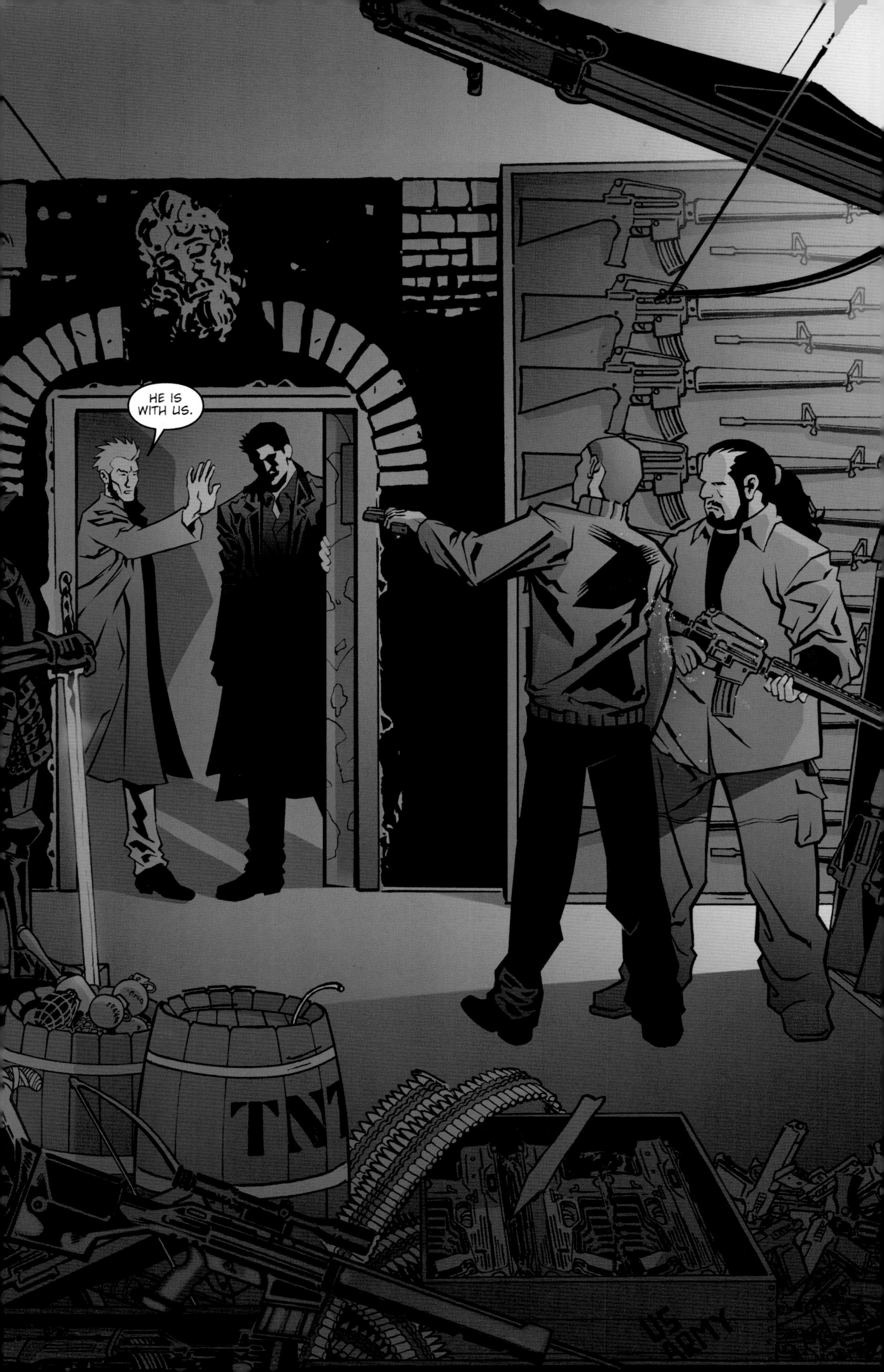
HE IS WITH US.
TNT
US ARMY

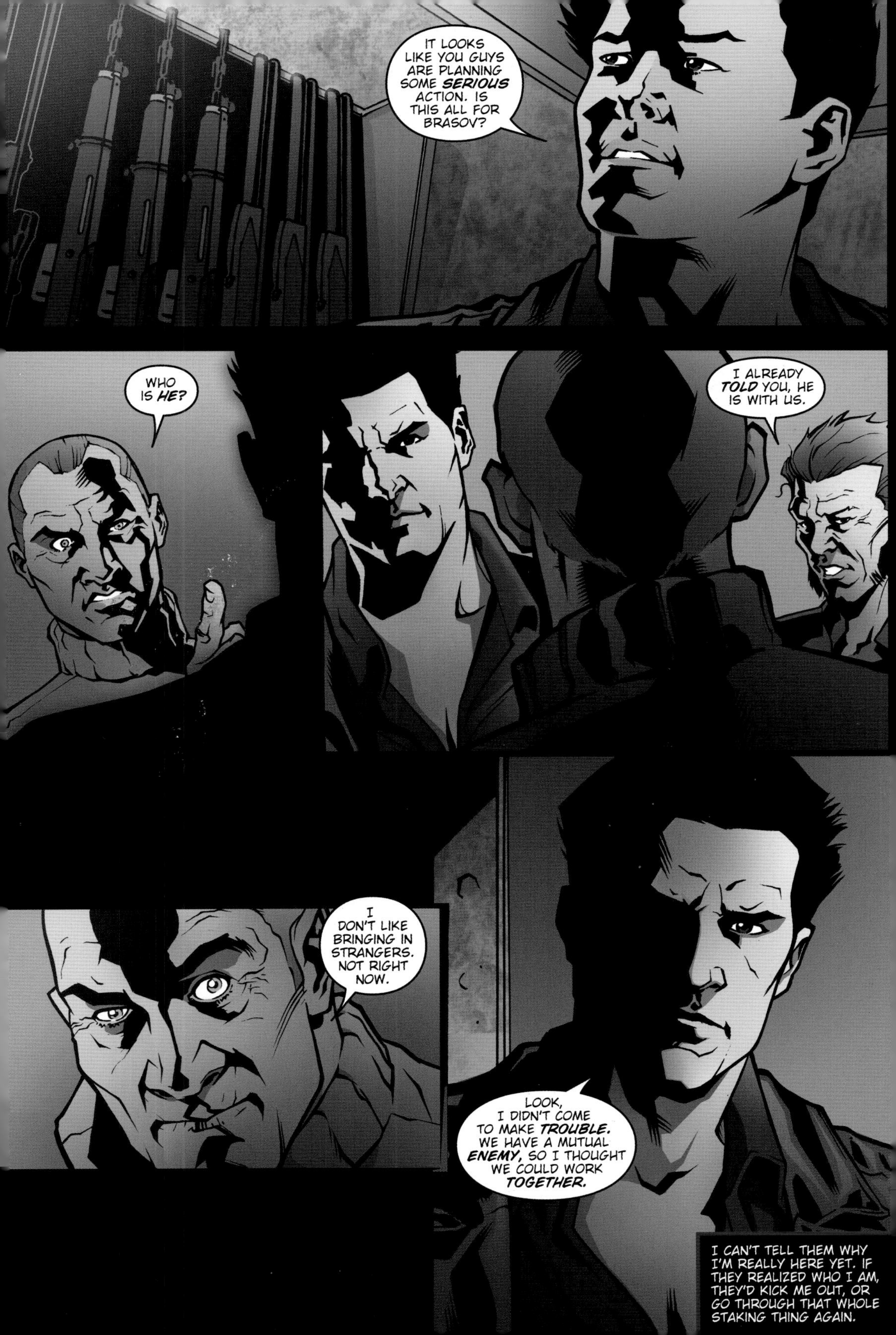

IT LOOKS LIKE YOU GUYS ARE PLANNING SOME SERIOUS ACTION. IS THIS ALL FOR BRASOV?
WHO IS HE?
I ALREADY TOLD YOU, HE IS WITH US.
I DON'T LIKE BRINGING IN STRANGERS. NOT RIGHT NOW.
LOOK, I DIDN'T COME TO MAKE TROUBLE. WE HAVE A MUTUAL ENEMY, SO I THOUGHT WE COULD WORK TOGETHER.
I CAN'T TELL THEM WHY I'M REALLY HERE YET. IF THEY REALIZED WHO I AM, THEY'D KICK ME OUT, OR GO THROUGH THAT WHOLE STAKING THING AGAIN.

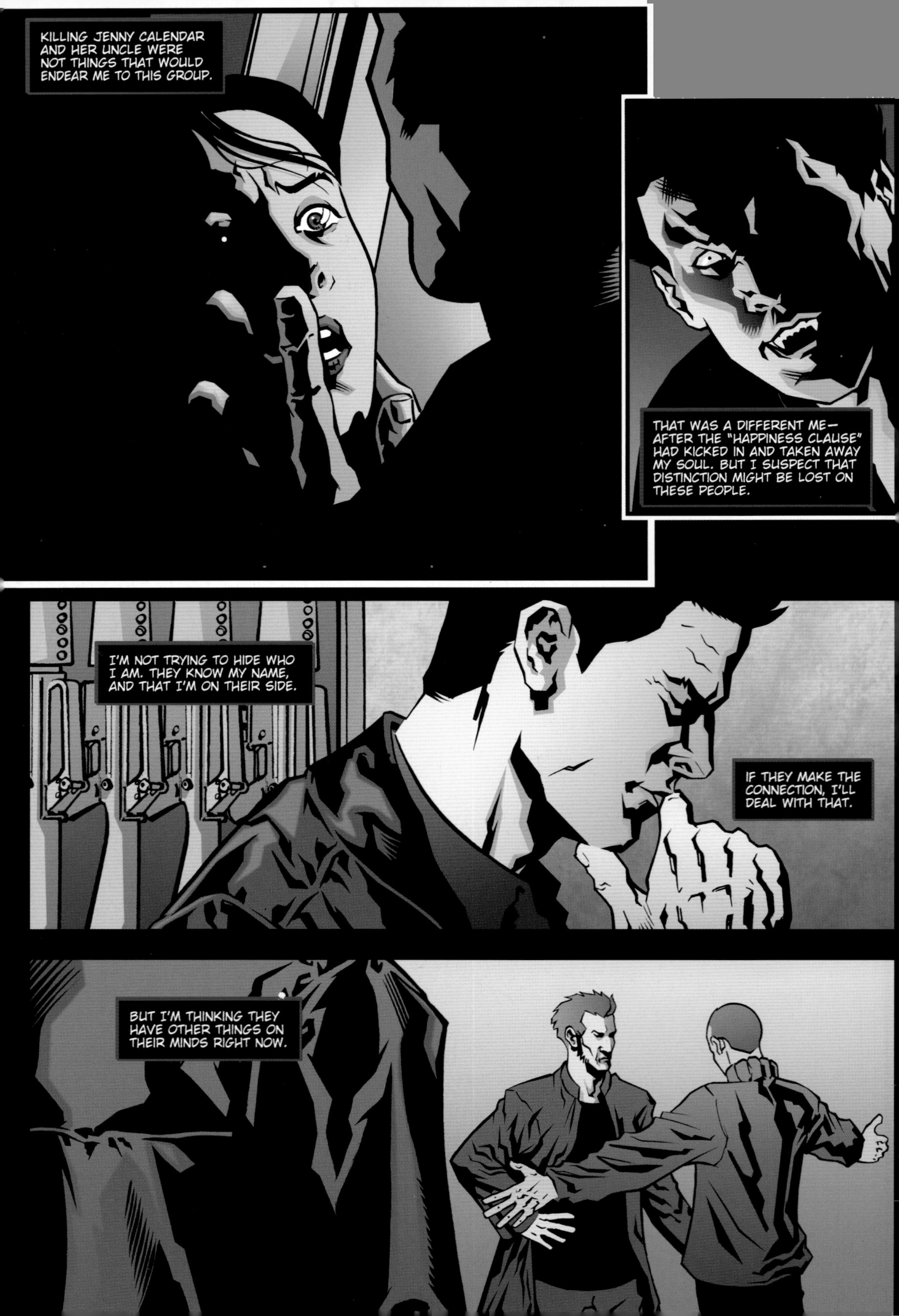
KILLING JENNY CALENDAR AND HER UNCLE WERE NOT THINGS THAT WOULD ENDEAR ME TO THIS GROUP.
THAT WAS A DIFFERENT ME— AFTER THE "HAPPINESS CLAUSE" HAD KICKED IN AND TAKEN AWAY MY SOUL. BUT I SUSPECT THAT DISTINCTION MIGHT BE LOST ON THESE PEOPLE.
I'M NOT TRYING TO HIDE WHO I AM. THEY KNOW MY NAME, AND THAT I'M ON THEIR SIDE.
IF THEY MAKE THE CONNECTION, I'LL DEAL WITH THAT.
BUT I'M THINKING THEY HAVE OTHER THINGS ON THEIR MINDS RIGHT NOW.

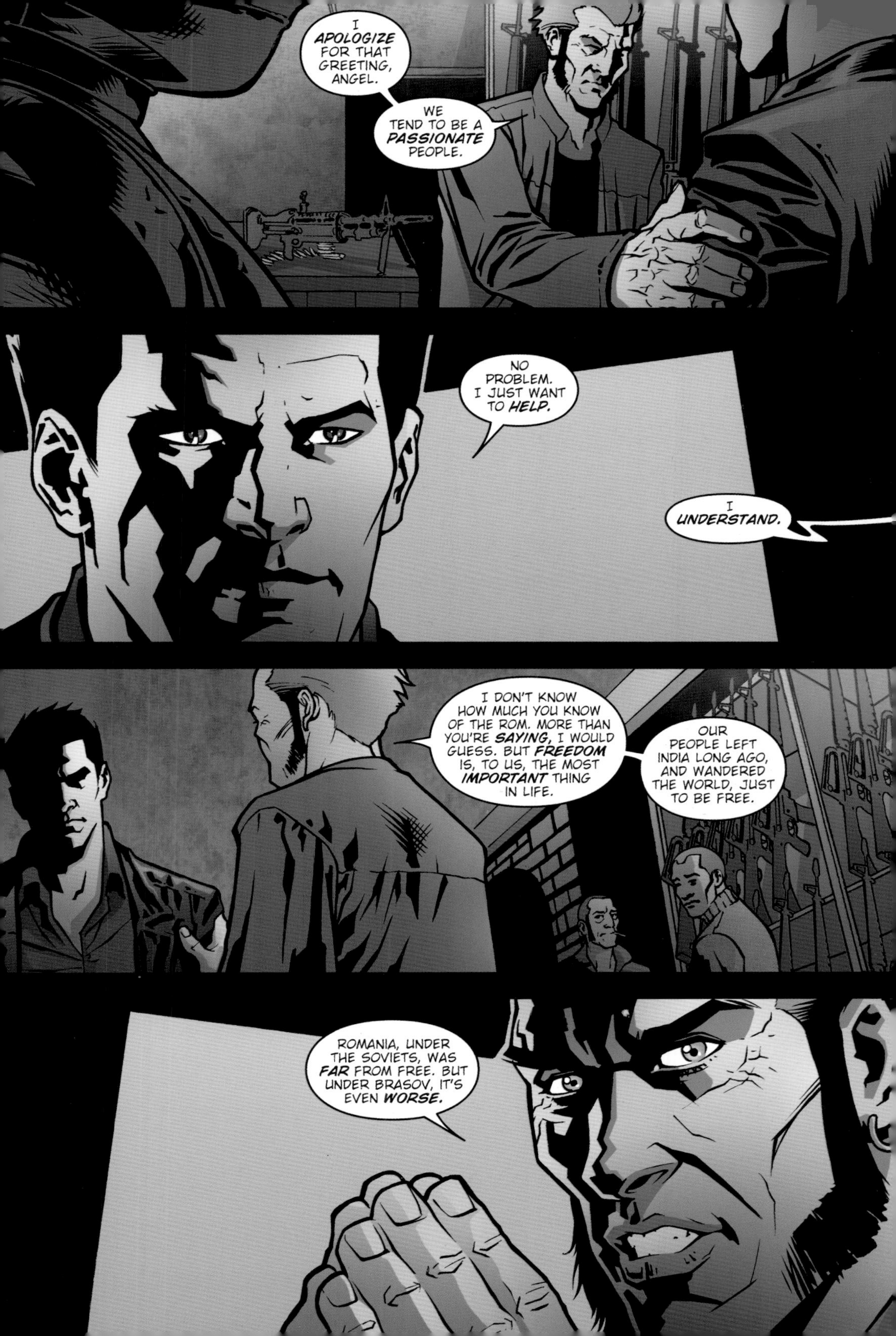
I APOLOGIZE FOR THAT GREETING, ANGEL.
WE TEND TO BE A PASSIONATE PEOPLE.
NO PROBLEM. I JUST WANT TO HELP.
I UNDERSTAND.
I DON'T KNOW HOW MUCH YOU KNOW OF THE ROM. MORE THAN YOU'RE SAYING, I WOULD GUESS. BUT FREEDOM IS, TO US, THE MOST IMPORTANT THING IN LIFE.
OUR PEOPLE LEFT INDIA LONG AGO, AND WANDERED THE WORLD, JUST TO BE FREE.
ROMANIA, UNDER THE SOVIETS, WAS FAR FROM FREE. BUT UNDER BRASOV, IT'S EVEN WORSE.

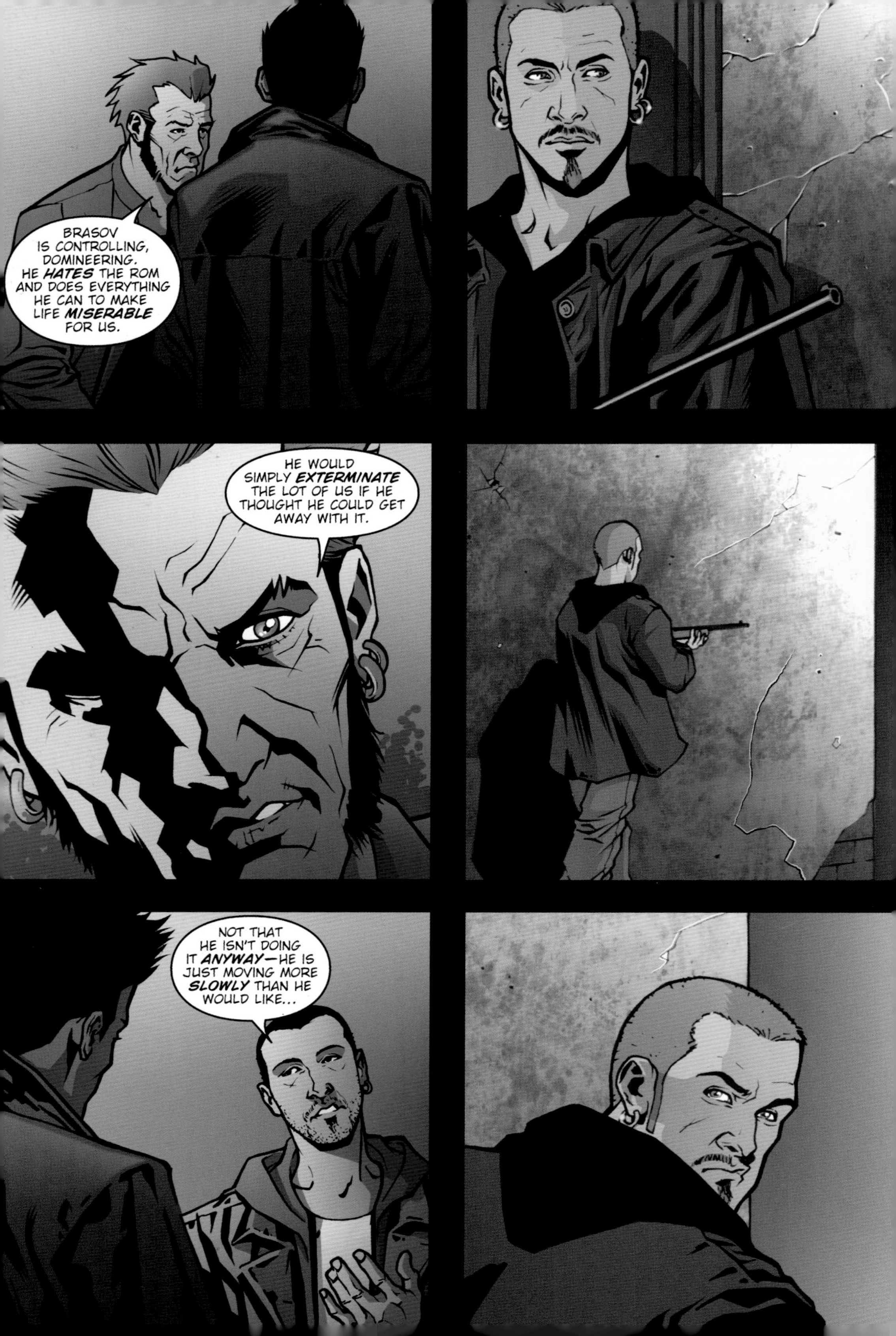
BRASOV IS CONTROLLING, DOMINEERING. HE HATES THE ROM AND DOES EVERYTHING HE CAN TO MAKE LIFE MISERABLE FOR US.
HE WOULD SIMPLY EXTERMINATE THE LOT OF US IF HE THOUGHT HE COULD GET AWAY WITH IT.
NOT THAT HE ISN'T DOING IT ANYWAY—HE IS JUST MOVING MORE SLOWLY THAN HE WOULD LIKE...

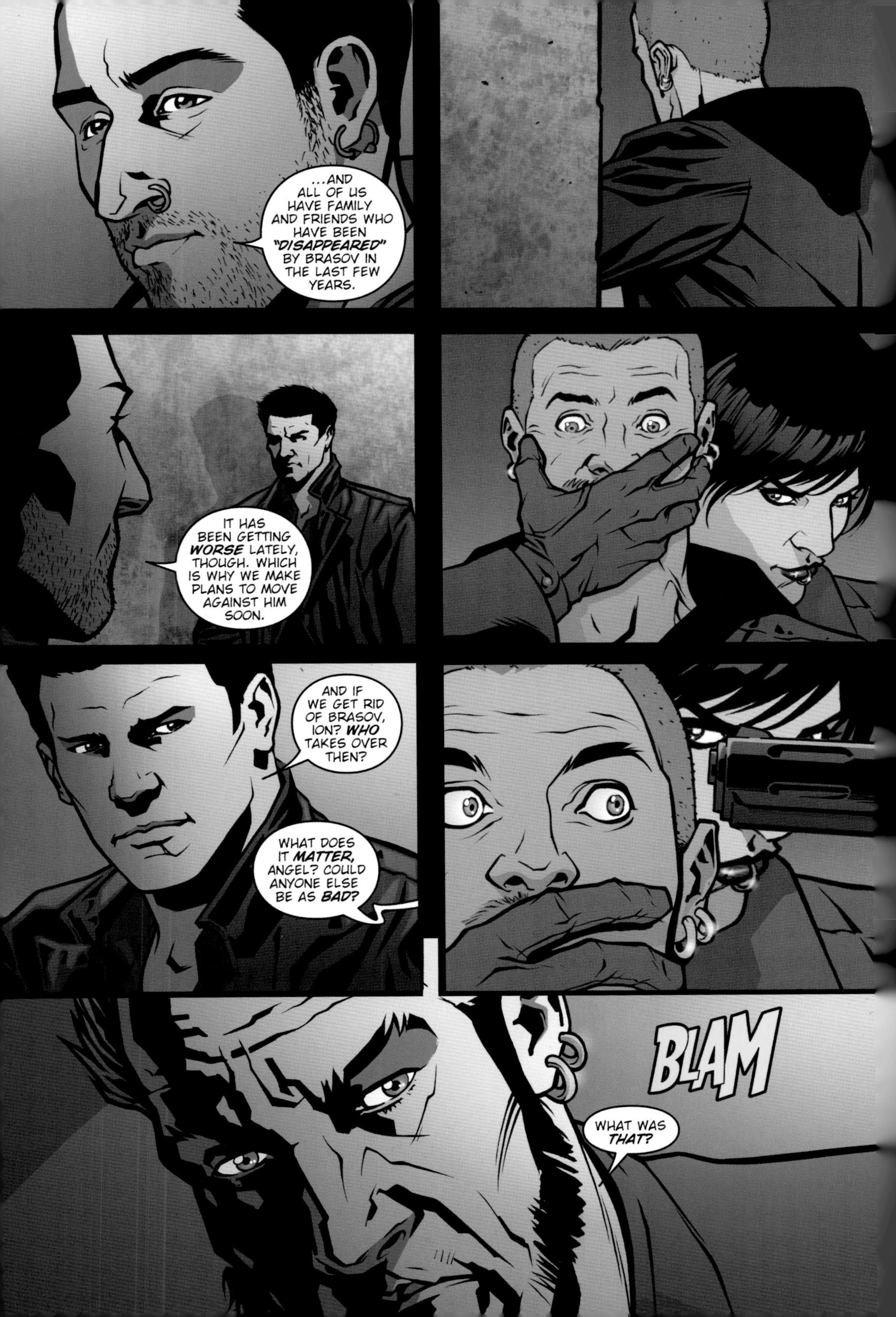
...AND ALL OF US HAVE FAMILY AND FRIENDS WHO HAVE BEEN "DISAPPEARED" BY BRASOV IN THE LAST FEW YEARS.
IT HAS BEEN GETTING WORSE LATELY, THOUGH. WHICH IS WHY WE MAKE PLANS TO MOVE AGAINST HIM SOON.
AND IF WE GET RID OF BRASOV, ION? WHO TAKES OVER THEN?
WHAT DOES IT MATTER, ANGEL? COULD ANYONE ELSE BE AS BAD?
BLAM
WHAT WAS THAT?

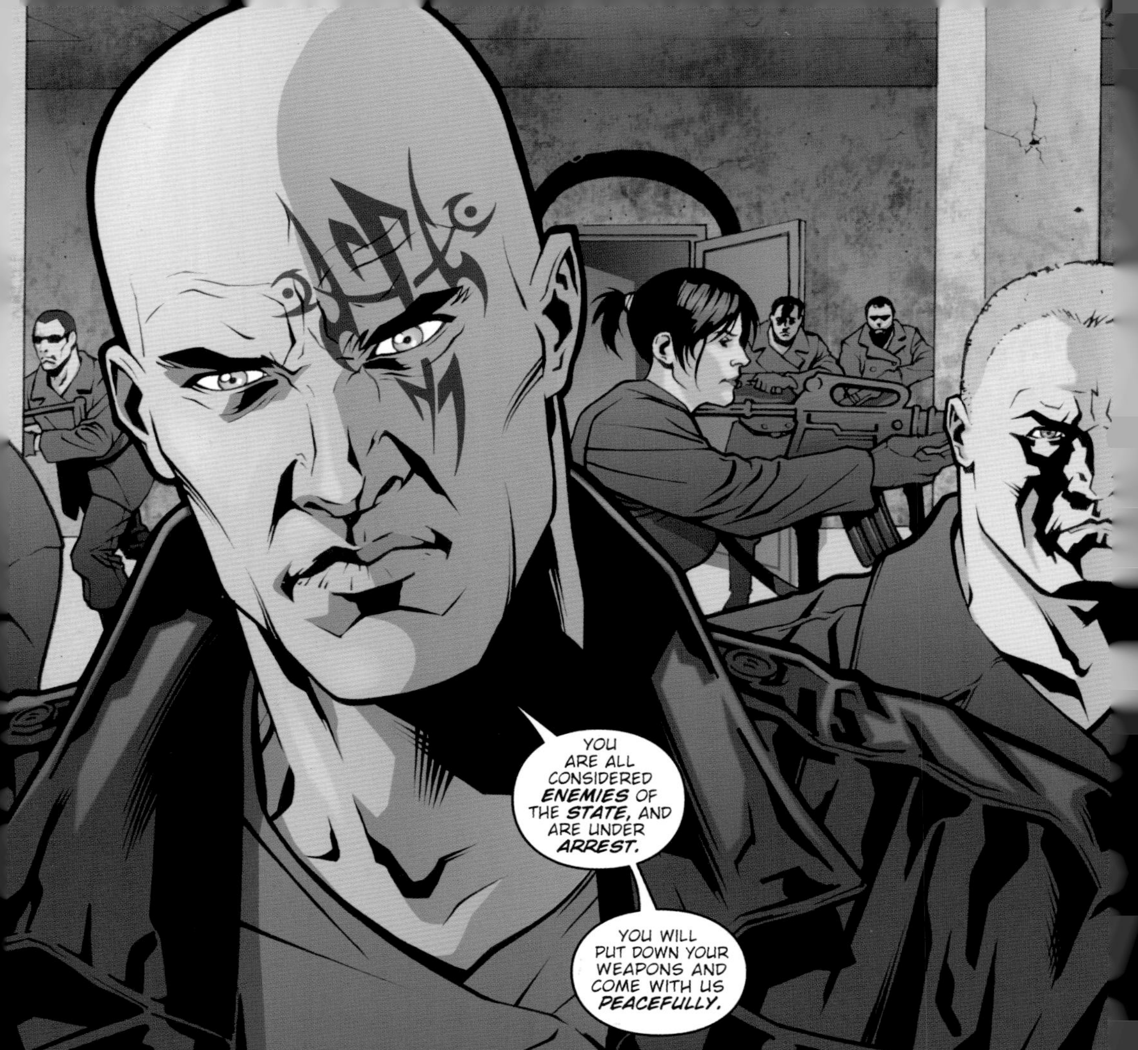
YOU ARE ALL CONSIDERED ENEMIES OF THE STATE, AND ARE UNDER ARREST.
YOU WILL PUT DOWN YOUR WEAPONS AND COME WITH US PEACEFULLY.

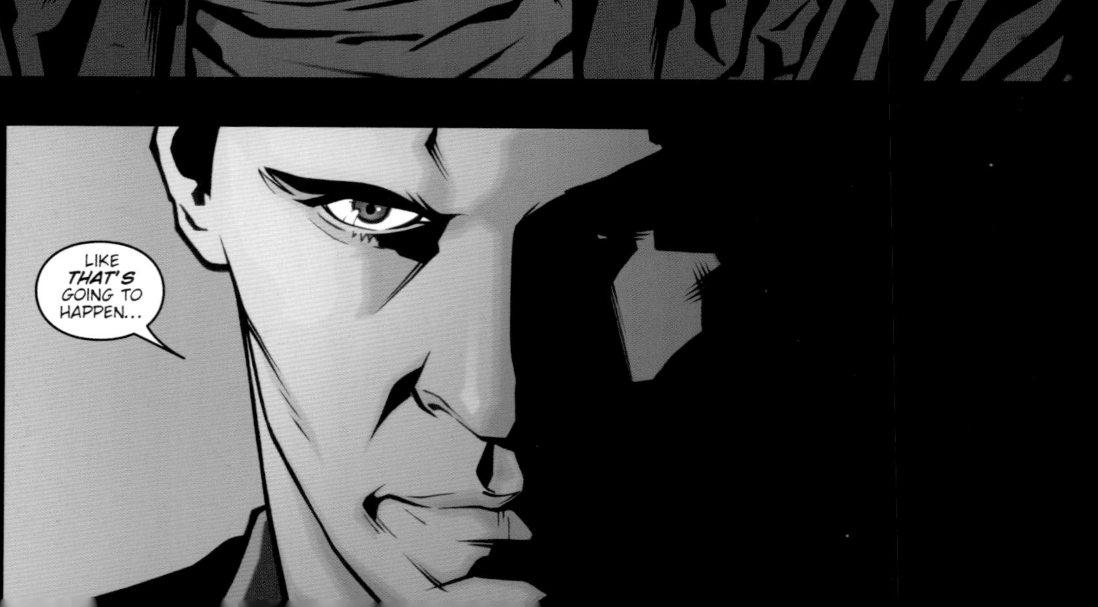
LIKE THAT'S GOING TO HAPPEN...

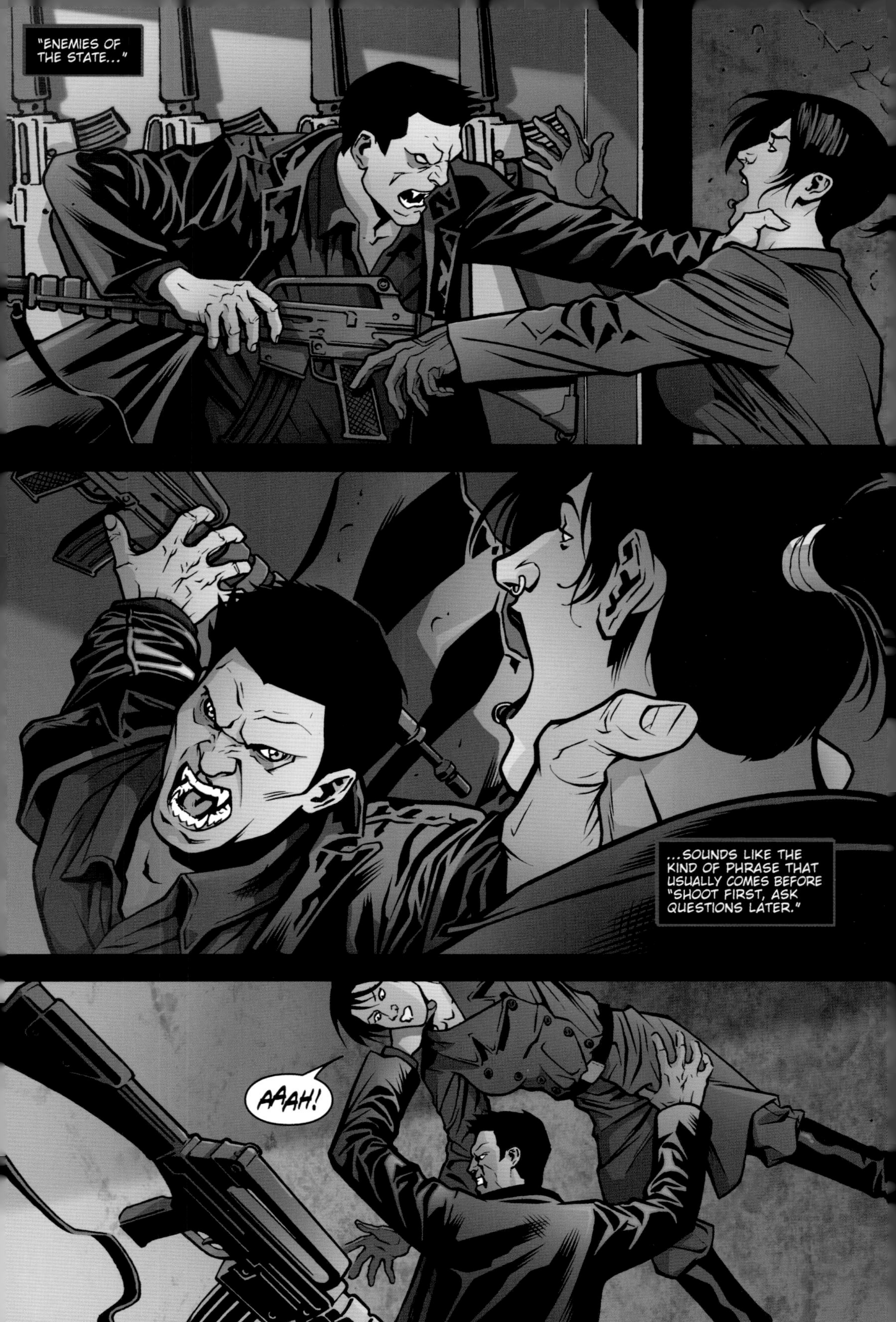
"ENEMIES OF THE STATE..."
...SOUNDS LIKE THE KIND OF PHRASE THAT USUALLY COMES BEFORE "SHOOT FIRST, ASK QUESTIONS LATER."
AAAH!

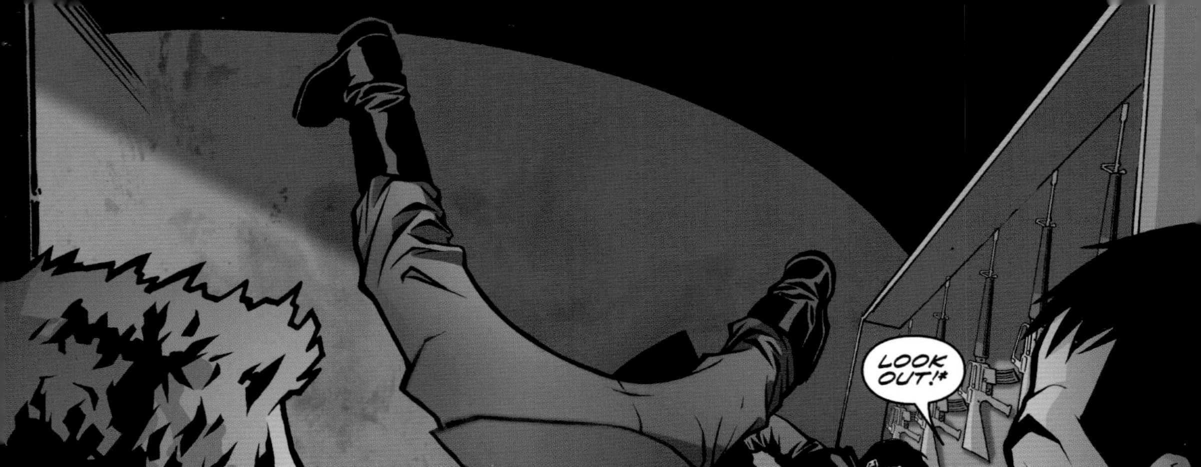
LOOK OUT!*
*ALL DIALOGUE TRANSLATED FROM THE ROMANIAN—ED.

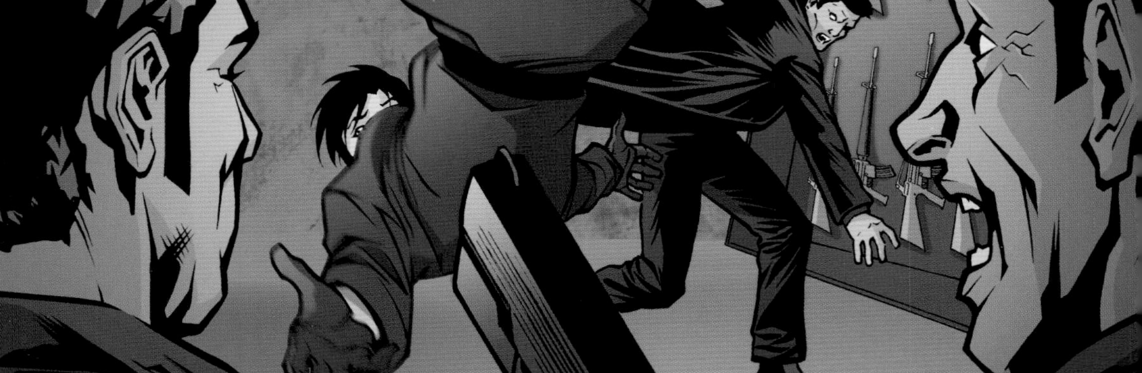
HEY!
OUT OF THE WAY!

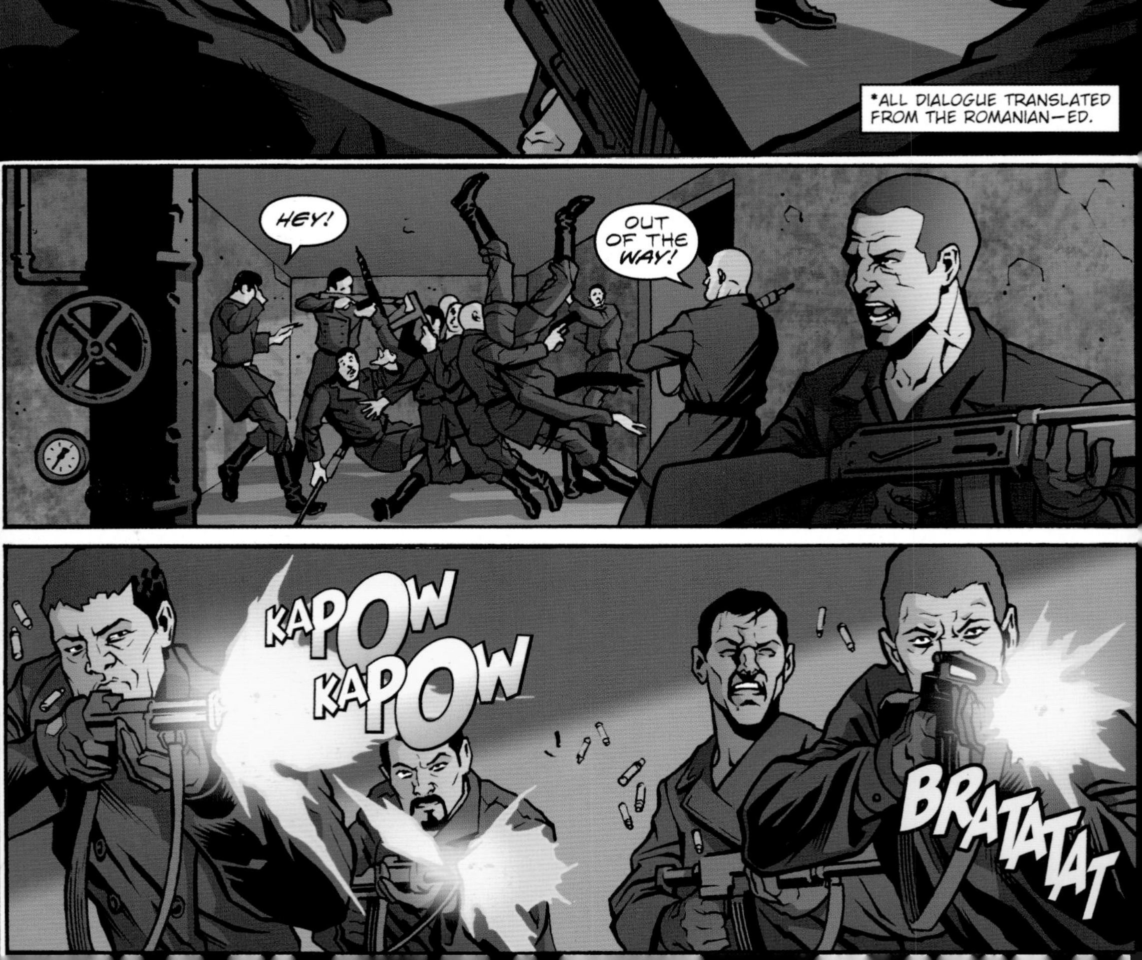
KAPOW KAPOW
BRATATAT

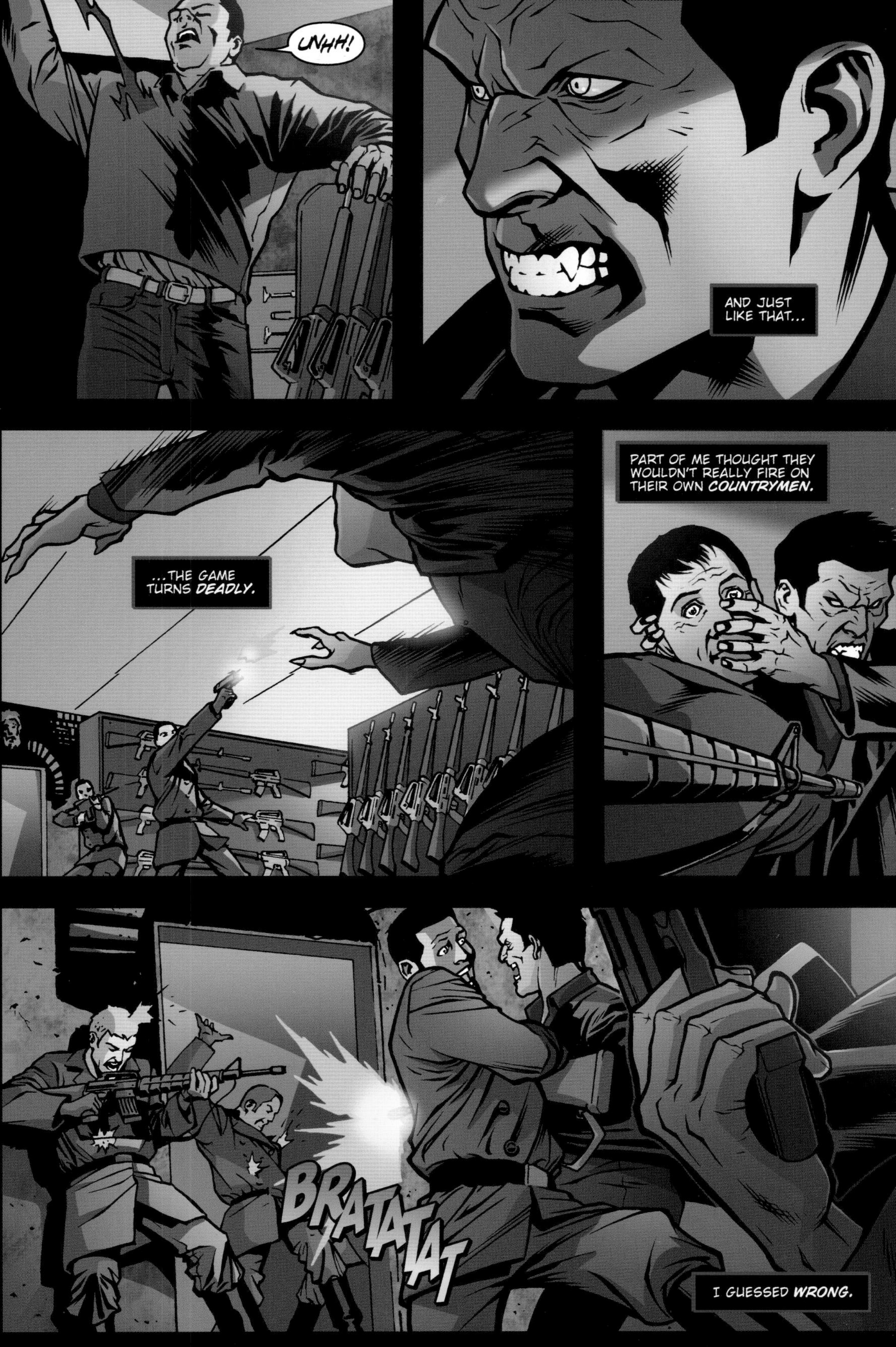
UNHH!
AND JUST LIKE THAT...
...THE GAME TURNS DEADLY.
PART OF ME THOUGHT THEY WOULDN'T REALLY FIRE ON THEIR OWN COUNTRYMEN.
BRATATATAT
I GUESSED WRONG.

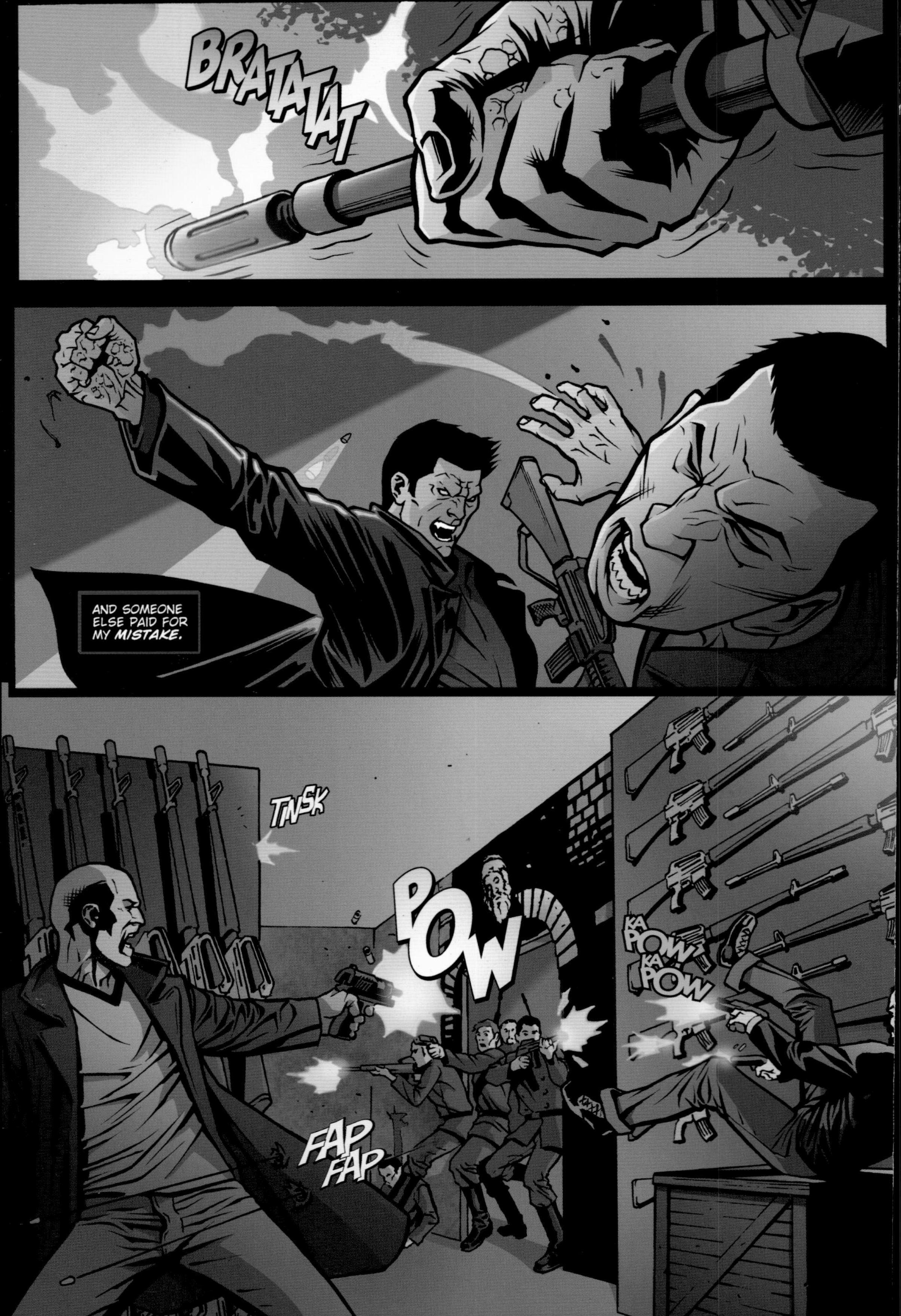
BRATATATAT
AND SOMEONE ELSE PAID FOR MY MISTAKE.
TINSK
POW
KA POW KA POW
FAP FAP

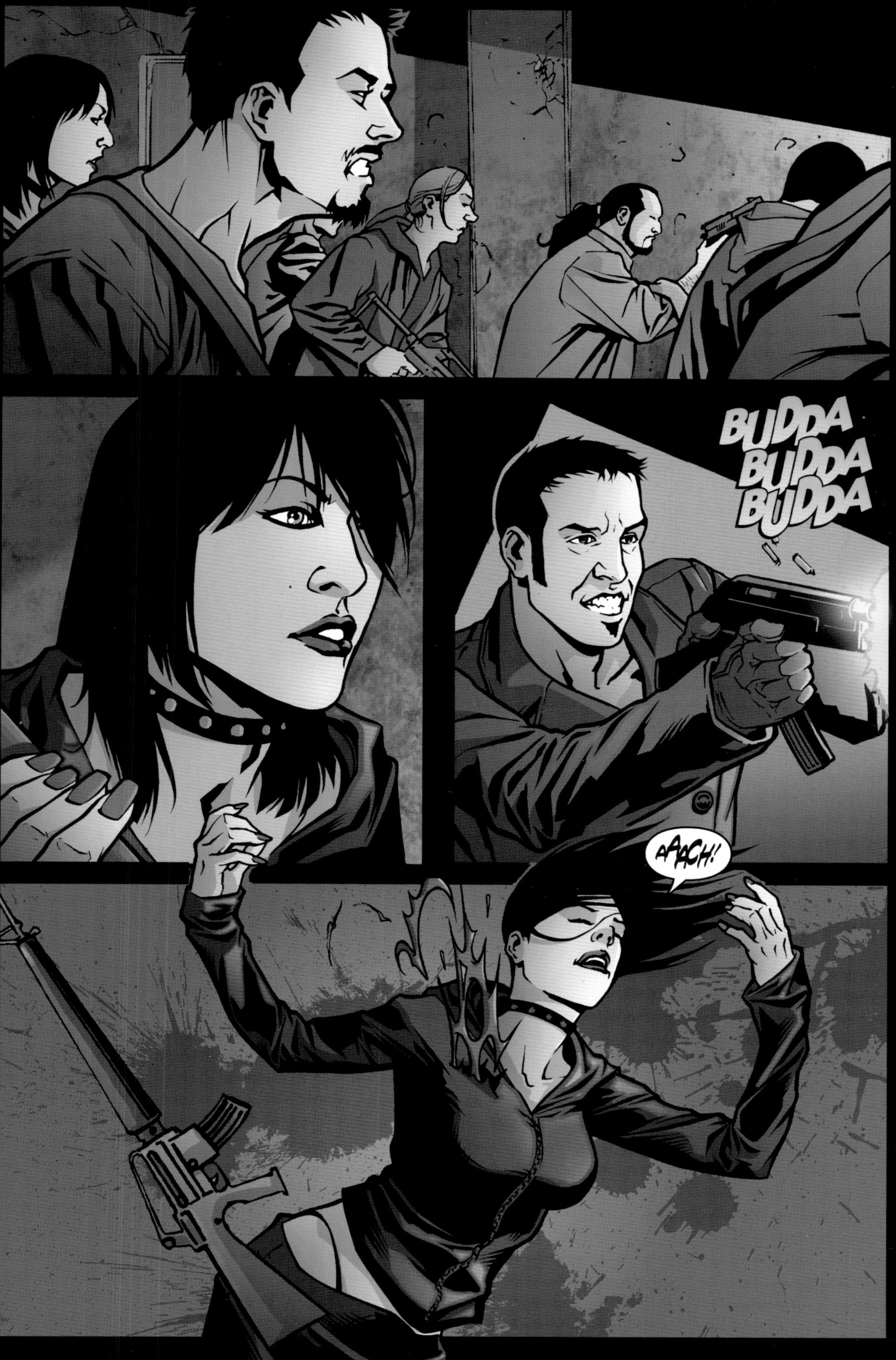

BUDDA
BUDDA
BUDDA
AAACH!

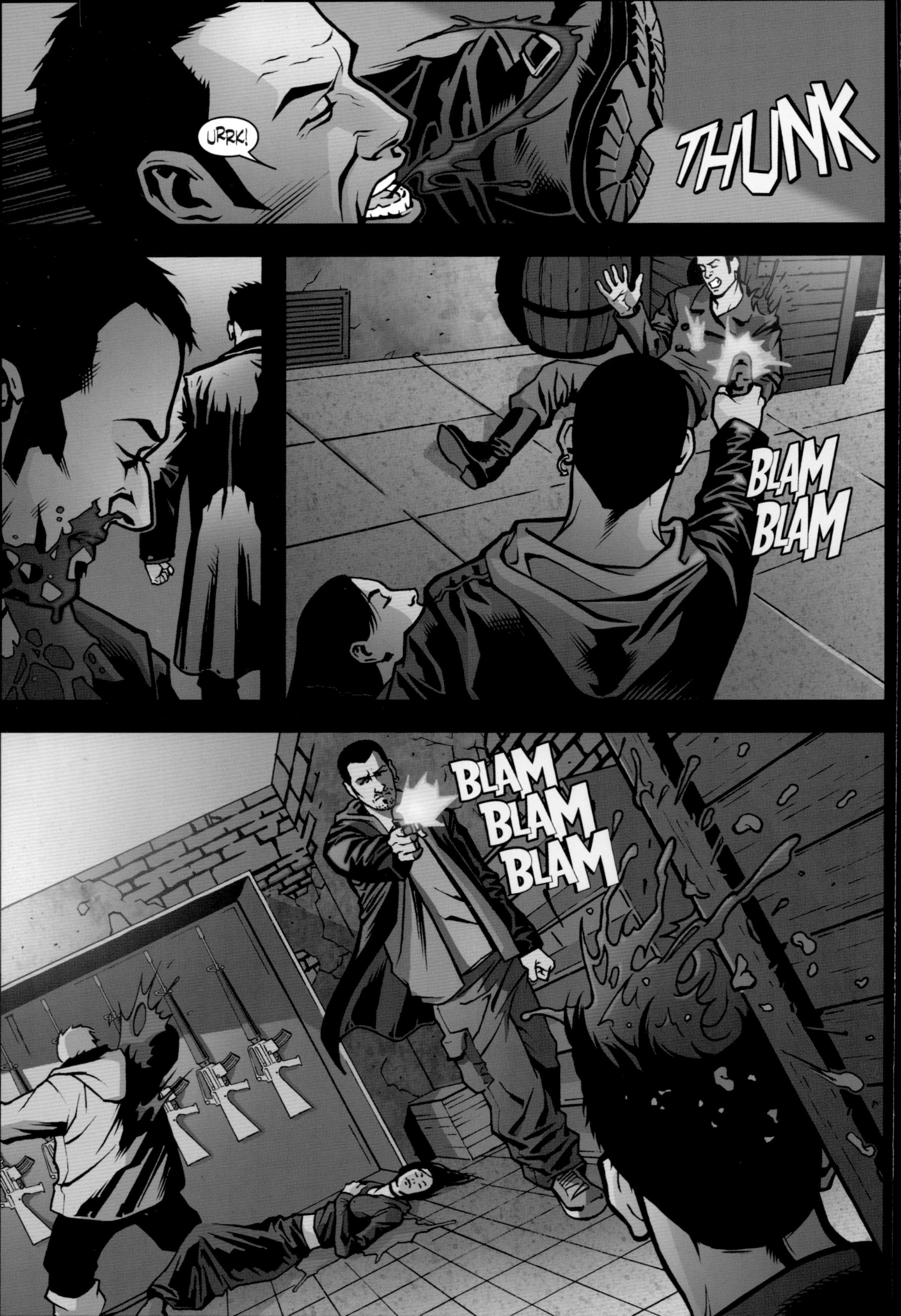
URRK!
THUNK
BLAM
BLAM
BLAM
BLAM
BLAM

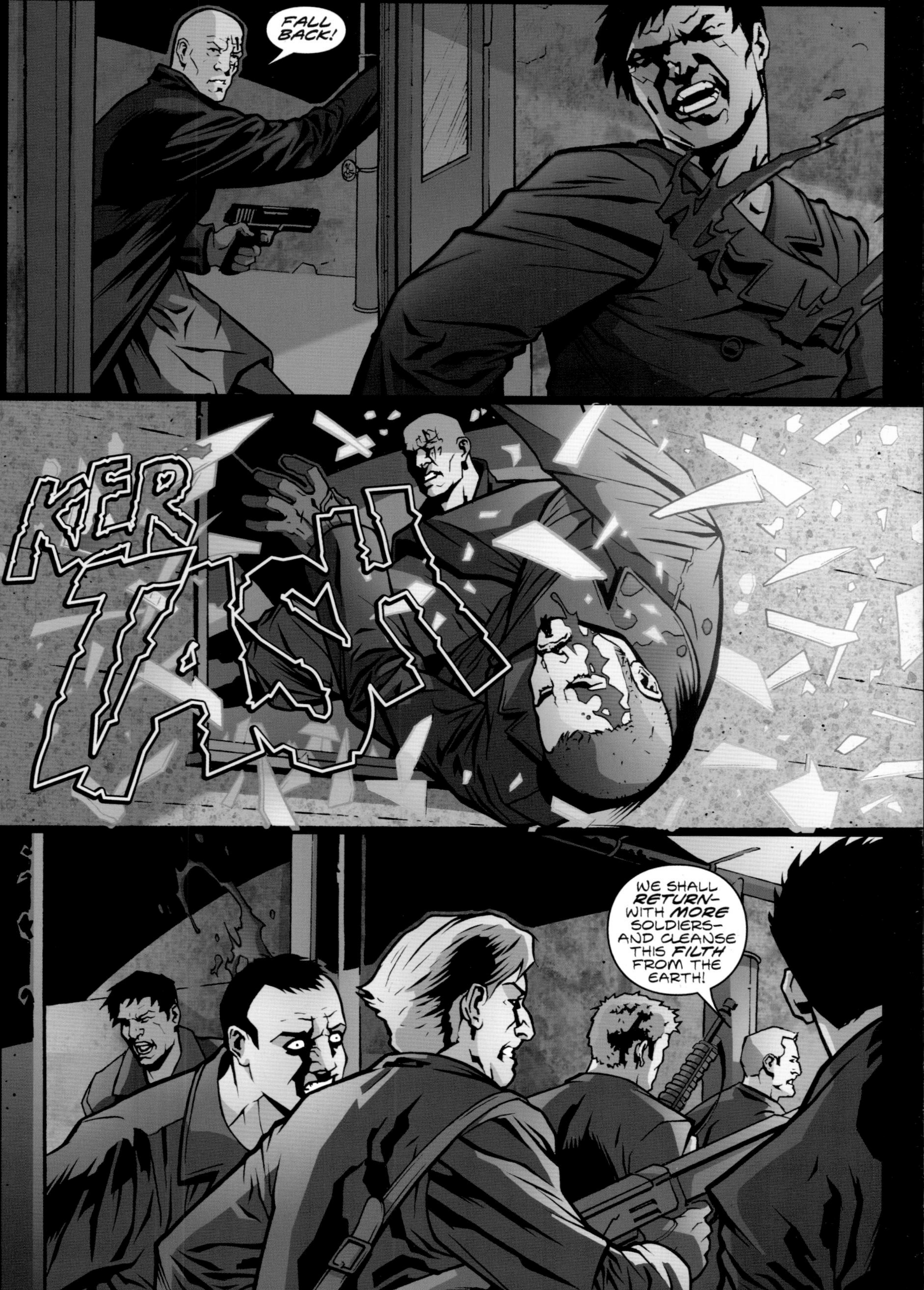
FALL BACK!
KER TASH
WE SHALL RETURN-WITH MORE SOLDIERS-AND CLEANSE THIS FILTH FROM THE EARTH!

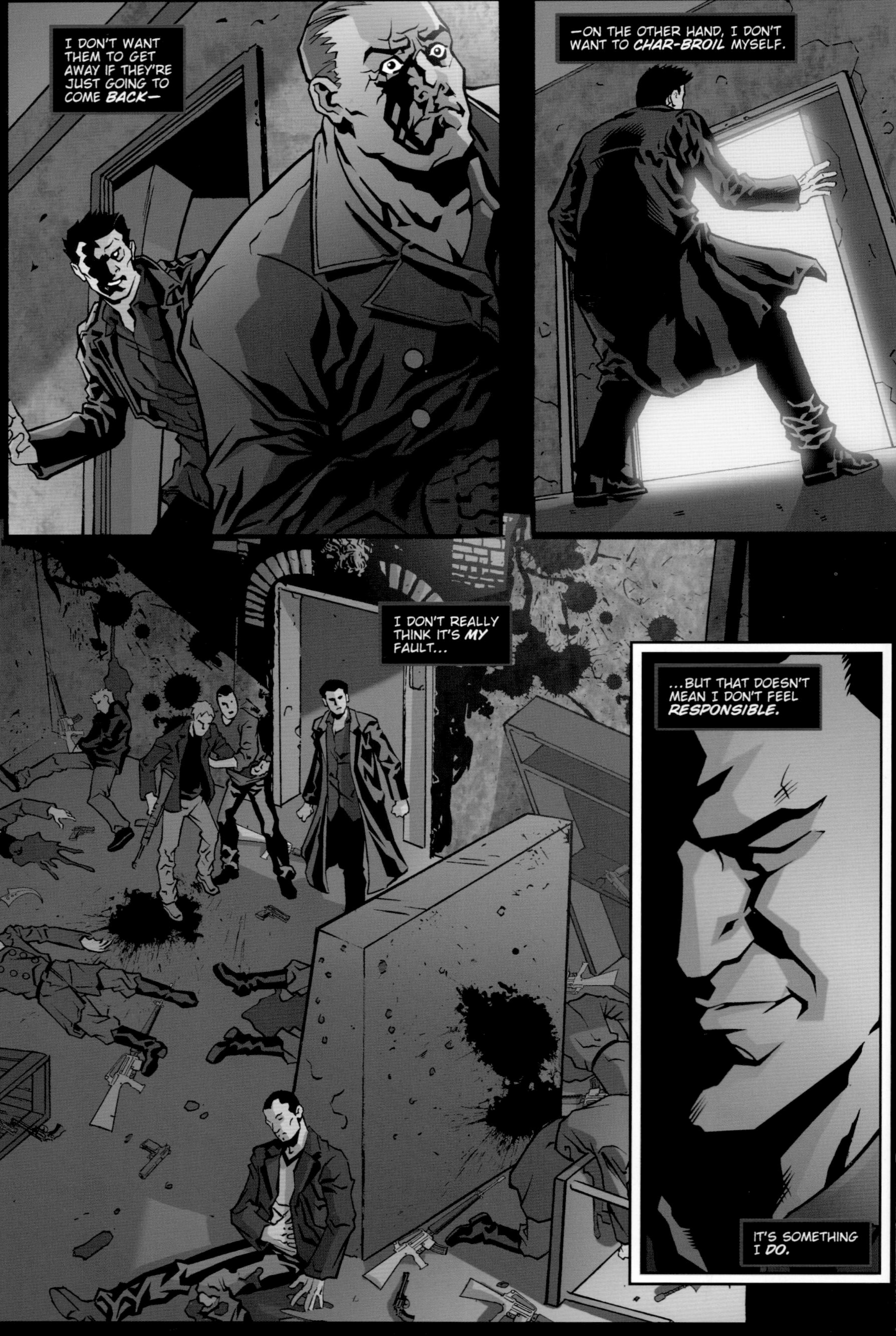
I DON'T WANT THEM TO GET AWAY IF THEY'RE JUST GOING TO COME BACK—
—ON THE OTHER HAND, I DON'T WANT TO CHAR-BROIL MYSELF.
I DON'T REALLY THINK IT'S MY FAULT...
...BUT THAT DOESN'T MEAN I DON'T FEEL RESPONSIBLE.
IT'S SOMETHING I DO.

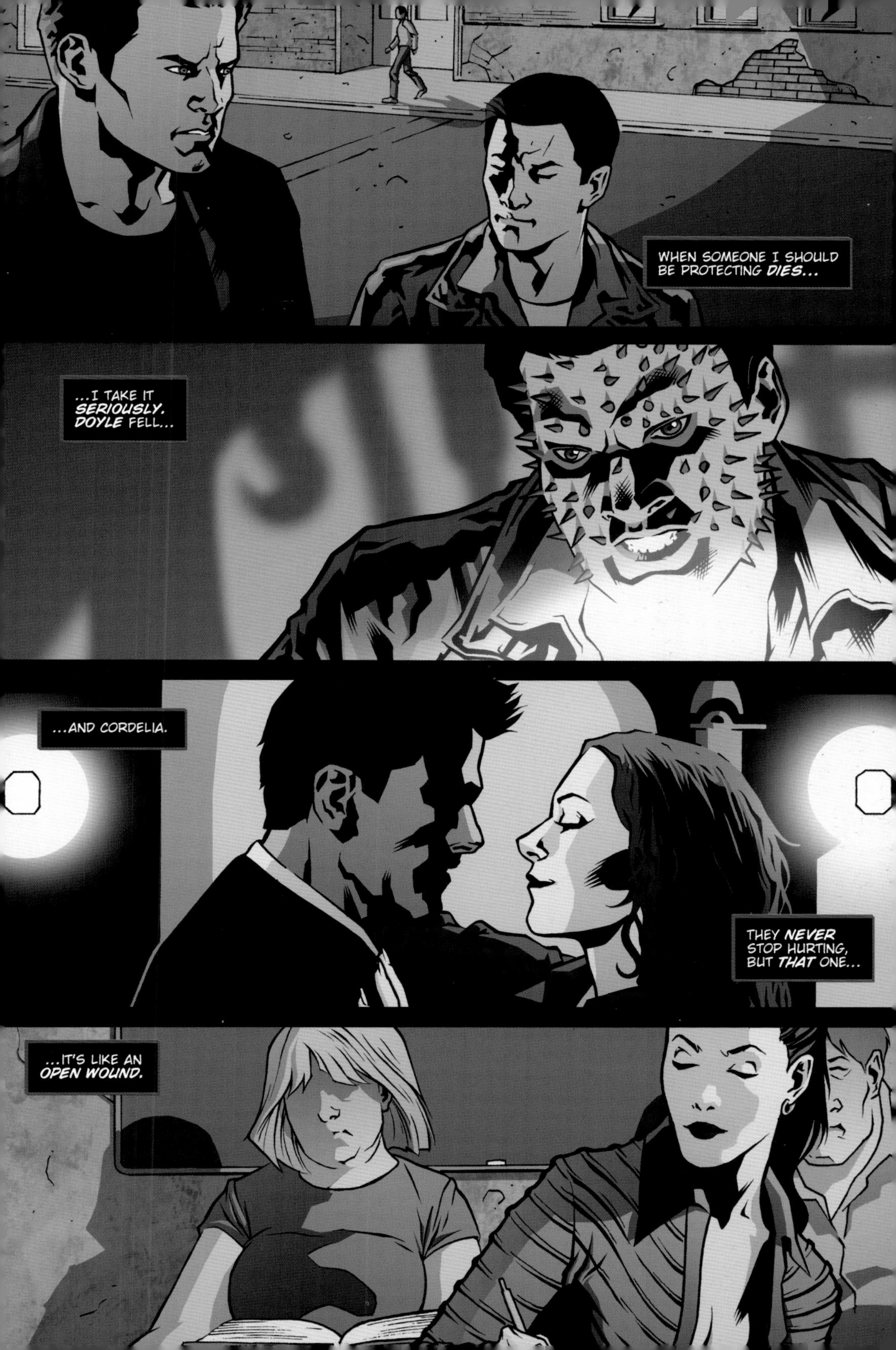
WHEN SOMEONE I SHOULD BE PROTECTING DIES...
...I TAKE IT SERIOUSLY. DOYLE FELL...
...AND CORDELIA.
THEY NEVER STOP HURTING, BUT THAT ONE...
...IT'S LIKE AN OPEN WOUND.

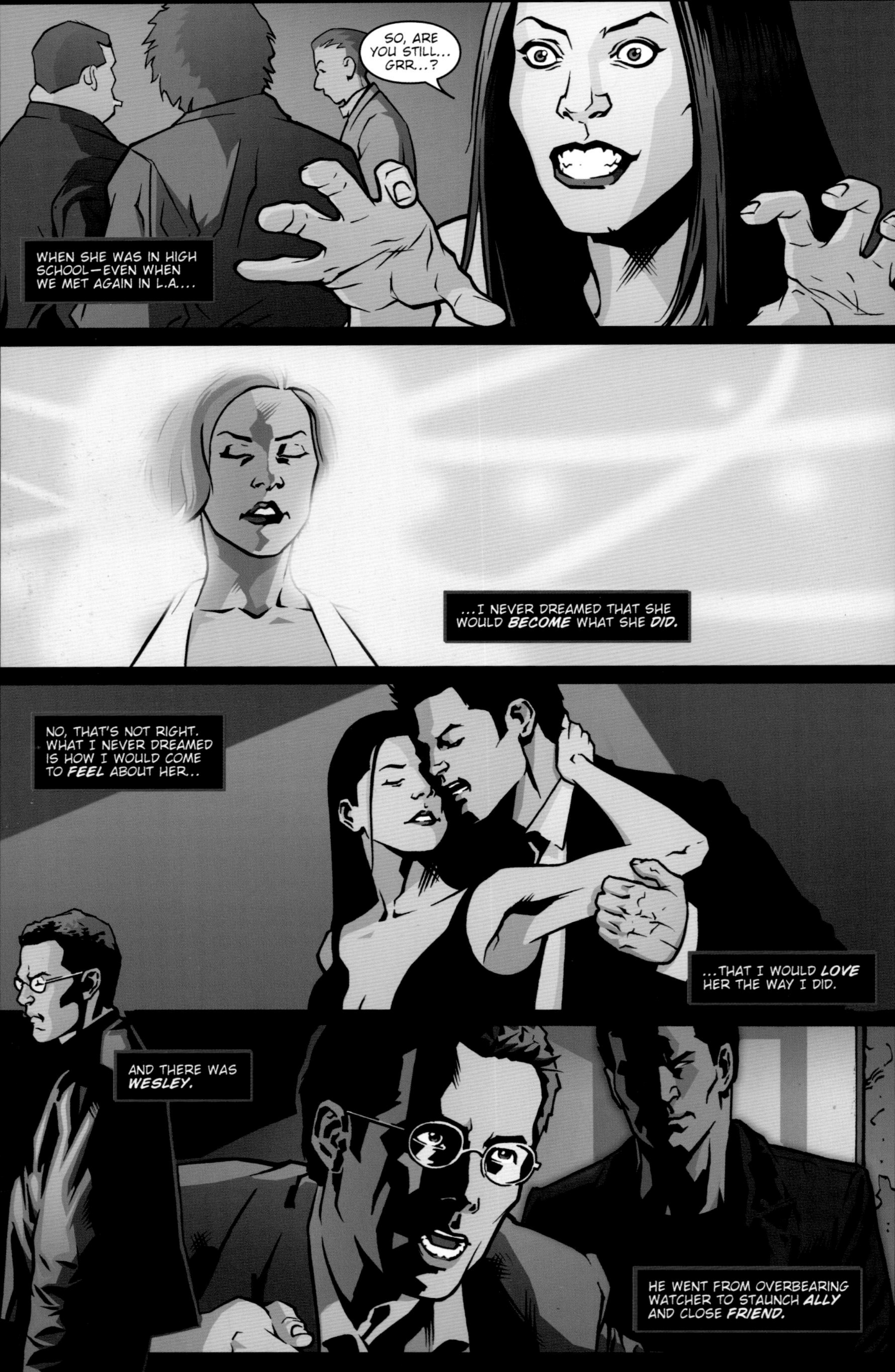
SO, ARE YOU STILL... GRR...?
WHEN SHE WAS IN HIGH SCHOOL—EVEN WHEN WE MET AGAIN IN L.A....
...I NEVER DREAMED THAT SHE WOULD BECOME WHAT SHE DID.
NO, THAT'S NOT RIGHT. WHAT I NEVER DREAMED IS HOW I WOULD COME TO FEEL ABOUT HER...
...THAT I WOULD LOVE HER THE WAY I DID.
AND THERE WAS WESLEY.
HE WENT FROM OVERBEARING WATCHER TO STAUNCH ALLY AND CLOSE FRIEND.

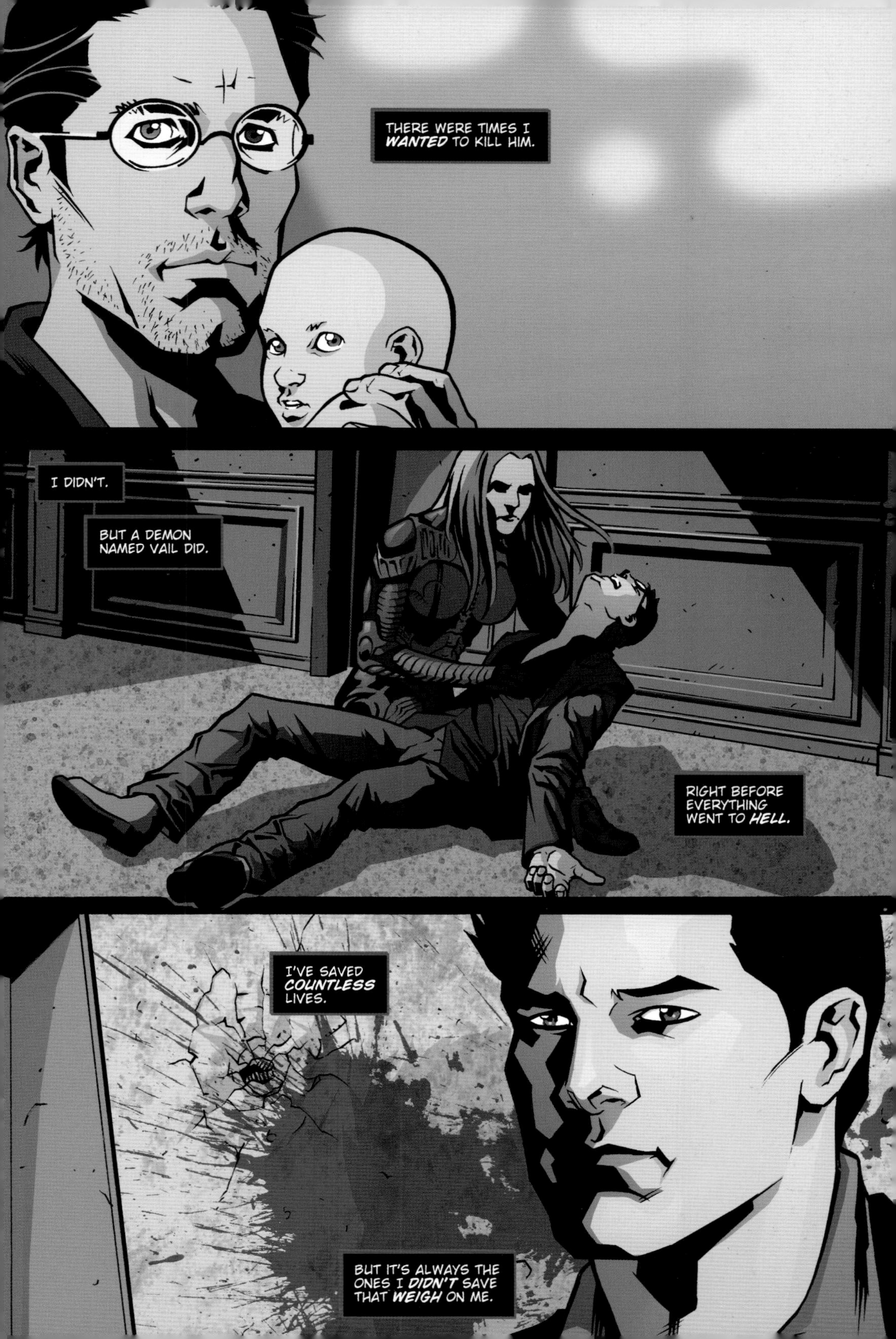
THERE WERE TIMES I *WANTED* TO KILL HIM.
I DIDN'T.
BUT A DEMON NAMED VAIL DID.
RIGHT BEFORE EVERYTHING WENT TO *HELL.*
I'VE SAVED *COUNTLESS* LIVES.
BUT IT'S ALWAYS THE ONES I *DIDN'T* SAVE THAT *WEIGH* ON ME.

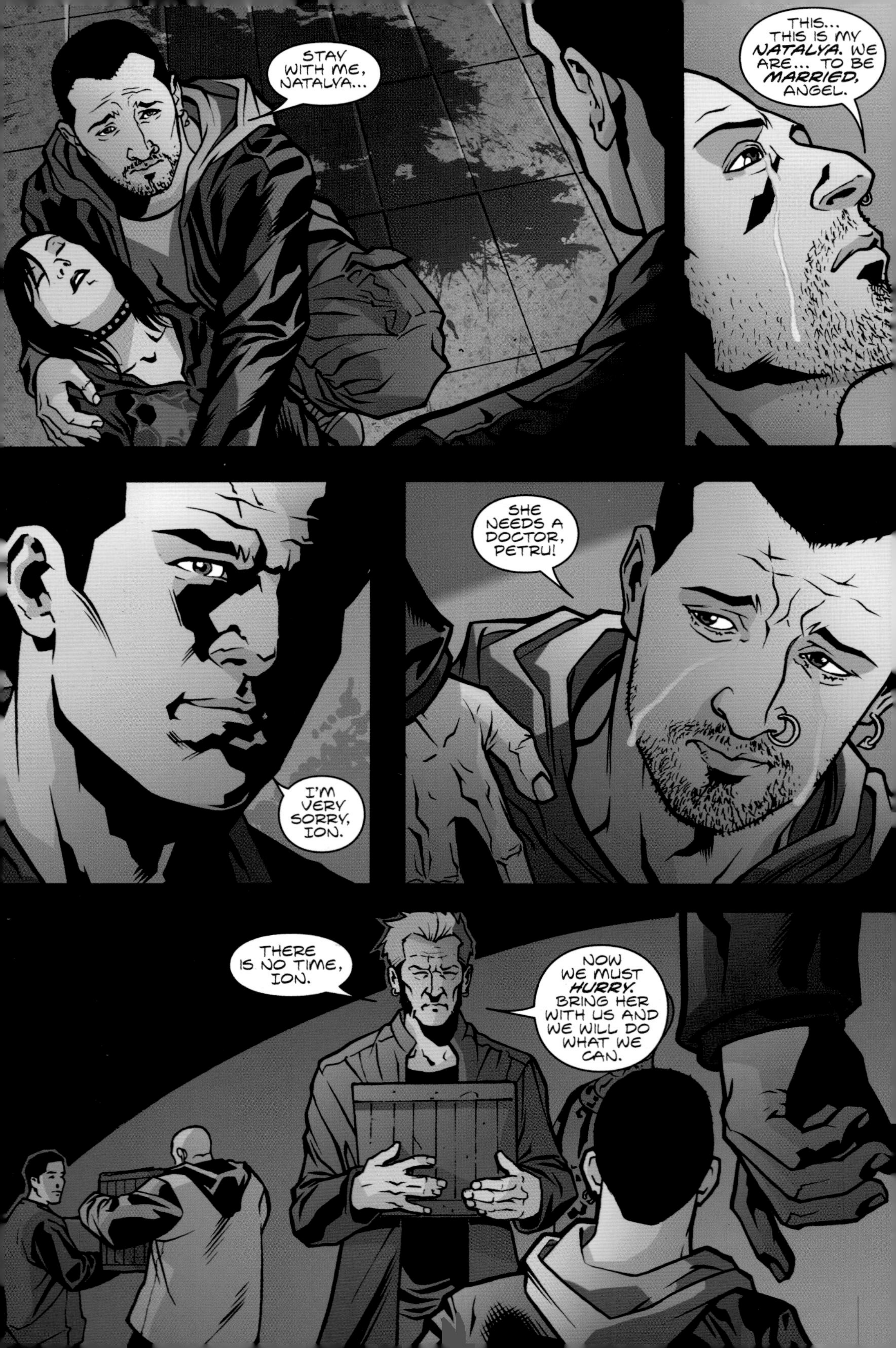
STAY WITH ME, NATALYA...
THIS... THIS IS MY NATALYA. WE ARE... TO BE MARRIED, ANGEL.
I'M VERY SORRY, ION.
SHE NEEDS A DOCTOR, PETRU!
THERE IS NO TIME, ION.
NOW WE MUST HURRY. BRING HER WITH US AND WE WILL DO WHAT WE CAN.

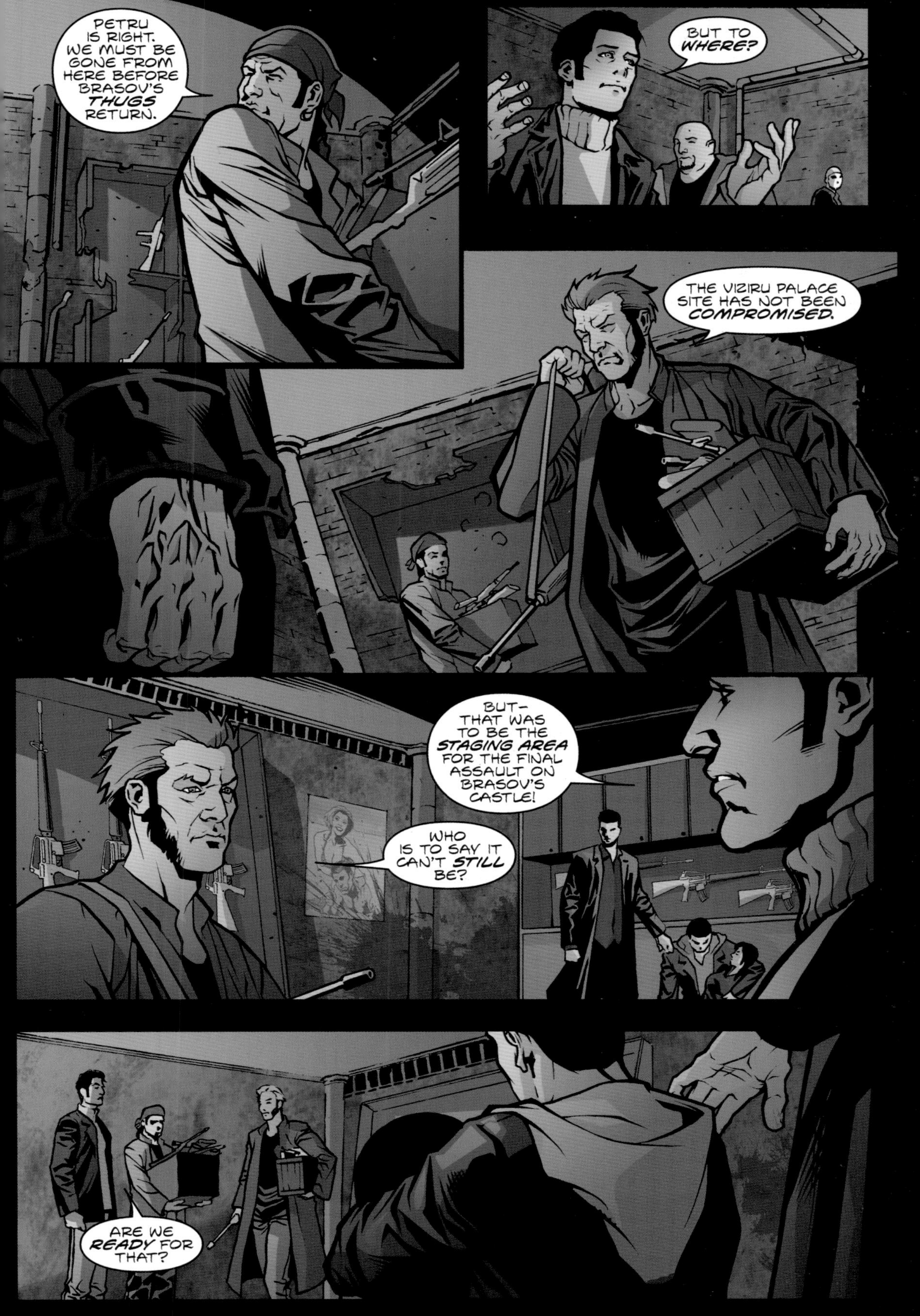
PETRU IS RIGHT. WE MUST BE GONE FROM HERE BEFORE BRASOV'S THUGS RETURN.
BUT TO WHERE?
THE VIZIRU PALACE SITE HAS NOT BEEN COMPROMISED.
BUT— THAT WAS TO BE THE STAGING AREA FOR THE FINAL ASSAULT ON BRASOV'S CASTLE!
WHO IS TO SAY IT CAN'T STILL BE?
ARE WE READY FOR THAT?

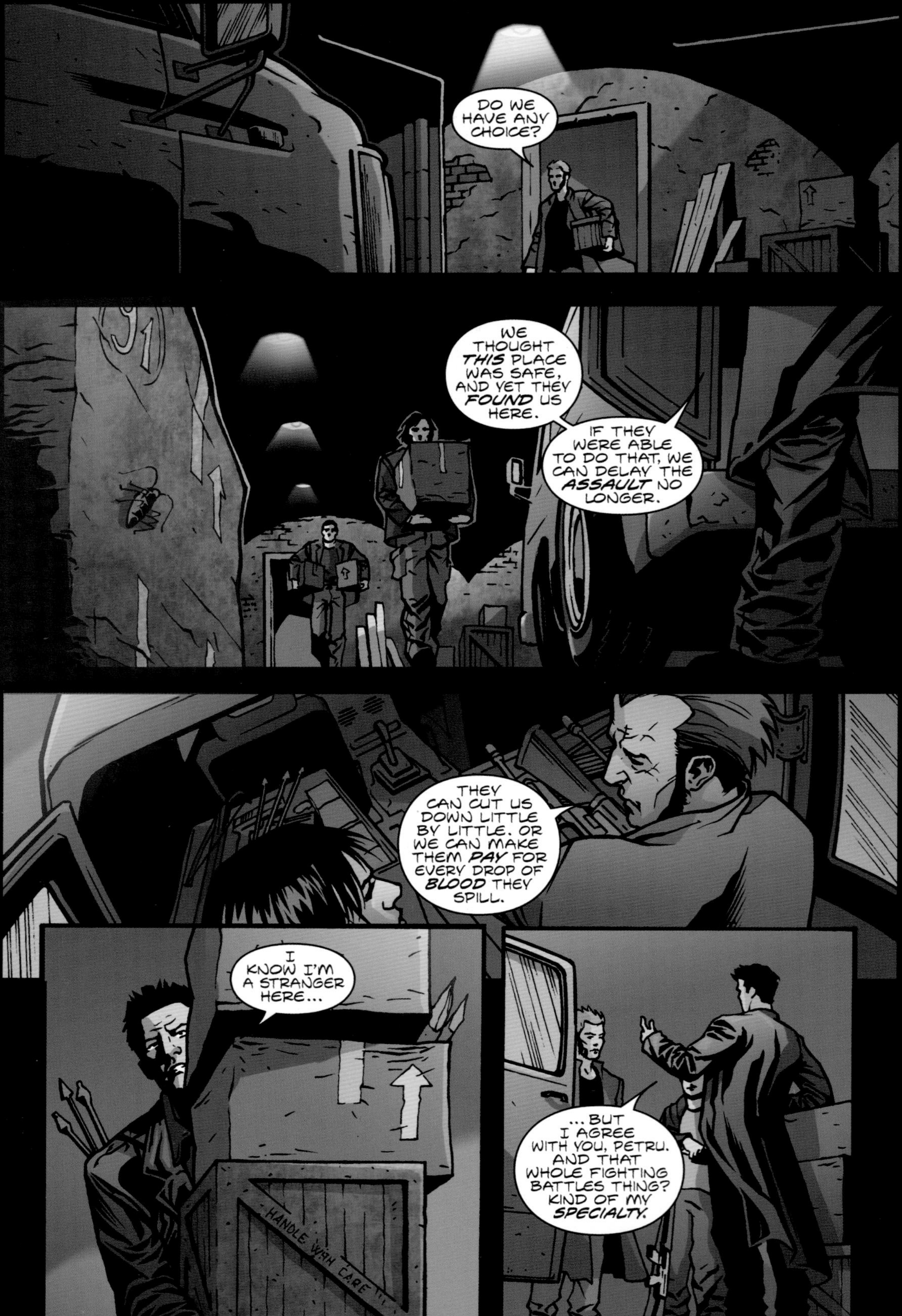
DO WE HAVE ANY CHOICE?
WE THOUGHT THIS PLACE WAS SAFE, AND YET THEY FOUND US HERE.
IF THEY WERE ABLE TO DO THAT, WE CAN DELAY THE ASSAULT NO LONGER.
THEY CAN CUT US DOWN LITTLE BY LITTLE. OR WE CAN MAKE THEM PAY FOR EVERY DROP OF BLOOD THEY SPILL.
I KNOW I'M A STRANGER HERE...
HANDLE WITH CARE
... BUT I AGREE WITH YOU, PETRU. AND THAT WHOLE FIGHTING BATTLES THING? KIND OF MY SPECIALTY.

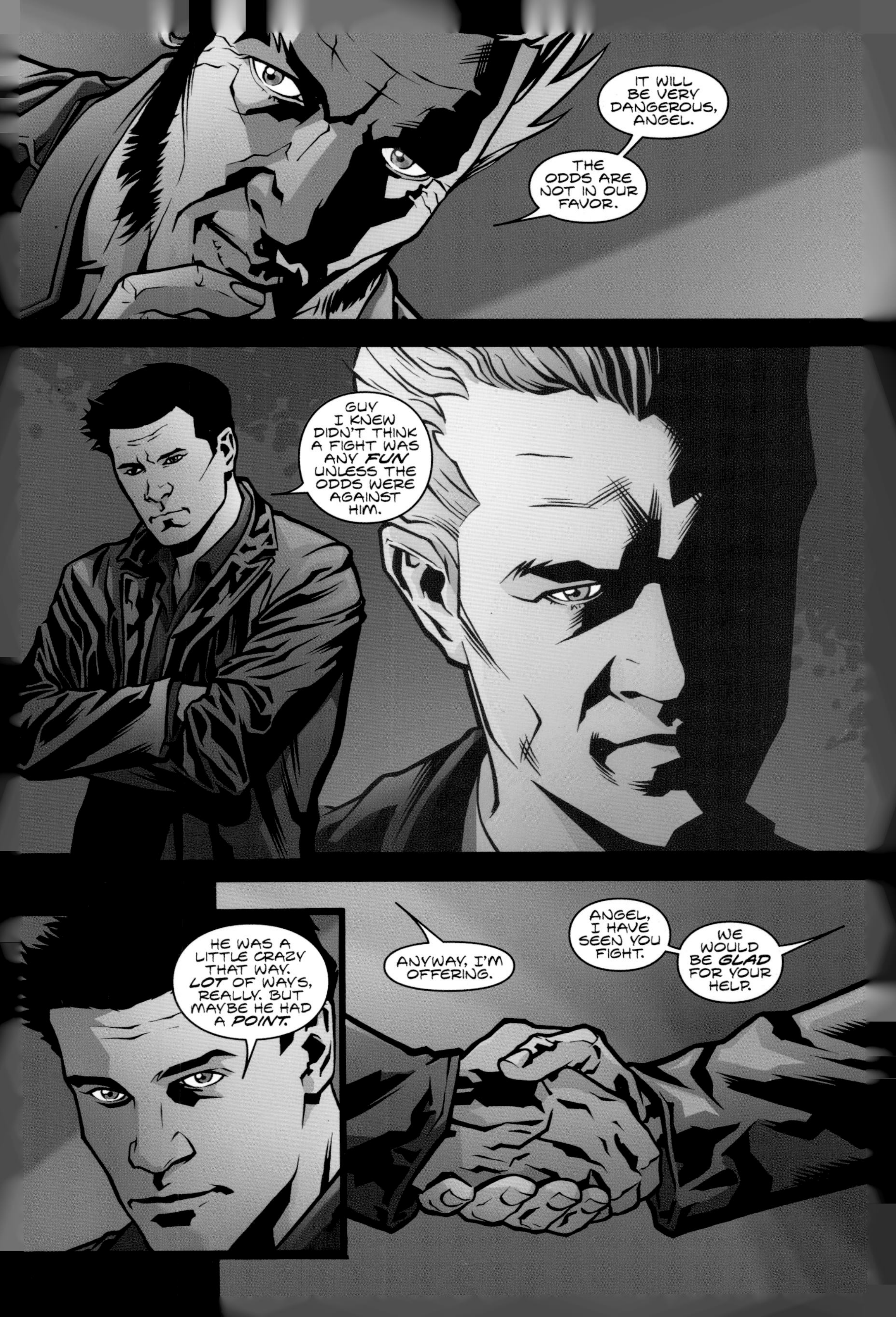
IT WILL BE VERY DANGEROUS, ANGEL.
THE ODDS ARE NOT IN OUR FAVOR.
GUY I KNEW DIDN'T THINK A FIGHT WAS ANY **FUN** UNLESS THE ODDS WERE AGAINST HIM.
HE WAS A LITTLE CRAZY THAT WAY. **LOT** OF WAYS, REALLY. BUT MAYBE HE HAD A **POINT.**
ANYWAY, I'M OFFERING.
ANGEL, I HAVE SEEN YOU FIGHT.
WE WOULD BE **GLAD** FOR YOUR HELP.

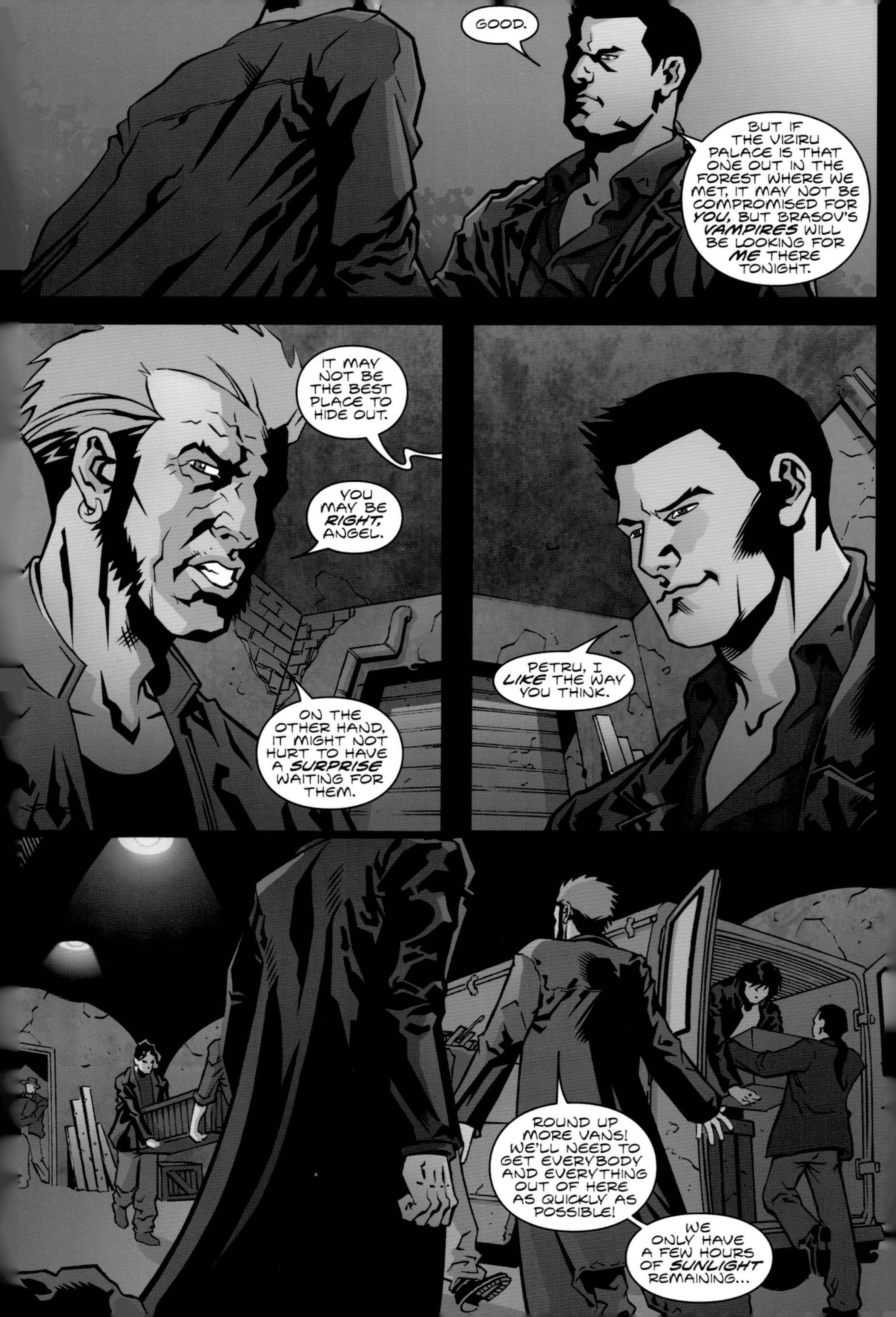
GOOD.
BUT IF THE VIZIRU PALACE IS THAT ONE OUT IN THE FOREST WHERE WE MET, IT MAY NOT BE COMPROMISED FOR YOU, BUT BRASOV'S VAMPIRES WILL BE LOOKING FOR ME THERE TONIGHT.
IT MAY NOT BE THE BEST PLACE TO HIDE OUT.
YOU MAY BE RIGHT, ANGEL.
ON THE OTHER HAND, IT MIGHT NOT HURT TO HAVE A SURPRISE WAITING FOR THEM.
PETRU, I LIKE THE WAY YOU THINK.
ROUND UP MORE VANS! WE'LL NEED TO GET EVERYBODY AND EVERYTHING OUT OF HERE AS QUICKLY AS POSSIBLE!
WE ONLY HAVE A FEW HOURS OF SUNLIGHT REMAINING...

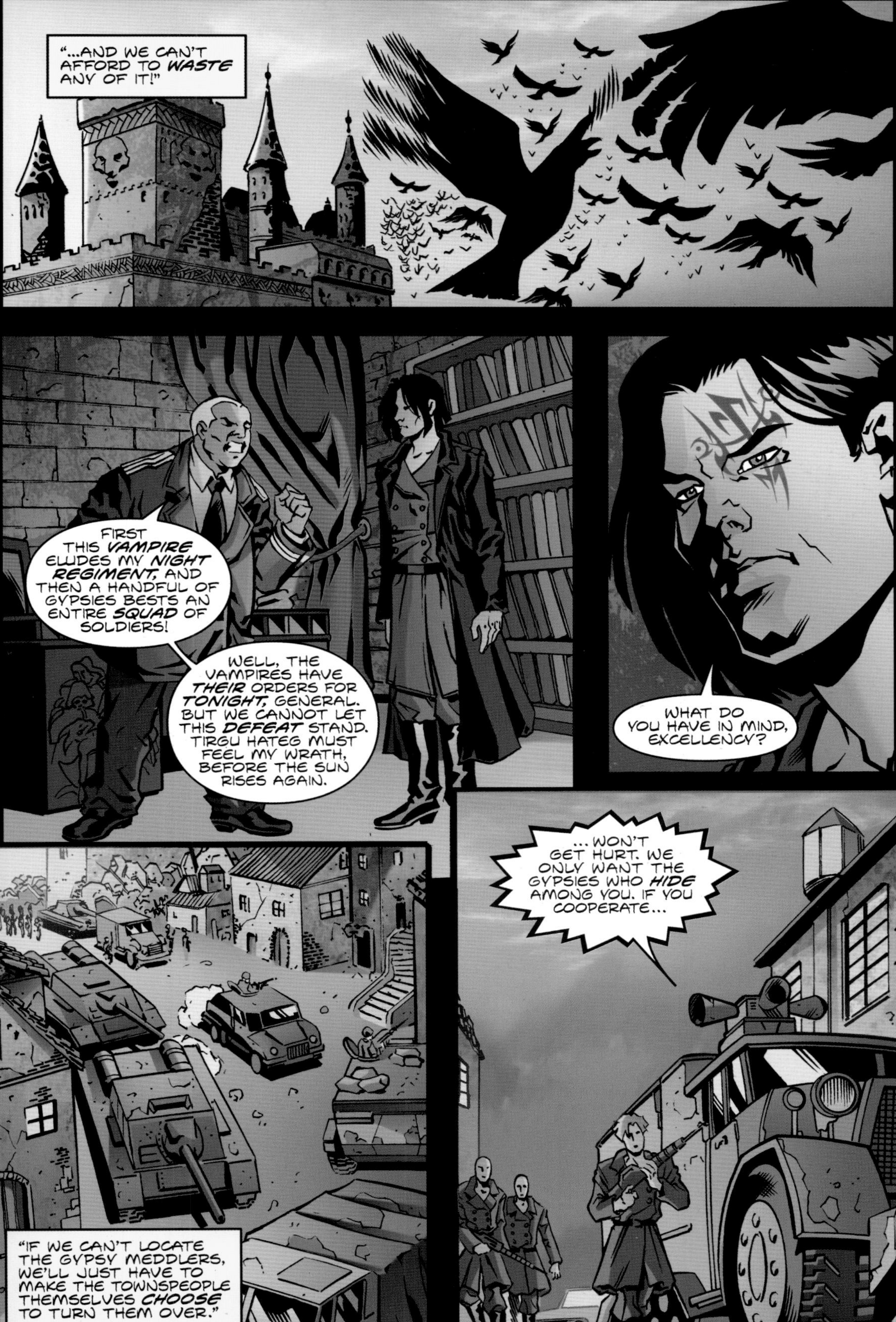
"...AND WE CAN'T AFFORD TO WASTE ANY OF IT!"
FIRST THIS VAMPIRE ELUDES MY NIGHT REGIMENT, AND THEN A HANDFUL OF GYPSIES BESTS AN ENTIRE SQUAD OF SOLDIERS!
WELL, THE VAMPIRES HAVE THEIR ORDERS FOR TONIGHT, GENERAL. BUT WE CANNOT LET THIS DEFEAT STAND. TIRGU HATEG MUST FEEL MY WRATH, BEFORE THE SUN RISES AGAIN.
WHAT DO YOU HAVE IN MIND, EXCELLENCY?
"IF WE CAN'T LOCATE THE GYPSY MEDDLERS, WE'LL JUST HAVE TO MAKE THE TOWNSPEOPLE THEMSELVES CHOOSE TO TURN THEM OVER."
...WON'T GET HURT. WE ONLY WANT THE GYPSIES WHO HIDE AMONG YOU. IF YOU COOPERATE...

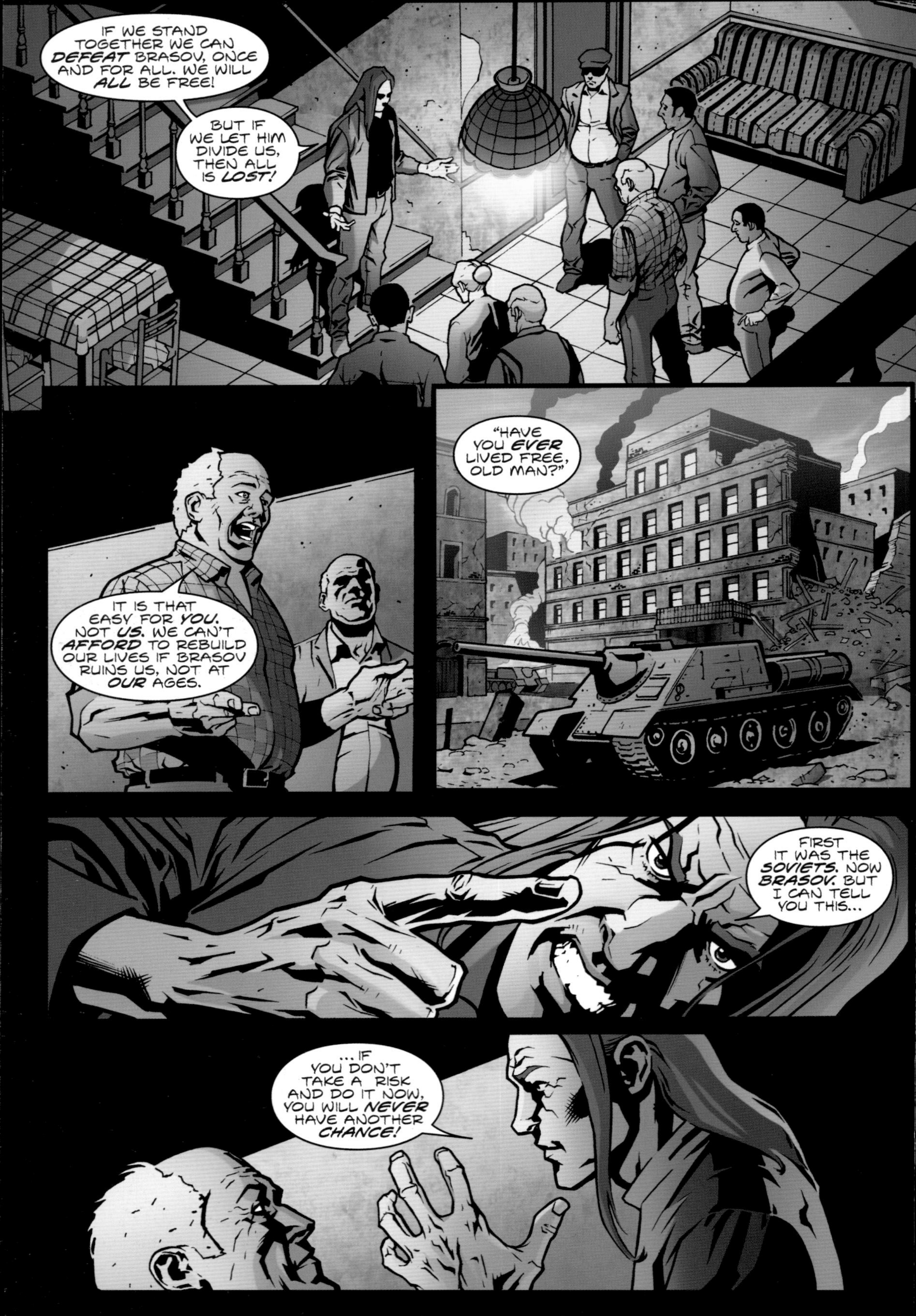
IF WE STAND TOGETHER WE CAN DEFEAT BRASOV, ONCE AND FOR ALL. WE WILL ALL BE FREE!
BUT IF WE LET HIM DIVIDE US, THEN ALL IS LOST!
IT IS THAT EASY FOR YOU. NOT US. WE CAN'T AFFORD TO REBUILD OUR LIVES IF BRASOV RUINS US, NOT AT OUR AGES.
"HAVE YOU EVER LIVED FREE, OLD MAN?"
FIRST IT WAS THE SOVIETS. NOW BRASOV. BUT I CAN TELL YOU THIS...
...IF YOU DON'T TAKE A RISK AND DO IT NOW, YOU WILL NEVER HAVE ANOTHER CHANCE!

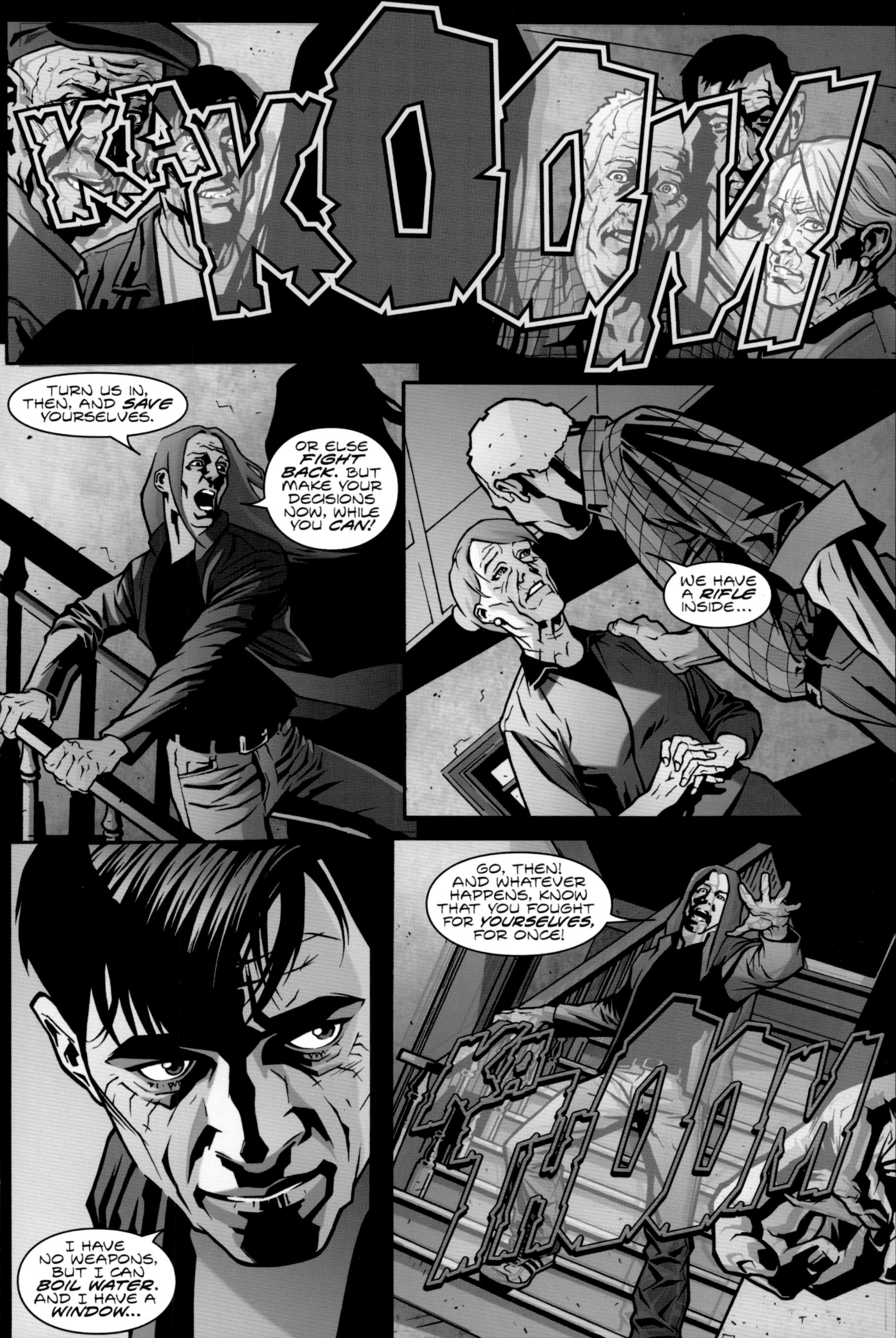
KRAKOOM
TURN US IN, THEN, AND SAVE YOURSELVES.
OR ELSE FIGHT BACK. BUT MAKE YOUR DECISIONS NOW, WHILE YOU CAN!
WE HAVE A RIFLE INSIDE...
I HAVE NO WEAPONS, BUT I CAN BOIL WATER. AND I HAVE A WINDOW...
GO, THEN! AND WHATEVER HAPPENS, KNOW THAT YOU FOUGHT FOR YOURSELVES, FOR ONCE!

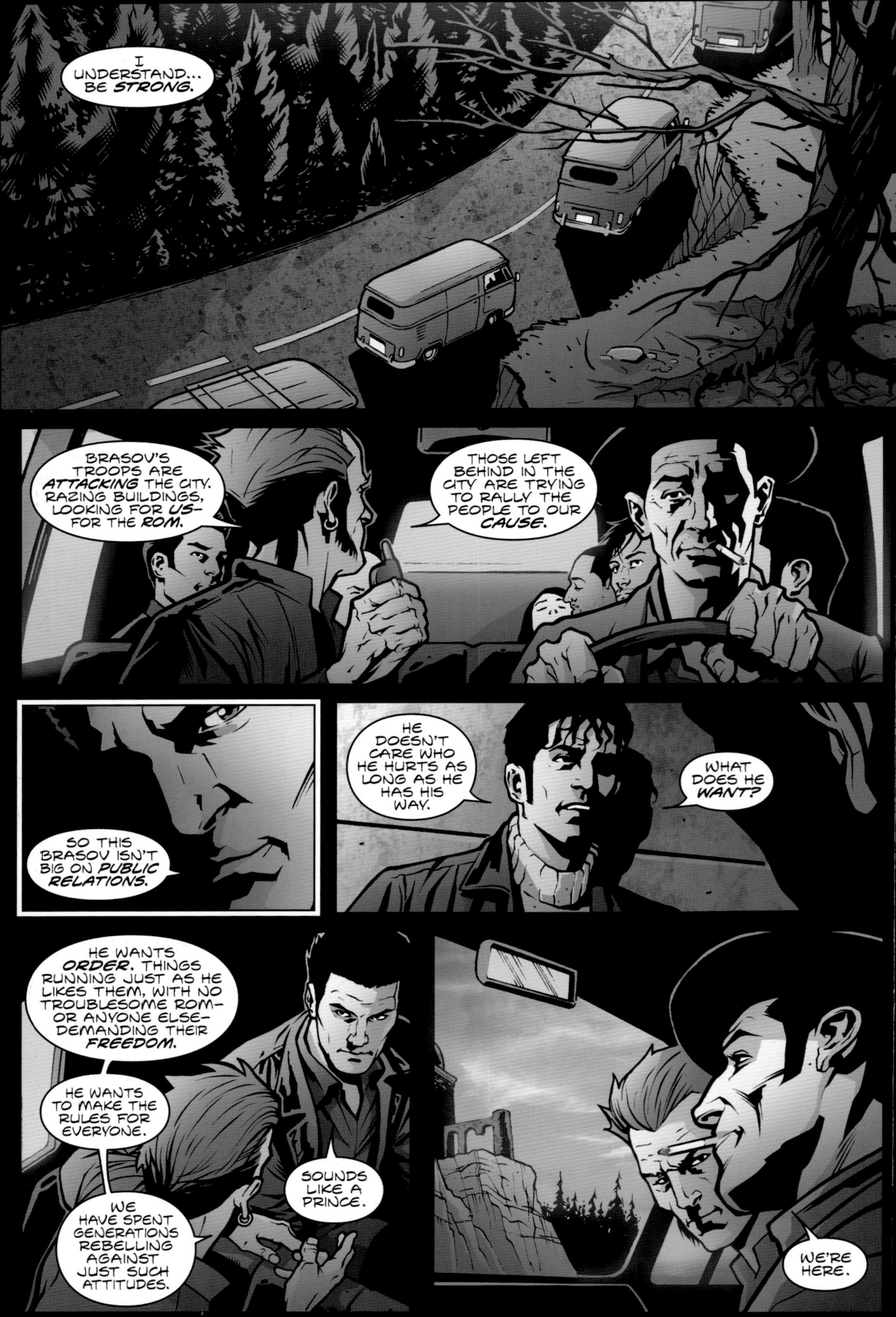
I UNDERSTAND... BE STRONG.
BRASOV'S TROOPS ARE ATTACKING THE CITY. RAZING BUILDINGS, LOOKING FOR US-FOR THE ROM.
THOSE LEFT BEHIND IN THE CITY ARE TRYING TO RALLY THE PEOPLE TO OUR CAUSE.
SO THIS BRASOV ISN'T BIG ON PUBLIC RELATIONS.
HE DOESN'T CARE WHO HE HURTS AS LONG AS HE HAS HIS WAY.
WHAT DOES HE WANT?
HE WANTS ORDER. THINGS RUNNING JUST AS HE LIKES THEM, WITH NO TROUBLESOME ROM-OR ANYONE ELSE-DEMANDING THEIR FREEDOM.
HE WANTS TO MAKE THE RULES FOR EVERYONE.
SOUNDS LIKE A PRINCE.
WE HAVE SPENT GENERATIONS REBELLING AGAINST JUST SUCH ATTITUDES.
WE'RE HERE.

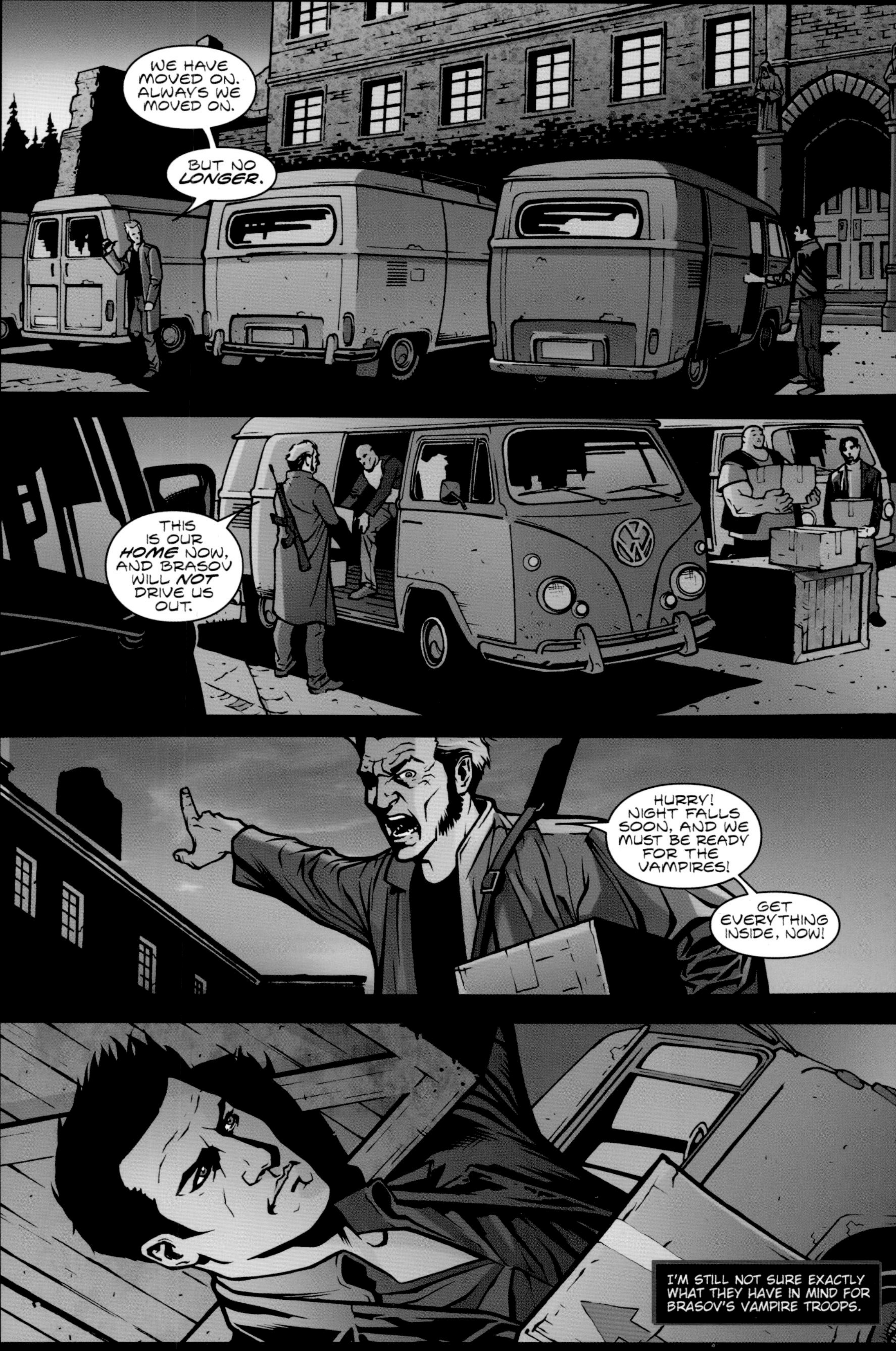
WE HAVE MOVED ON. ALWAYS WE MOVED ON.
BUT NO *LONGER*.
THIS IS OUR *HOME* NOW, AND BRASOV WILL *NOT* DRIVE US OUT.
HURRY! NIGHT FALLS SOON, AND WE MUST BE READY FOR THE VAMPIRES!
GET EVERYTHING INSIDE, NOW!
I'M STILL NOT SURE EXACTLY WHAT THEY HAVE IN MIND FOR BRASOV'S VAMPIRE TROOPS.

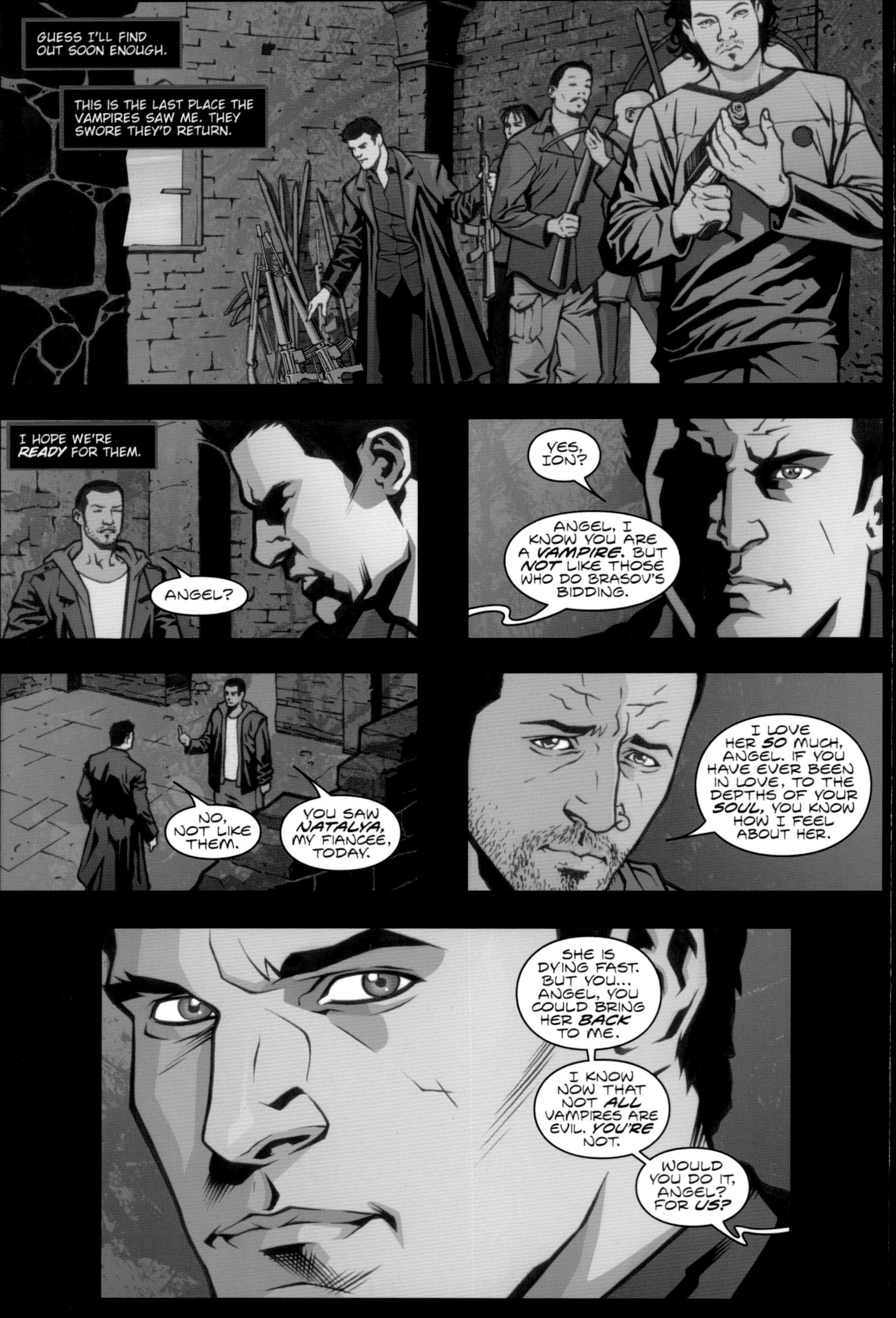
GUESS I'LL FIND OUT SOON ENOUGH.
THIS IS THE LAST PLACE THE VAMPIRES SAW ME. THEY SWORE THEY'D RETURN.
I HOPE WE'RE READY FOR THEM.
ANGEL?
YES, ION?
ANGEL, I KNOW YOU ARE A VAMPIRE. BUT NOT LIKE THOSE WHO DO BRASOV'S BIDDING.
NO, NOT LIKE THEM.
YOU SAW NATALYA, MY FIANCEE, TODAY.
I LOVE HER SO MUCH, ANGEL. IF YOU HAVE EVER BEEN IN LOVE, TO THE DEPTHS OF YOUR SOUL, YOU KNOW HOW I FEEL ABOUT HER.
SHE IS DYING FAST. BUT YOU... ANGEL, YOU COULD BRING HER BACK TO ME.
I KNOW NOW THAT NOT ALL VAMPIRES ARE EVIL. YOU'RE NOT.
WOULD YOU DO IT, ANGEL? FOR US?

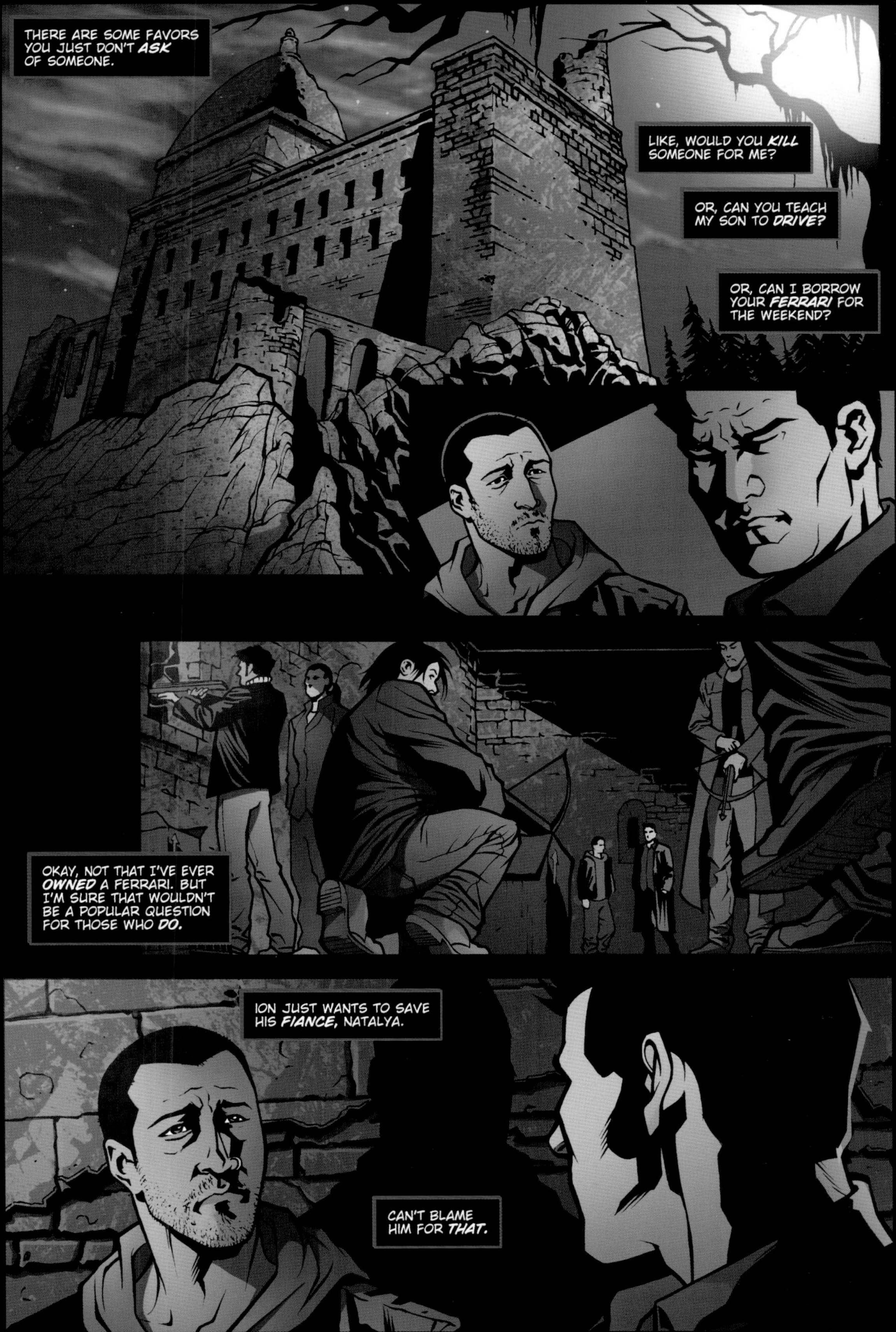
THERE ARE SOME FAVORS YOU JUST DON'T ASK OF SOMEONE.
LIKE, WOULD YOU KILL SOMEONE FOR ME?
OR, CAN YOU TEACH MY SON TO DRIVE?
OR, CAN I BORROW YOUR FERRARI FOR THE WEEKEND?
OKAY, NOT THAT I'VE EVER OWNED A FERRARI. BUT I'M SURE THAT WOULDN'T BE A POPULAR QUESTION FOR THOSE WHO DO.
ION JUST WANTS TO SAVE HIS FIANCE, NATALYA.
CAN'T BLAME HIM FOR THAT.

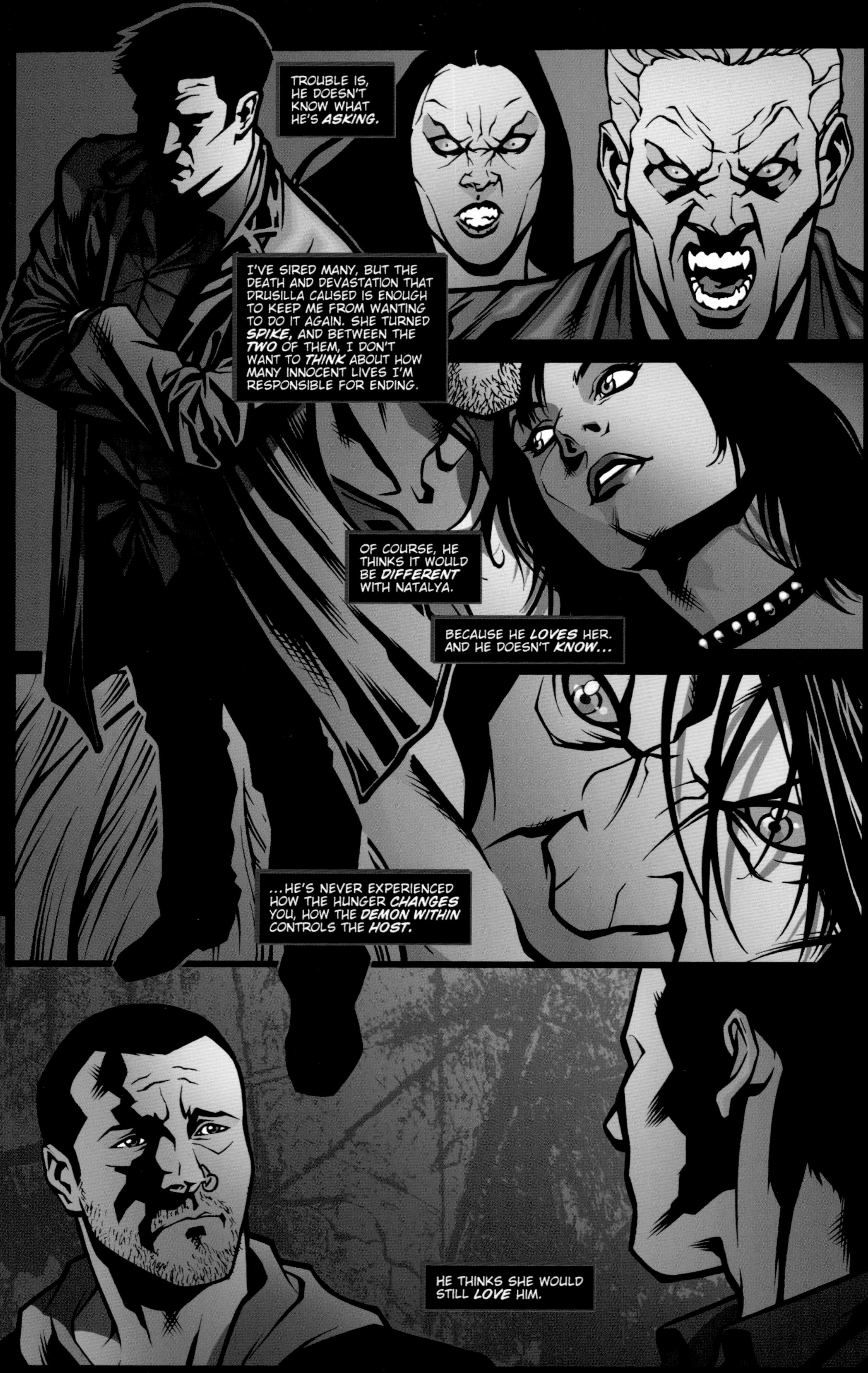
TROUBLE IS, HE DOESN'T KNOW WHAT HE'S ASKING.
I'VE SIRED MANY, BUT THE DEATH AND DEVASTATION THAT DRUSILLA CAUSED IS ENOUGH TO KEEP ME FROM WANTING TO DO IT AGAIN. SHE TURNED SPIKE, AND BETWEEN THE TWO OF THEM, I DON'T WANT TO THINK ABOUT HOW MANY INNOCENT LIVES I'M RESPONSIBLE FOR ENDING.
OF COURSE, HE THINKS IT WOULD BE DIFFERENT WITH NATALYA.
BECAUSE HE LOVES HER. AND HE DOESN'T KNOW...
...HE'S NEVER EXPERIENCED HOW THE HUNGER CHANGES YOU, HOW THE DEMON WITHIN CONTROLS THE HOST.
HE THINKS SHE WOULD STILL LOVE HIM.

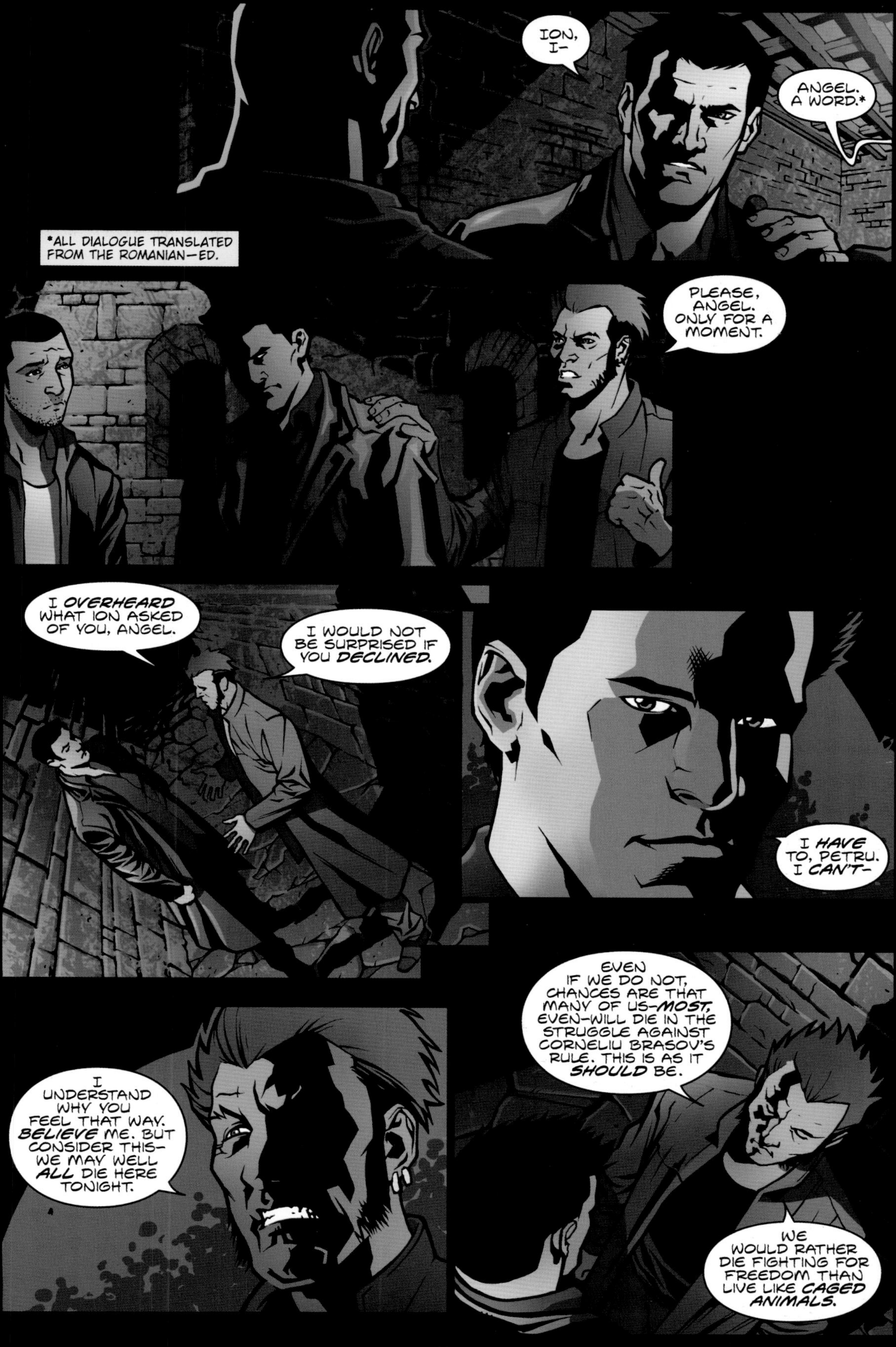
ION, I–
ANGEL. A WORD.*
*ALL DIALOGUE TRANSLATED FROM THE ROMANIAN—ED.
PLEASE, ANGEL. ONLY FOR A MOMENT.
I OVERHEARD WHAT ION ASKED OF YOU, ANGEL.
I WOULD NOT BE SURPRISED IF YOU DECLINED.
I HAVE TO, PETRU. I CAN'T–
I UNDERSTAND WHY YOU FEEL THAT WAY. BELIEVE ME. BUT CONSIDER THIS– WE MAY WELL ALL DIE HERE TONIGHT.
EVEN IF WE DO NOT, CHANCES ARE THAT MANY OF US–MOST, EVEN–WILL DIE IN THE STRUGGLE AGAINST CORNELIU BRASOV'S RULE. THIS IS AS IT SHOULD BE.
WE WOULD RATHER DIE FIGHTING FOR FREEDOM THAN LIVE LIKE CAGED ANIMALS.

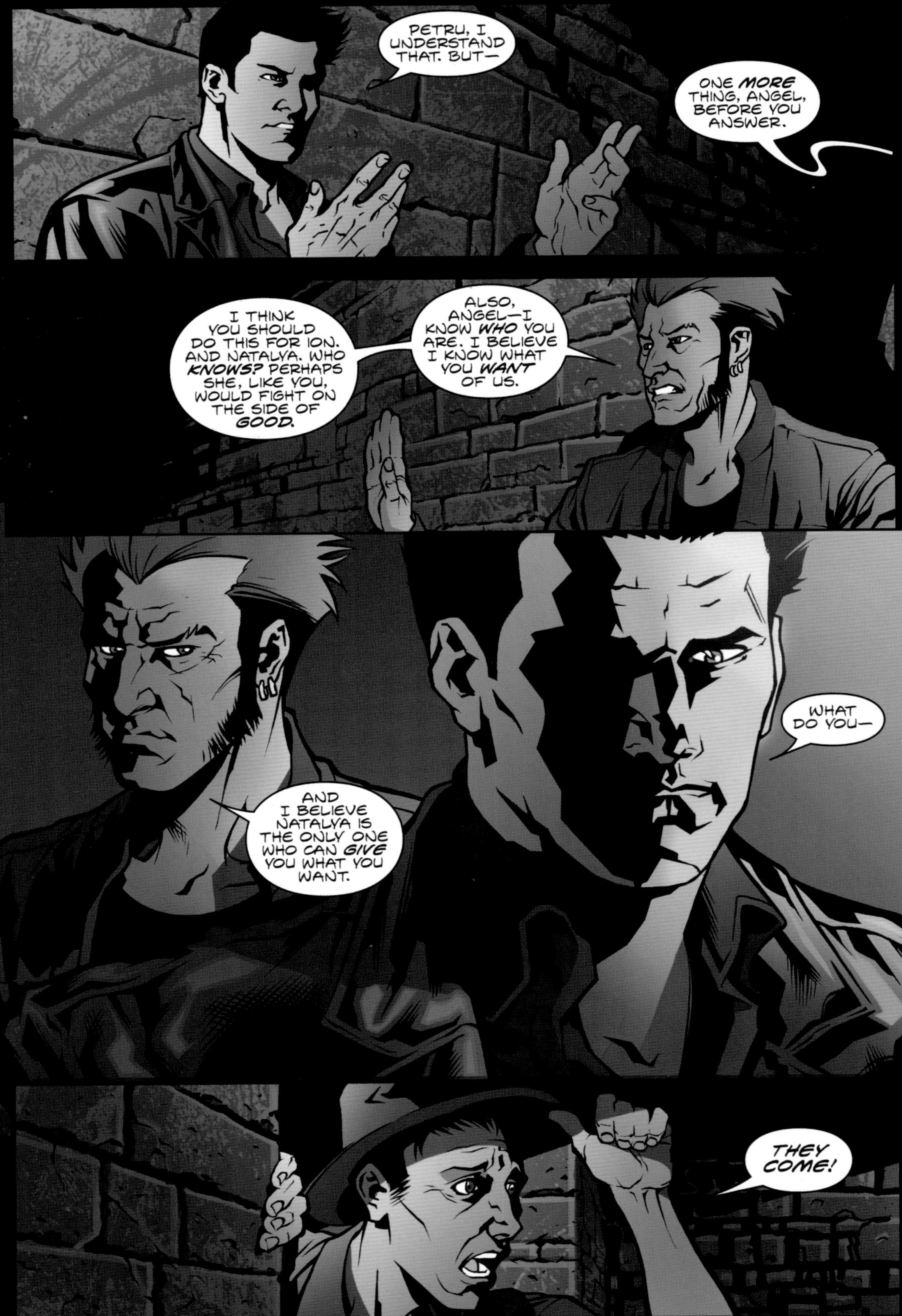
PETRU, I UNDERSTAND THAT. BUT—
ONE MORE THING, ANGEL, BEFORE YOU ANSWER.
ALSO, ANGEL—I KNOW WHO YOU ARE. I BELIEVE I KNOW WHAT YOU WANT OF US.
I THINK YOU SHOULD DO THIS FOR ION. AND NATALYA. WHO KNOWS? PERHAPS SHE, LIKE YOU, WOULD FIGHT ON THE SIDE OF GOOD.
WHAT DO YOU—
AND I BELIEVE NATALYA IS THE ONLY ONE WHO CAN GIVE YOU WHAT YOU WANT.
THEY COME!

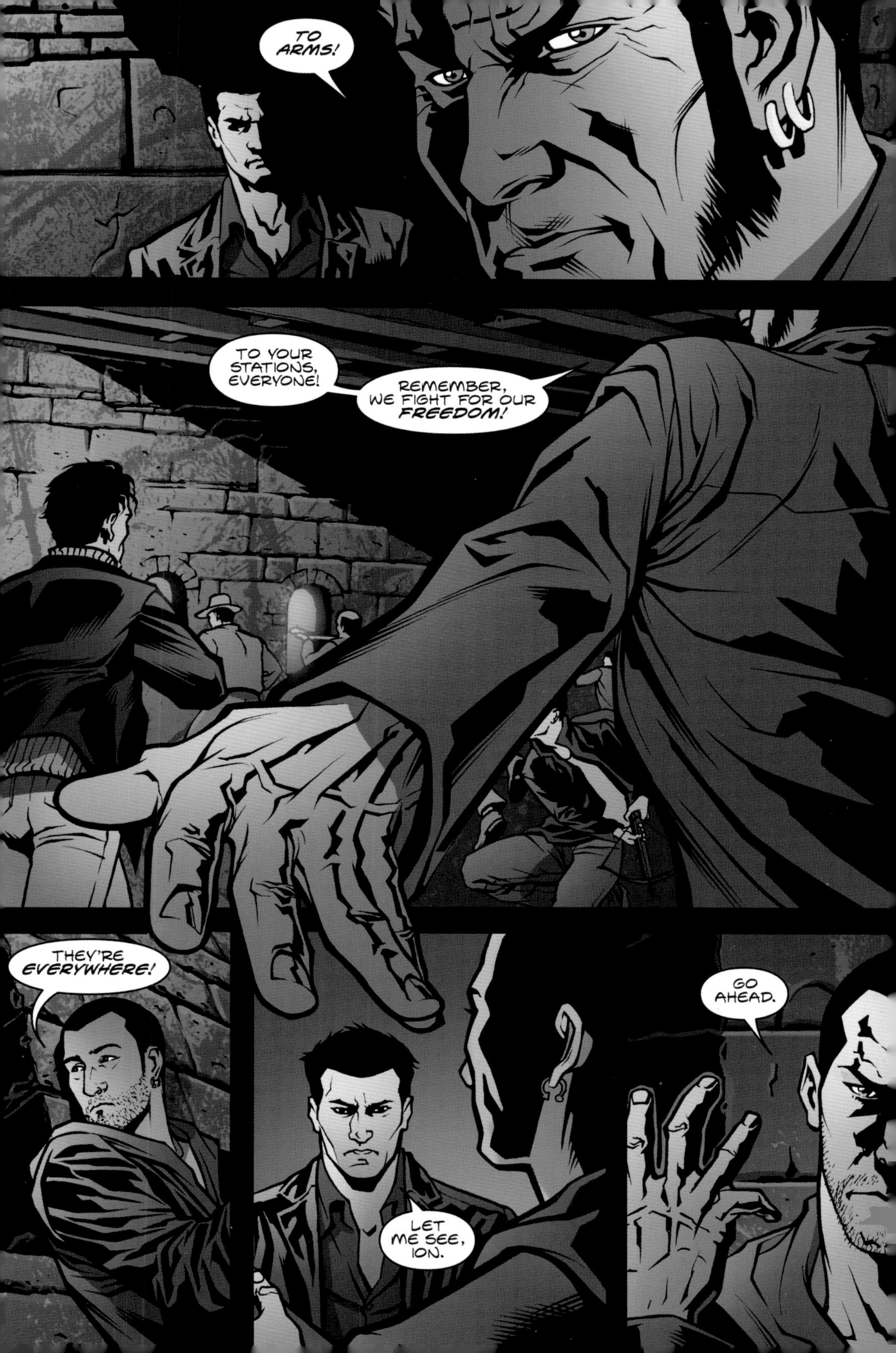
TO ARMS!
TO YOUR STATIONS, EVERYONE!
REMEMBER, WE FIGHT FOR OUR FREEDOM!
THEY'RE EVERYWHERE!
LET ME SEE, ION.
GO AHEAD.

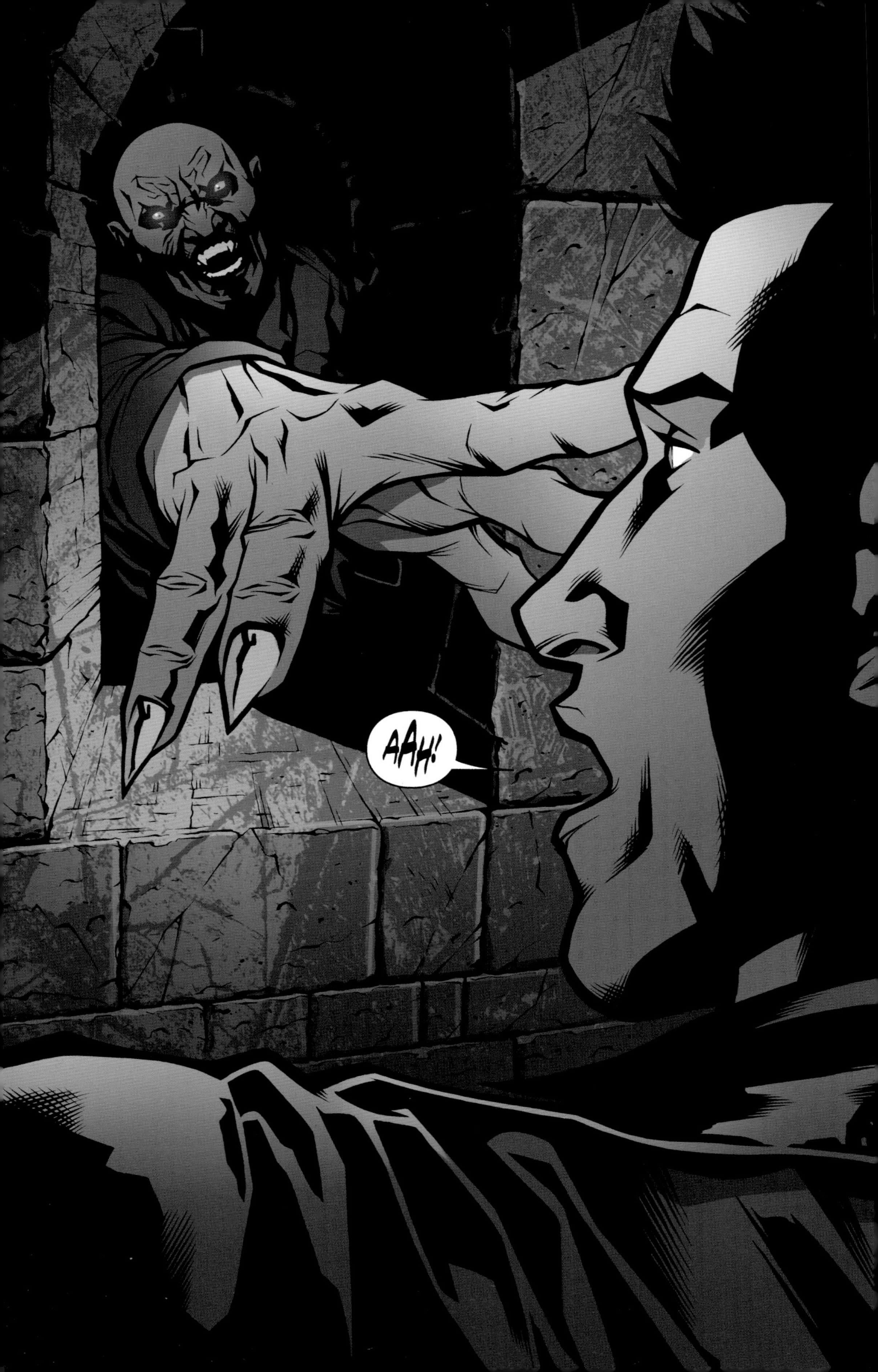
AAH!

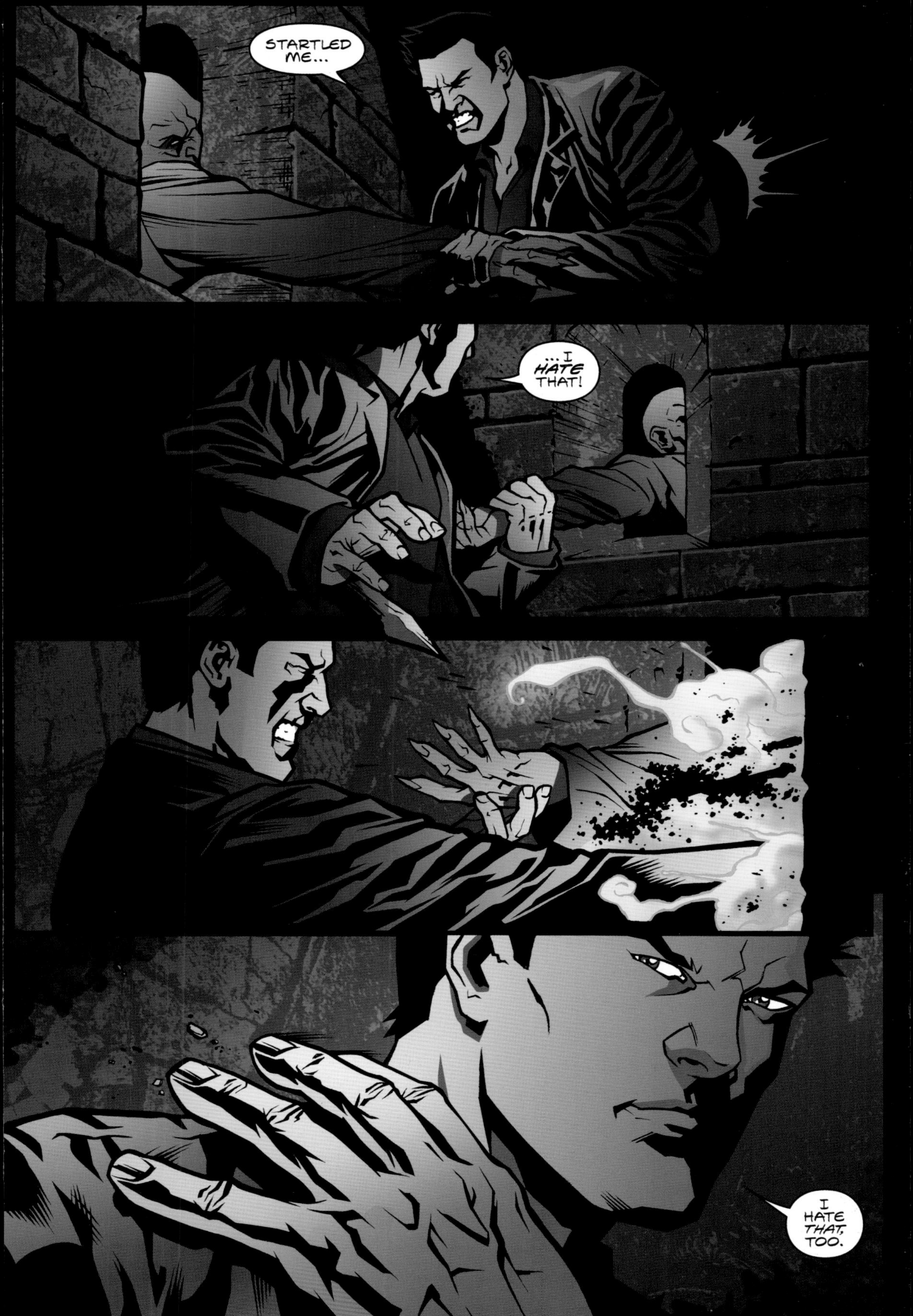
STARTLED ME...
...I *HATE* THAT!
I HATE *THAT,* TOO.

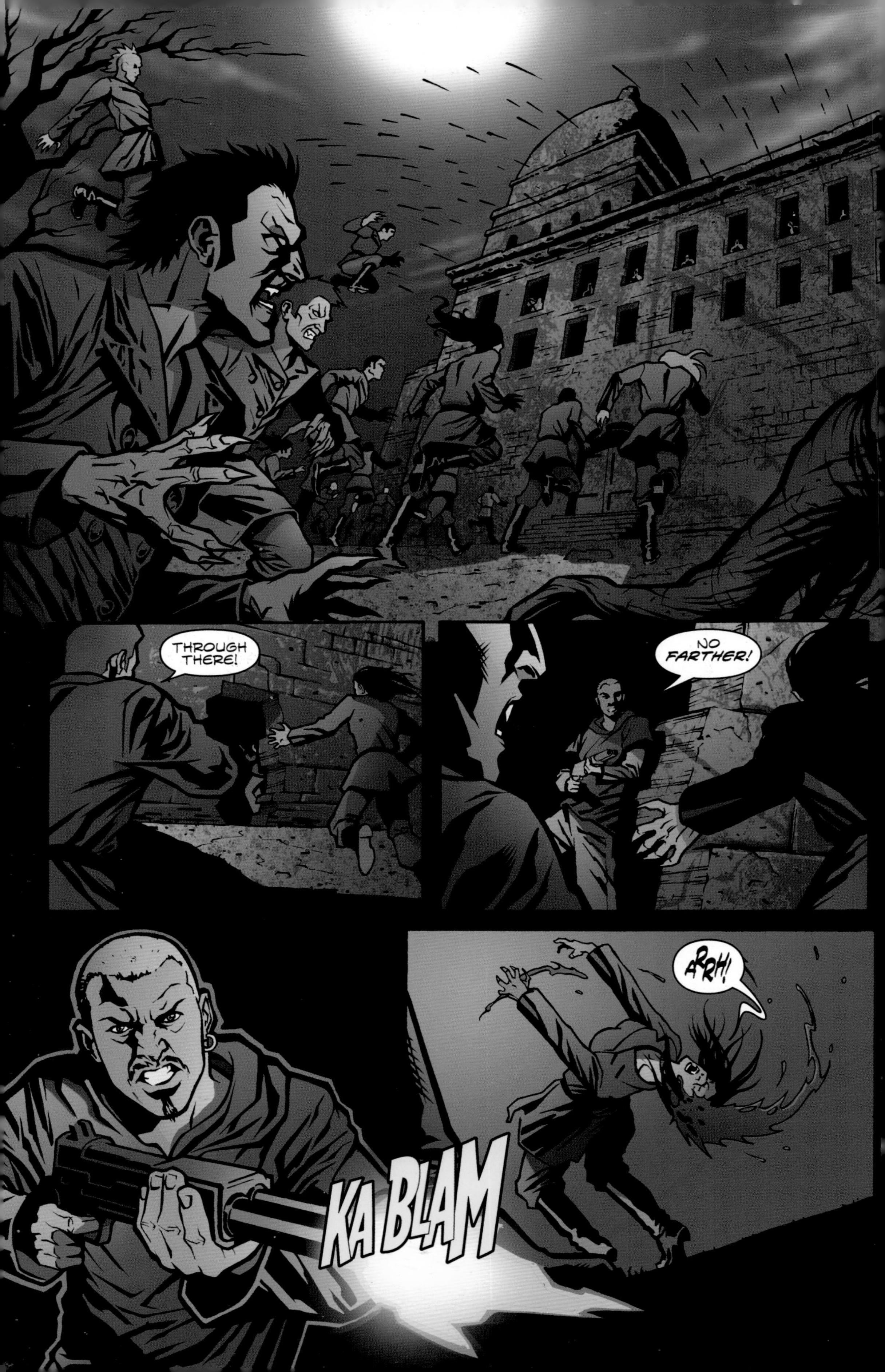
THROUGH THERE!
NO FARTHER!
KA BLAM
ARRH!

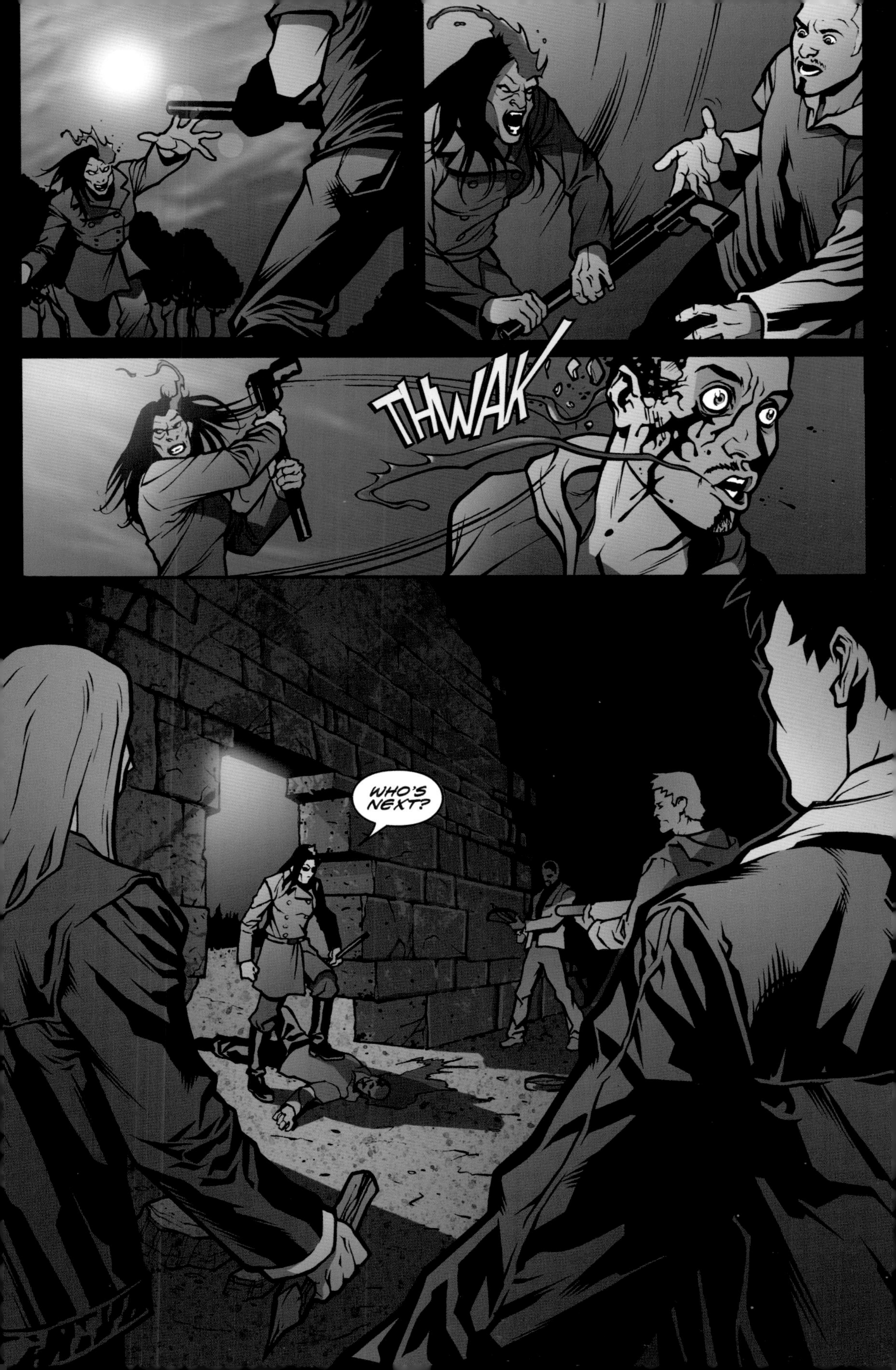
THWAK!
WHO'S NEXT?

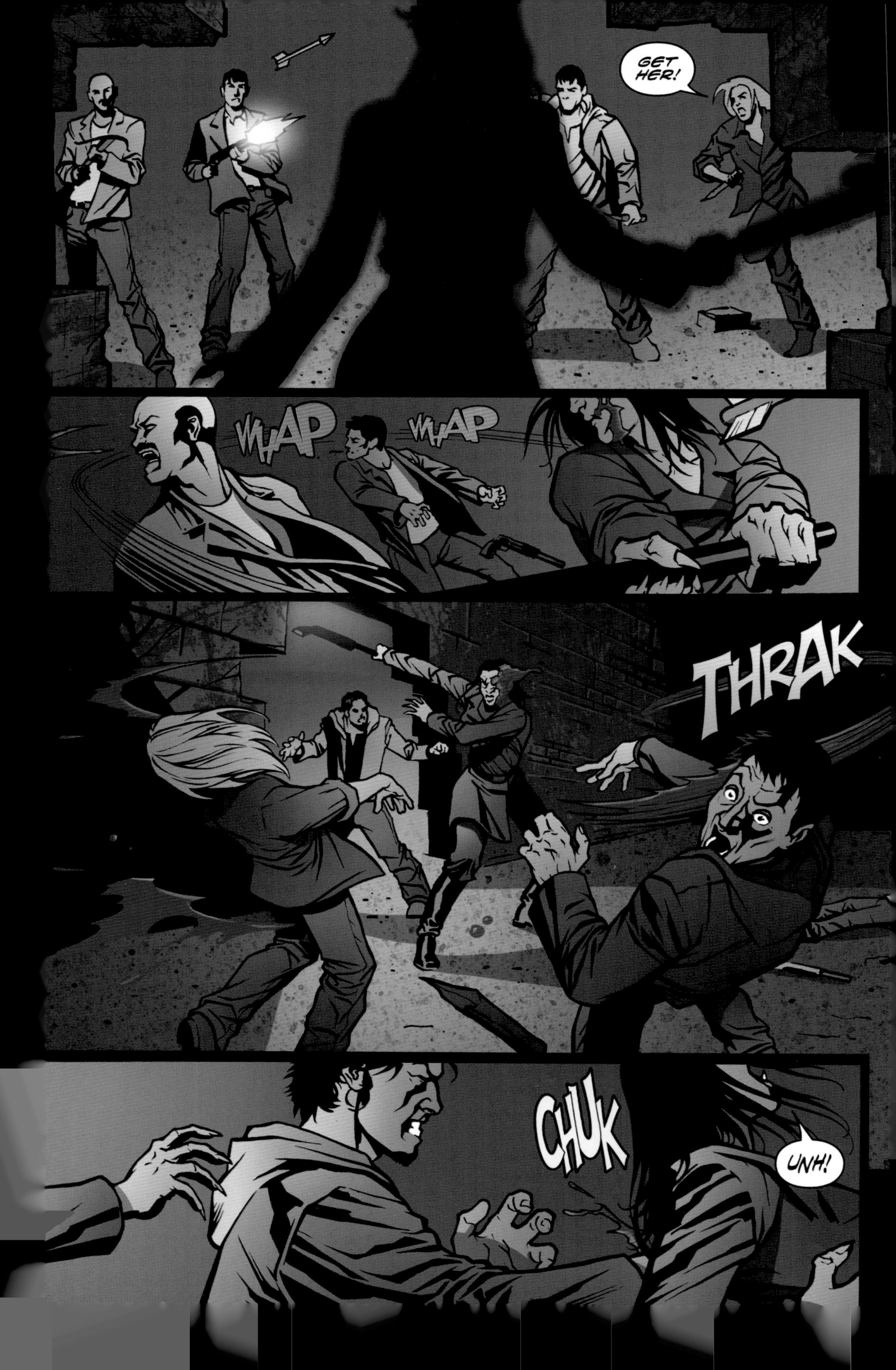
GET HER!
WHAP
WHAP
THRAK
CHUK
UNH!

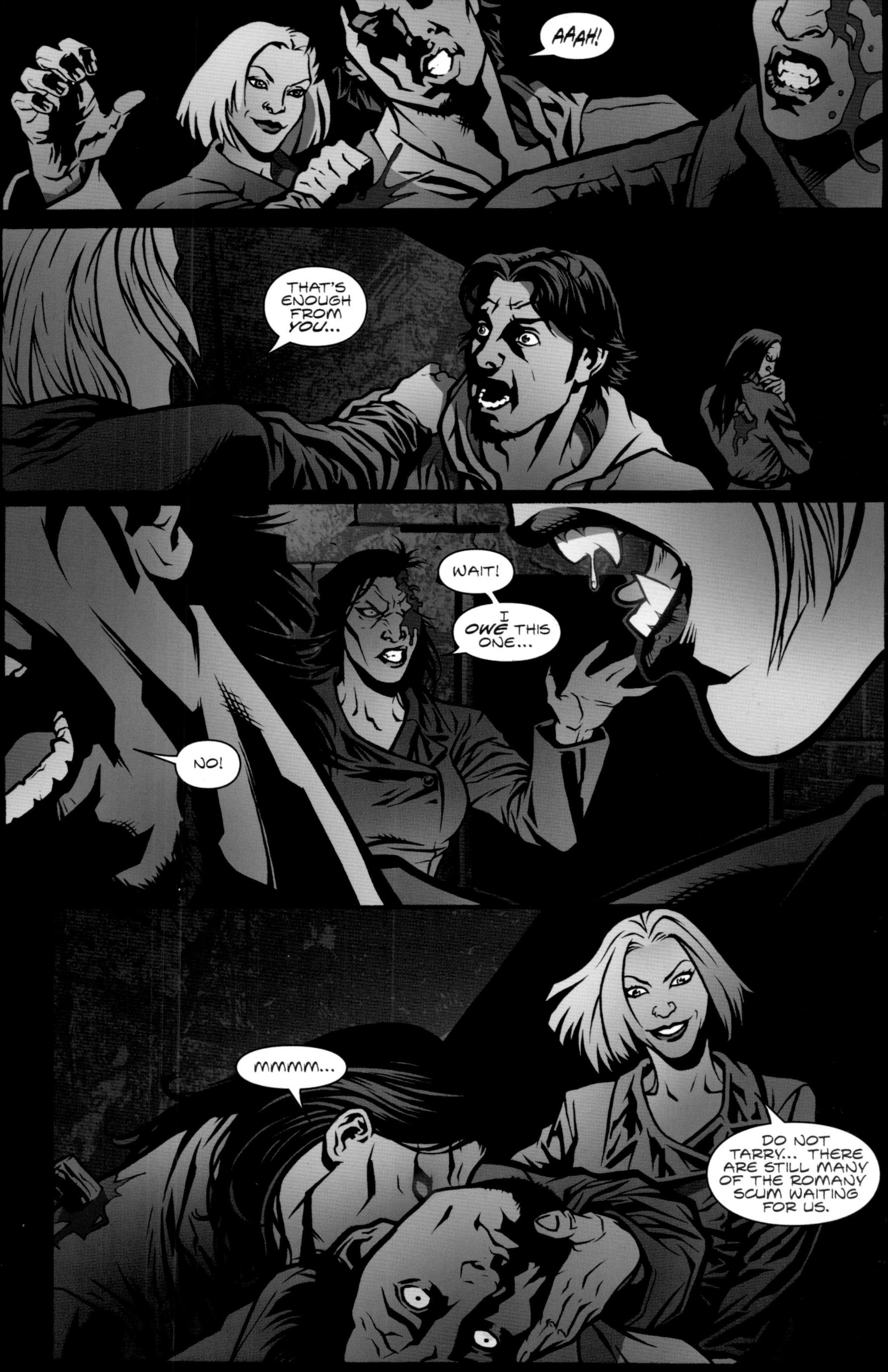
AAAH!
THAT'S ENOUGH FROM YOU...
WAIT!
I OWE THIS ONE...
NO!
MMMM...
DO NOT TARRY... THERE ARE STILL MANY OF THE ROMANY SCUM WAITING FOR US.

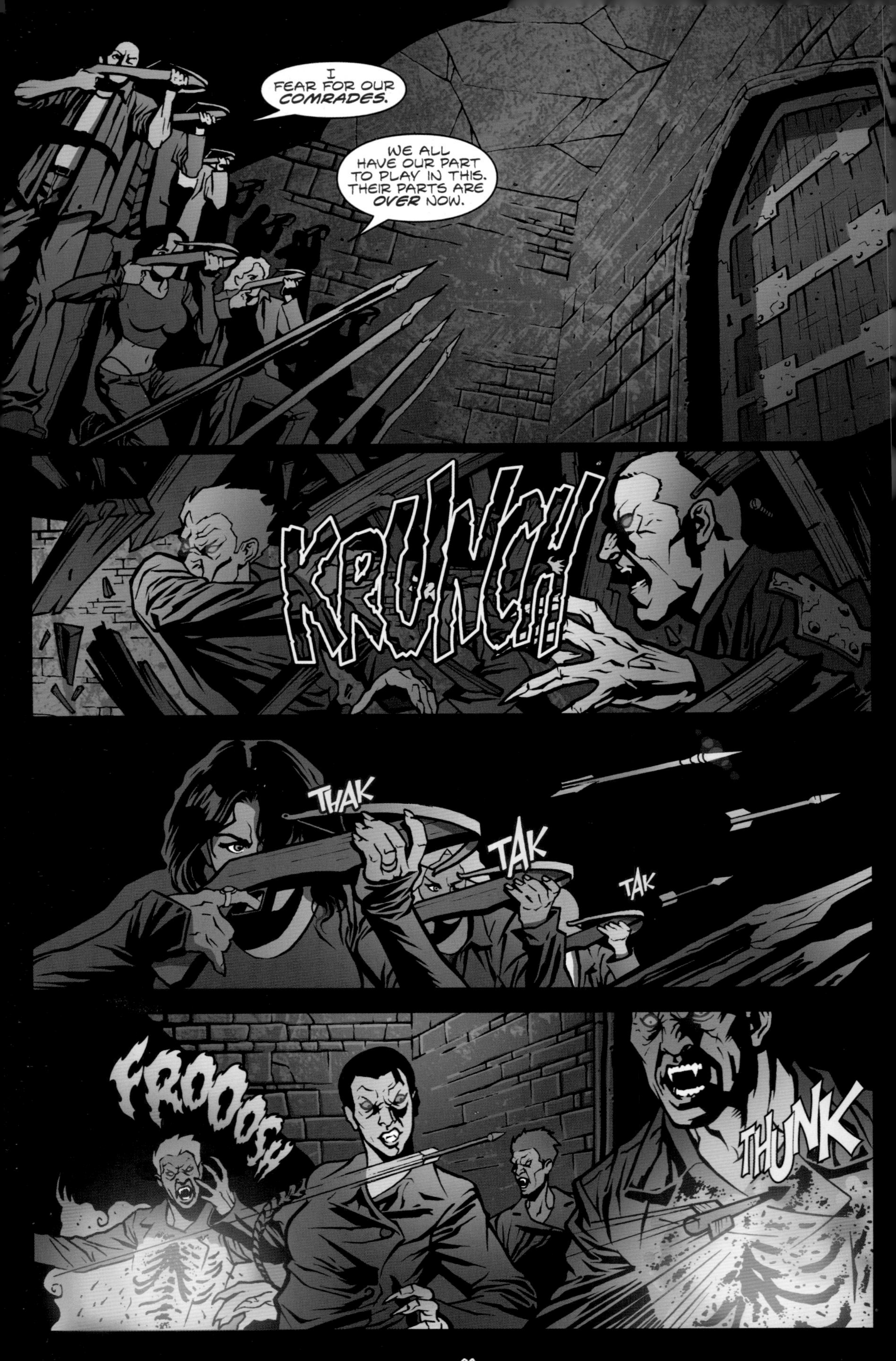
I FEAR FOR OUR *COMRADES.*
WE ALL HAVE OUR PART TO PLAY IN THIS. THEIR PARTS ARE *OVER* NOW.
KRUNCH
THAK
TAK
TAK
FROOOSH
THUNK

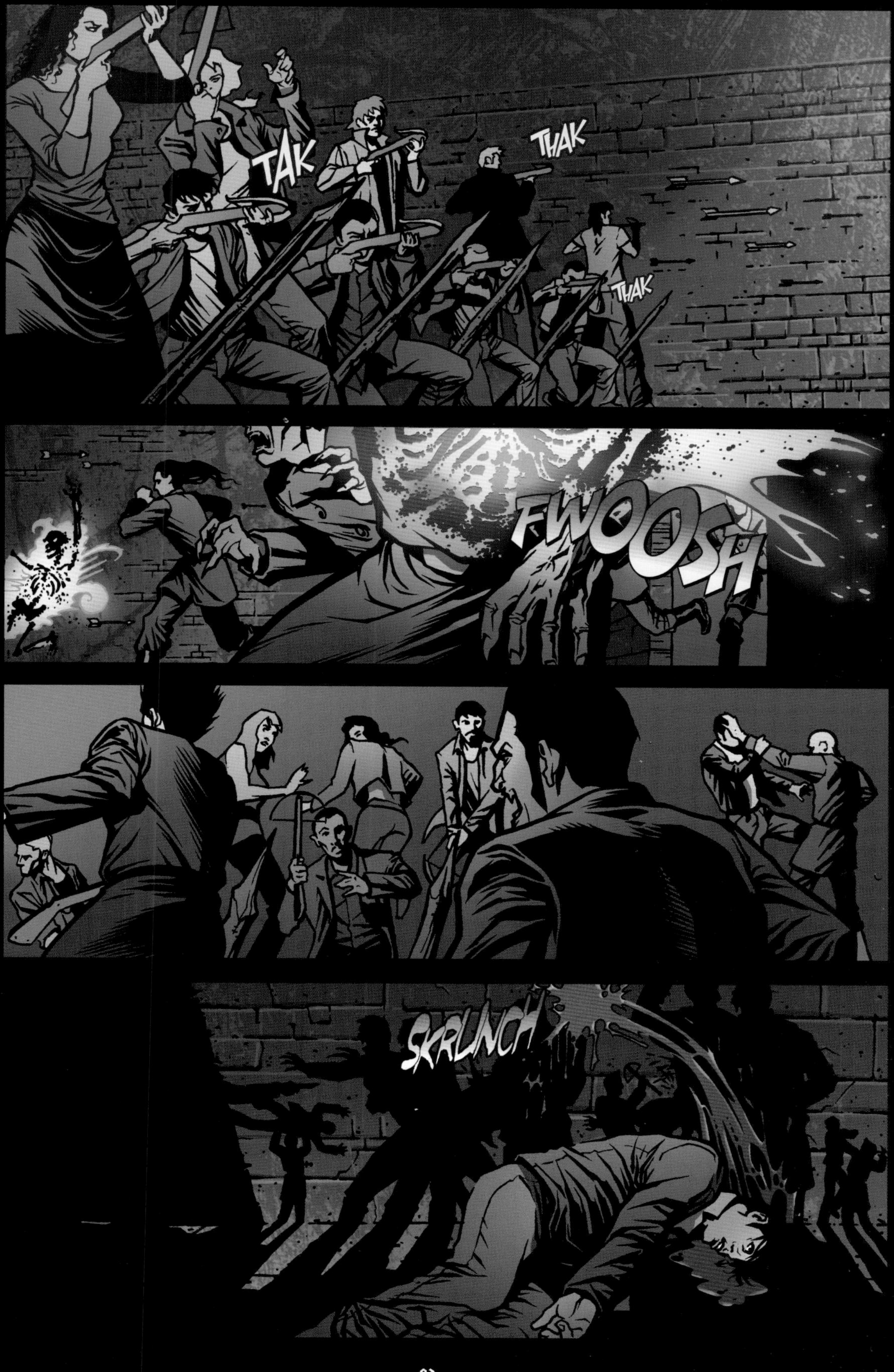
TAK
THAK
THAK
FWOOSH
SKRUNCH

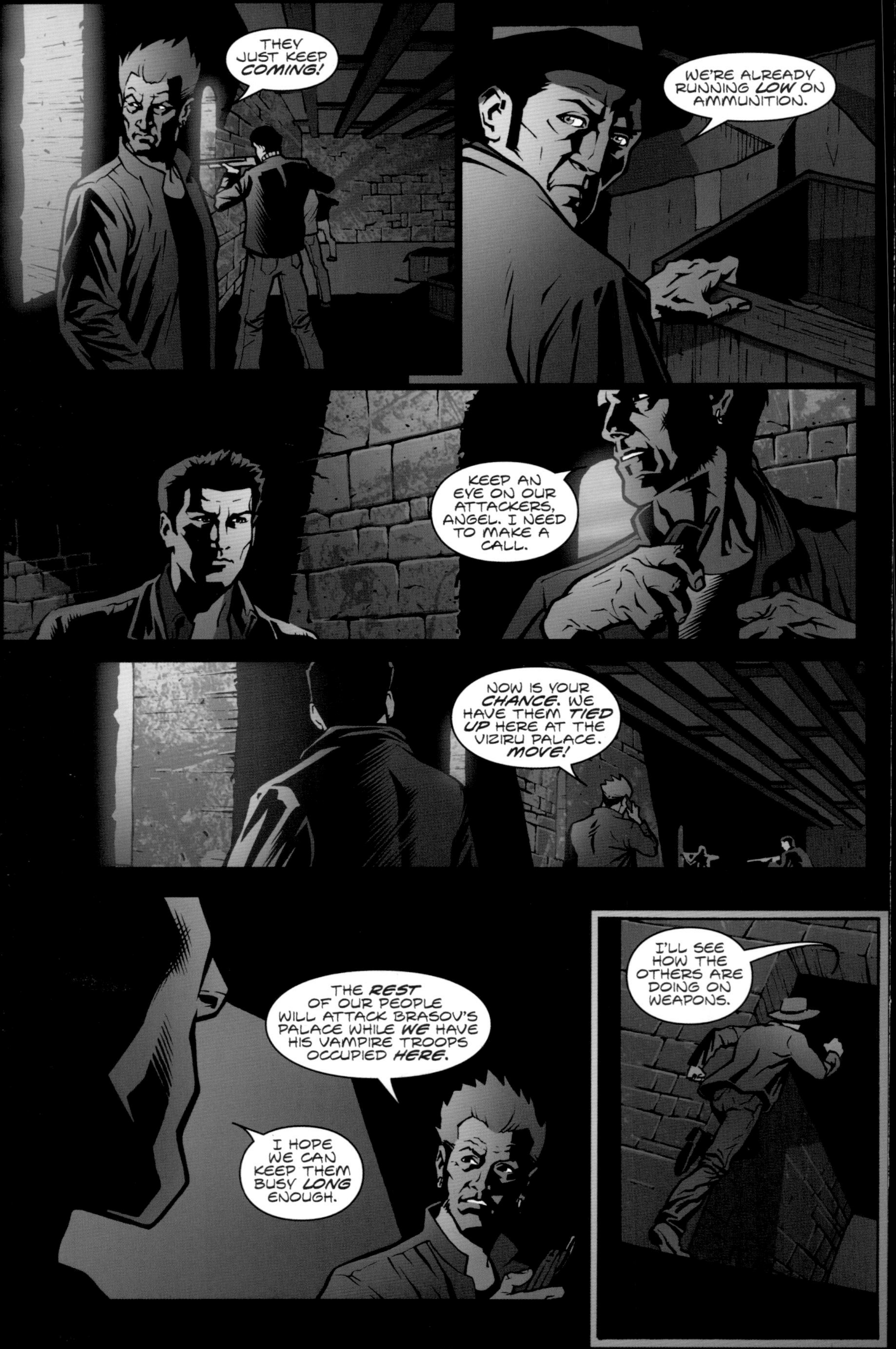
THEY JUST KEEP COMING!
WE'RE ALREADY RUNNING LOW ON AMMUNITION.
KEEP AN EYE ON OUR ATTACKERS, ANGEL. I NEED TO MAKE A CALL.
NOW IS YOUR CHANCE. WE HAVE THEM TIED UP HERE AT THE VIZIRU PALACE. MOVE!
THE REST OF OUR PEOPLE WILL ATTACK BRASOV'S PALACE WHILE WE HAVE HIS VAMPIRE TROOPS OCCUPIED HERE.
I HOPE WE CAN KEEP THEM BUSY LONG ENOUGH.
I'LL SEE HOW THE OTHERS ARE DOING ON WEAPONS.

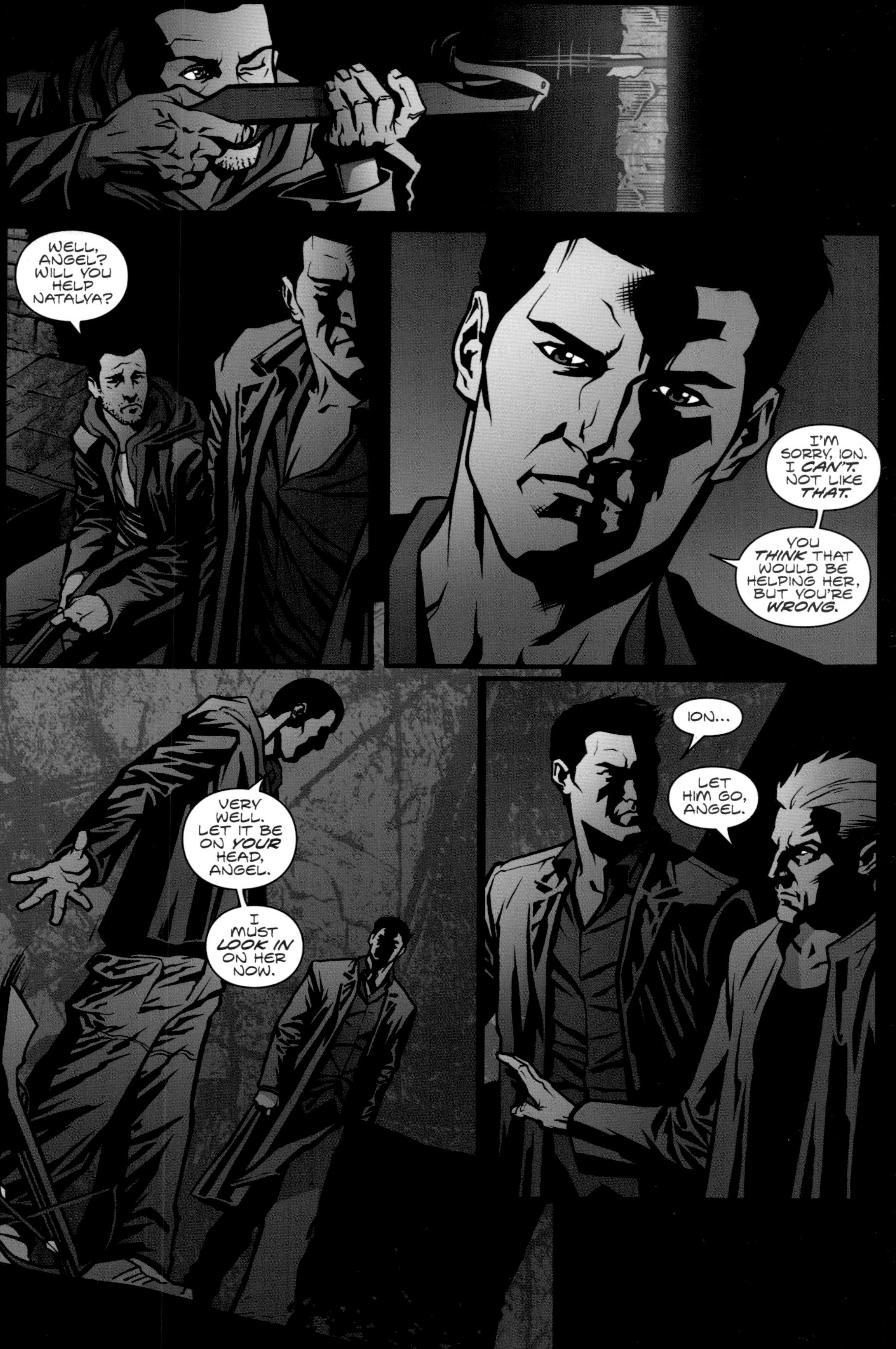
WELL, ANGEL? WILL YOU HELP NATALYA?
I'M SORRY, ION. I CAN'T. NOT LIKE THAT.
YOU THINK THAT WOULD BE HELPING HER, BUT YOU'RE WRONG.
VERY WELL. LET IT BE ON YOUR HEAD, ANGEL.
I MUST LOOK IN ON HER NOW.
ION...
LET HIM GO, ANGEL.

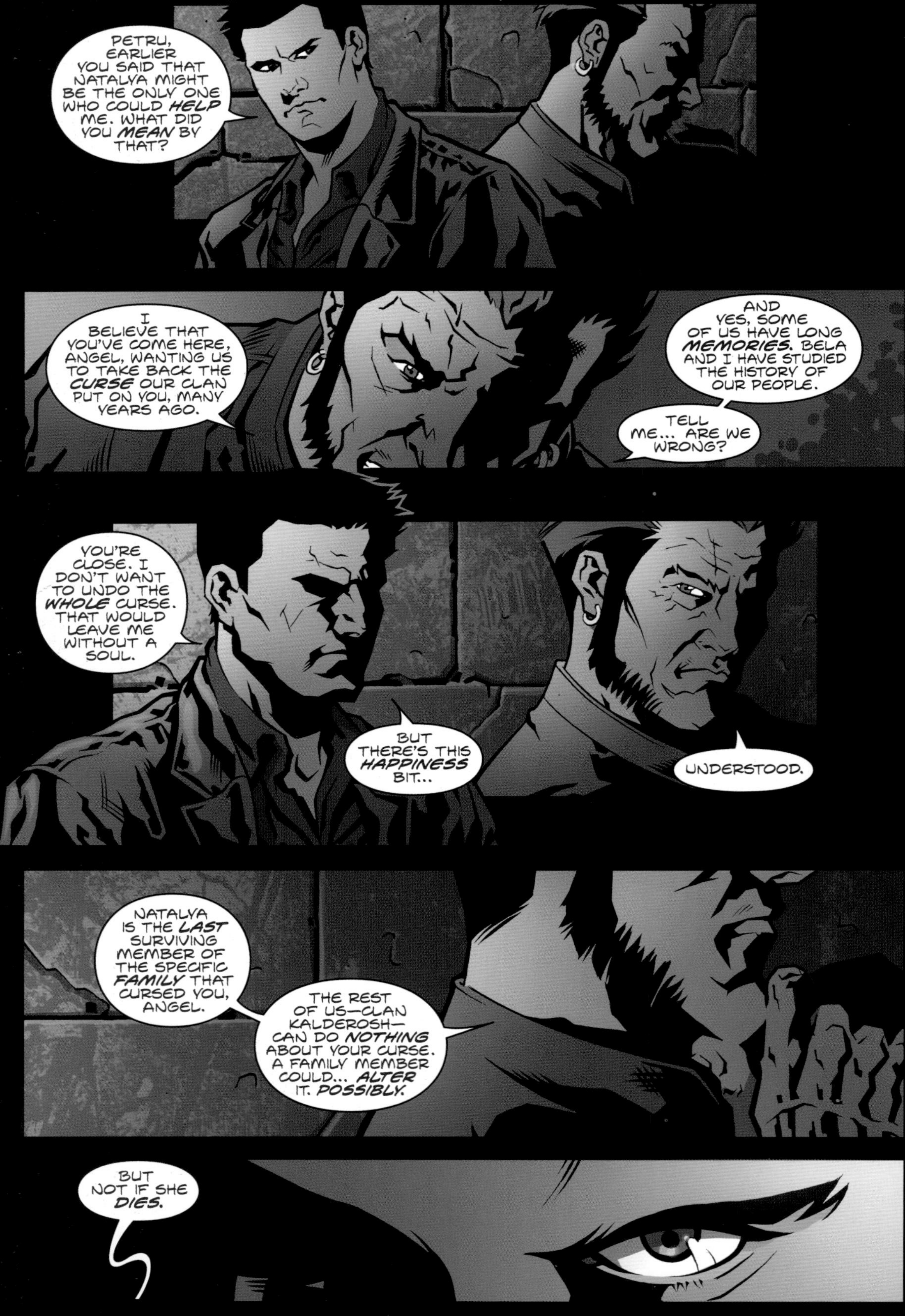

PETRU, EARLIER YOU SAID THAT NATALYA MIGHT BE THE ONLY ONE WHO COULD HELP ME. WHAT DID YOU MEAN BY THAT?
I BELIEVE THAT YOU'VE COME HERE, ANGEL, WANTING US TO TAKE BACK THE CURSE OUR CLAN PUT ON YOU, MANY YEARS AGO.
AND YES, SOME OF US HAVE LONG MEMORIES. BELA AND I HAVE STUDIED THE HISTORY OF OUR PEOPLE.
TELL ME... ARE WE WRONG?
YOU'RE CLOSE. I DON'T WANT TO UNDO THE WHOLE CURSE. THAT WOULD LEAVE ME WITHOUT A SOUL.
BUT THERE'S THIS HAPPINESS BIT...
UNDERSTOOD.
NATALYA IS THE LAST SURVIVING MEMBER OF THE SPECIFIC FAMILY THAT CURSED YOU, ANGEL.
THE REST OF US—CLAN KALDEROSH—CAN DO NOTHING ABOUT YOUR CURSE. A FAMILY MEMBER COULD... ALTER IT. POSSIBLY.
BUT NOT IF SHE DIES.

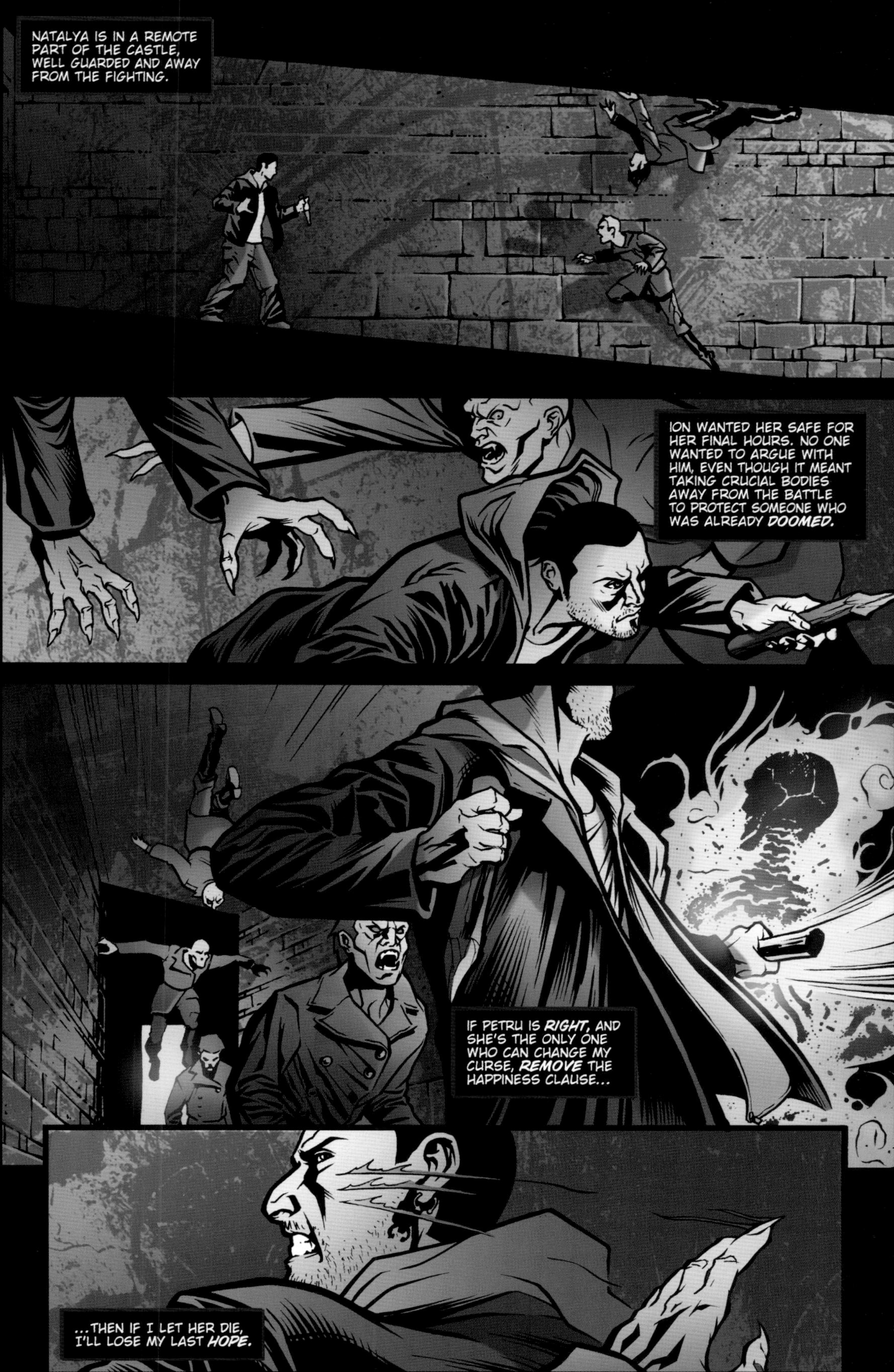
NATALYA IS IN A REMOTE PART OF THE CASTLE, WELL GUARDED AND AWAY FROM THE FIGHTING.
ION WANTED HER SAFE FOR HER FINAL HOURS. NO ONE WANTED TO ARGUE WITH HIM, EVEN THOUGH IT MEANT TAKING CRUCIAL BODIES AWAY FROM THE BATTLE TO PROTECT SOMEONE WHO WAS ALREADY DOOMED.
IF PETRU IS RIGHT, AND SHE'S THE ONLY ONE WHO CAN CHANGE MY CURSE, REMOVE THE HAPPINESS CLAUSE...
...THEN IF I LET HER DIE, I'LL LOSE MY LAST HOPE.

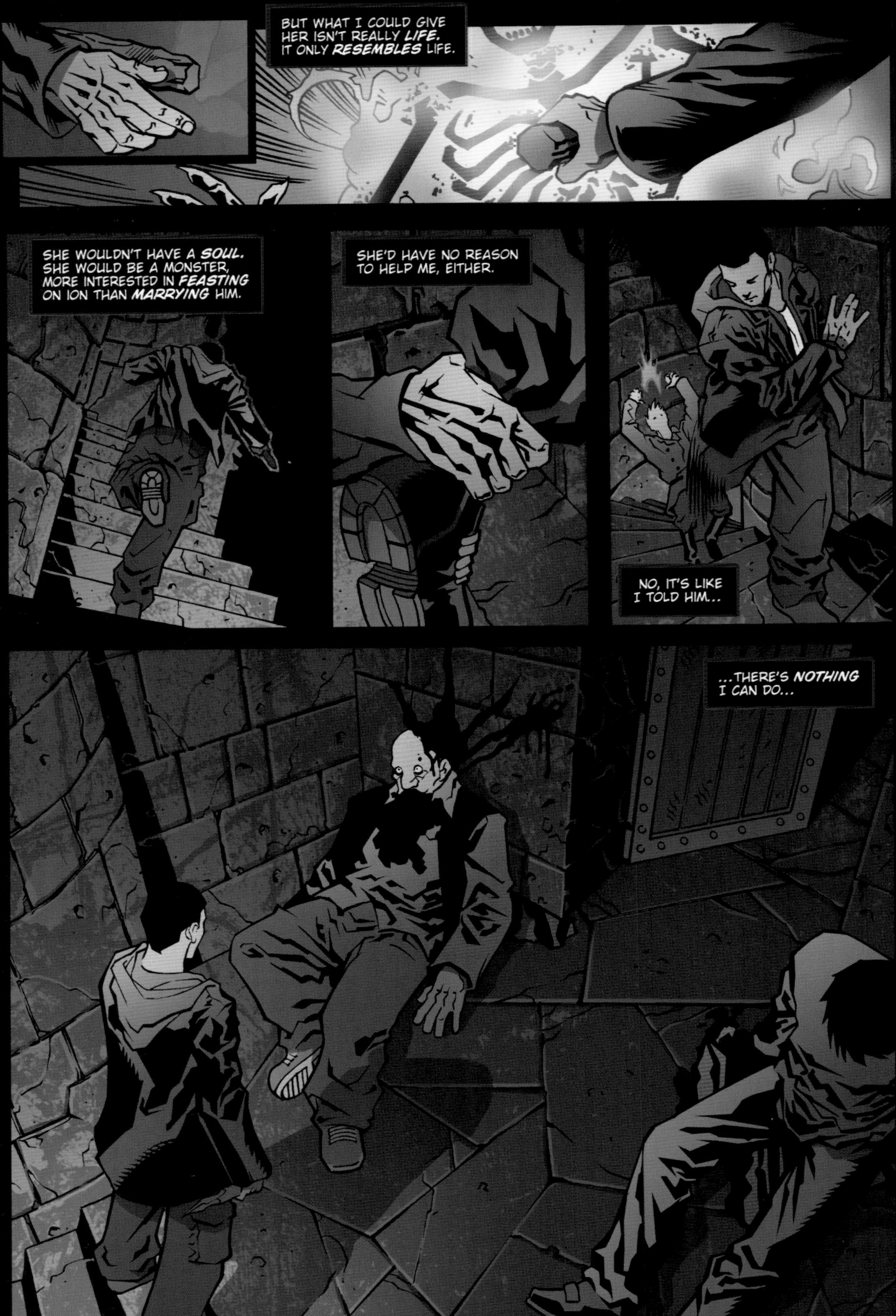
BUT WHAT I COULD GIVE HER ISN'T REALLY *LIFE*. IT ONLY *RESEMBLES* LIFE.
SHE WOULDN'T HAVE A *SOUL*. SHE WOULD BE A MONSTER, MORE INTERESTED IN *FEASTING* ON ION THAN *MARRYING* HIM.
SHE'D HAVE NO REASON TO HELP ME, EITHER.
NO, IT'S LIKE I TOLD HIM...
...THERE'S *NOTHING* I CAN DO...

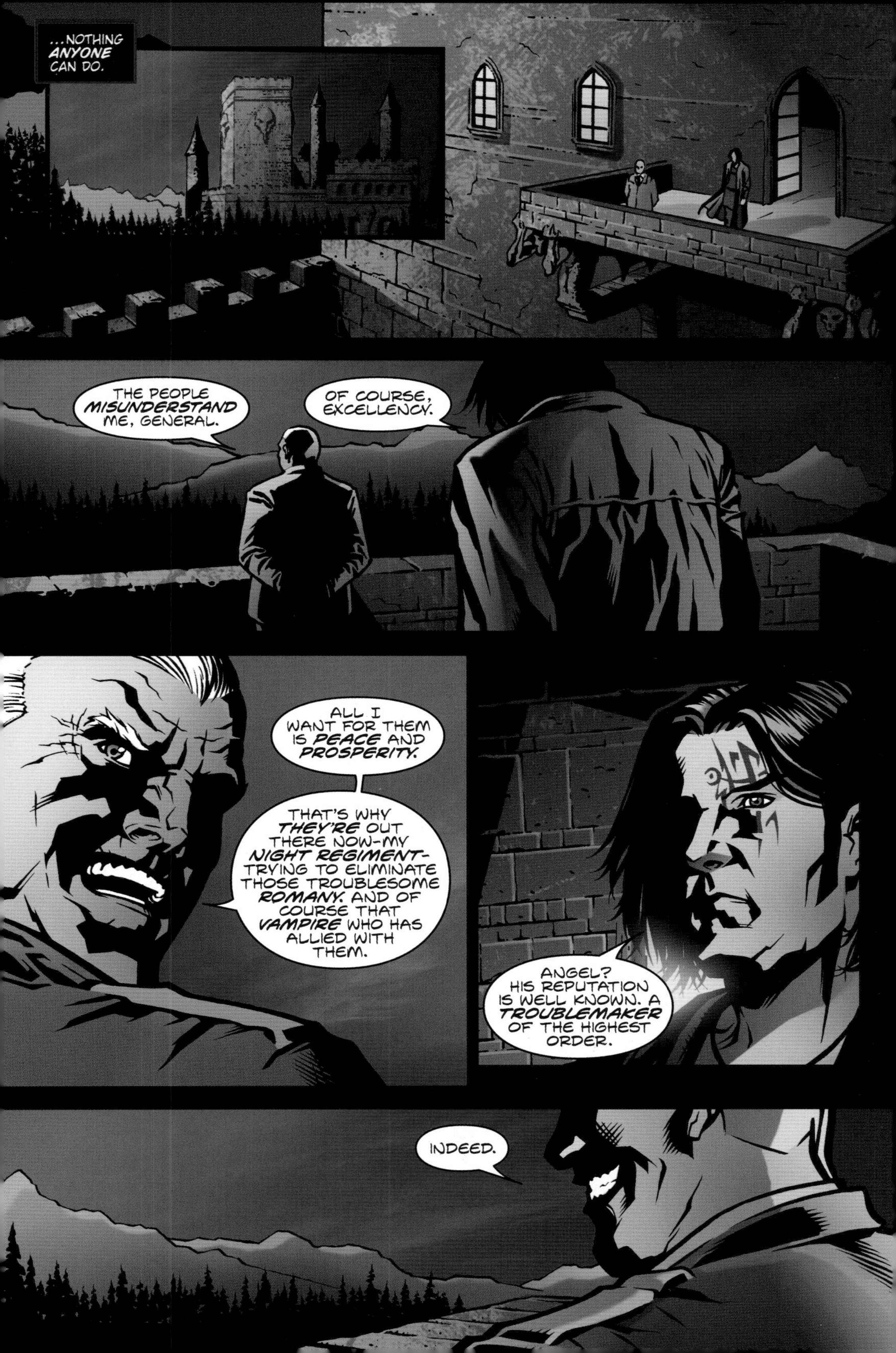
...NOTHING ANYONE CAN DO.
THE PEOPLE MISUNDERSTAND ME, GENERAL.
OF COURSE, EXCELLENCY.
ALL I WANT FOR THEM IS PEACE AND PROSPERITY.
THAT'S WHY THEY'RE OUT THERE NOW-MY NIGHT REGIMENT-TRYING TO ELIMINATE THOSE TROUBLESOME ROMANY. AND OF COURSE THAT VAMPIRE WHO HAS ALLIED WITH THEM.
ANGEL? HIS REPUTATION IS WELL KNOWN. A TROUBLEMAKER OF THE HIGHEST ORDER.
INDEED.

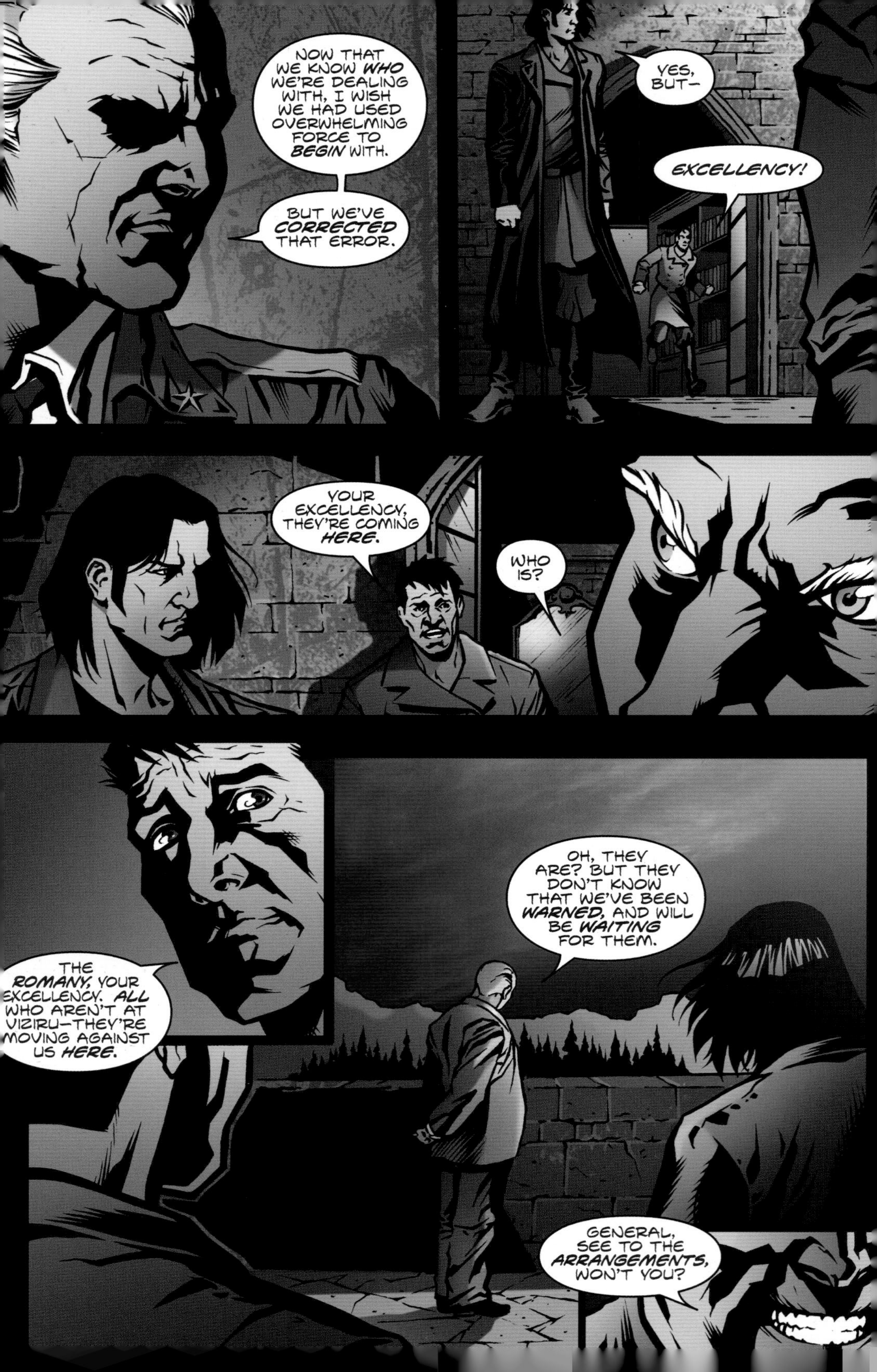
NOW THAT WE KNOW WHO WE'RE DEALING WITH, I WISH WE HAD USED OVERWHELMING FORCE TO BEGIN WITH.
BUT WE'VE CORRECTED THAT ERROR.
YES, BUT—
EXCELLENCY!
YOUR EXCELLENCY, THEY'RE COMING HERE.
WHO IS?
THE ROMANY, YOUR EXCELLENCY. ALL WHO AREN'T AT VIZIRU—THEY'RE MOVING AGAINST US HERE.
OH, THEY ARE? BUT THEY DON'T KNOW THAT WE'VE BEEN WARNED, AND WILL BE WAITING FOR THEM.
GENERAL, SEE TO THE ARRANGEMENTS, WON'T YOU?

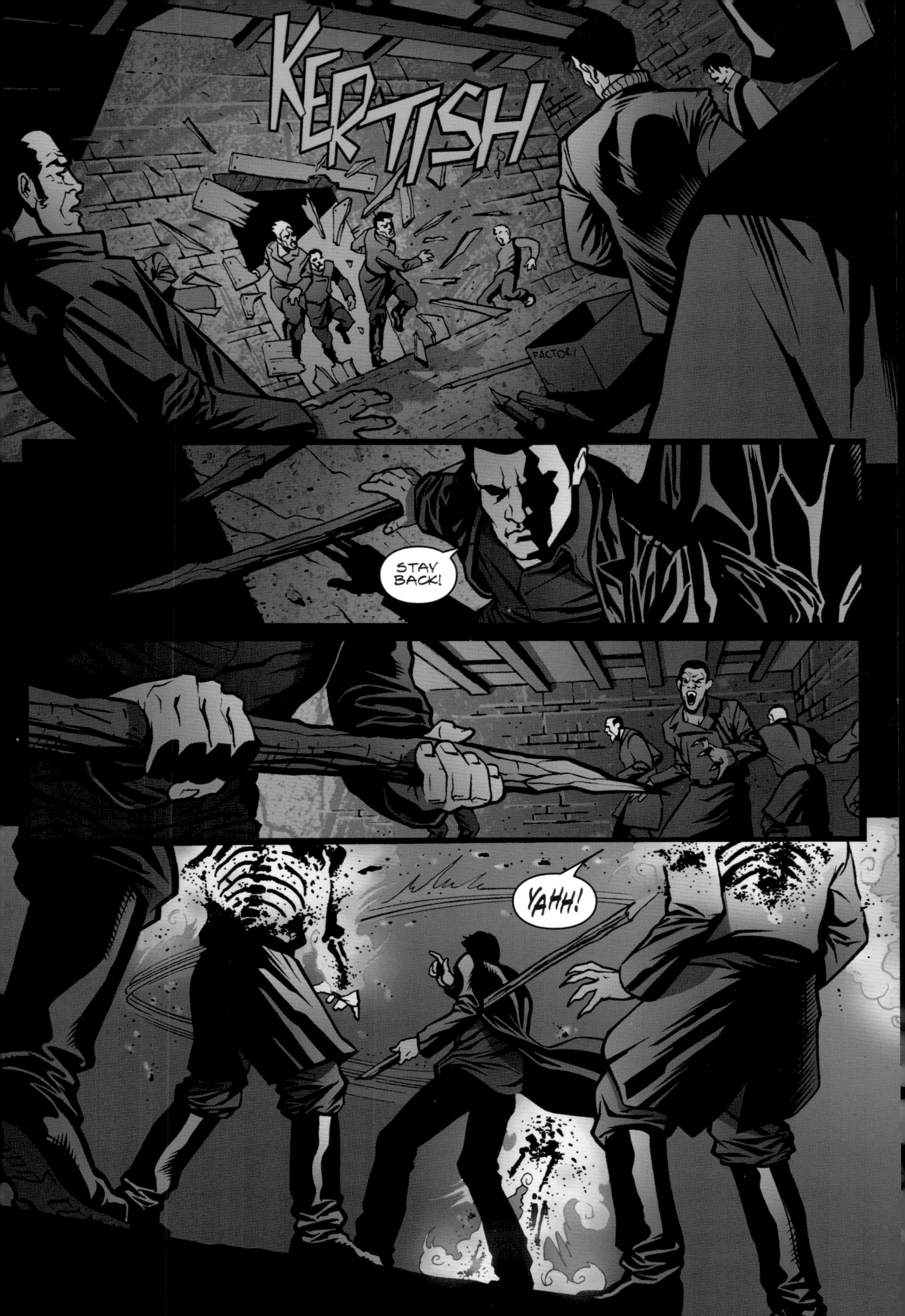
KER-TISH
FACTORY
STAY BACK!
YAHH!

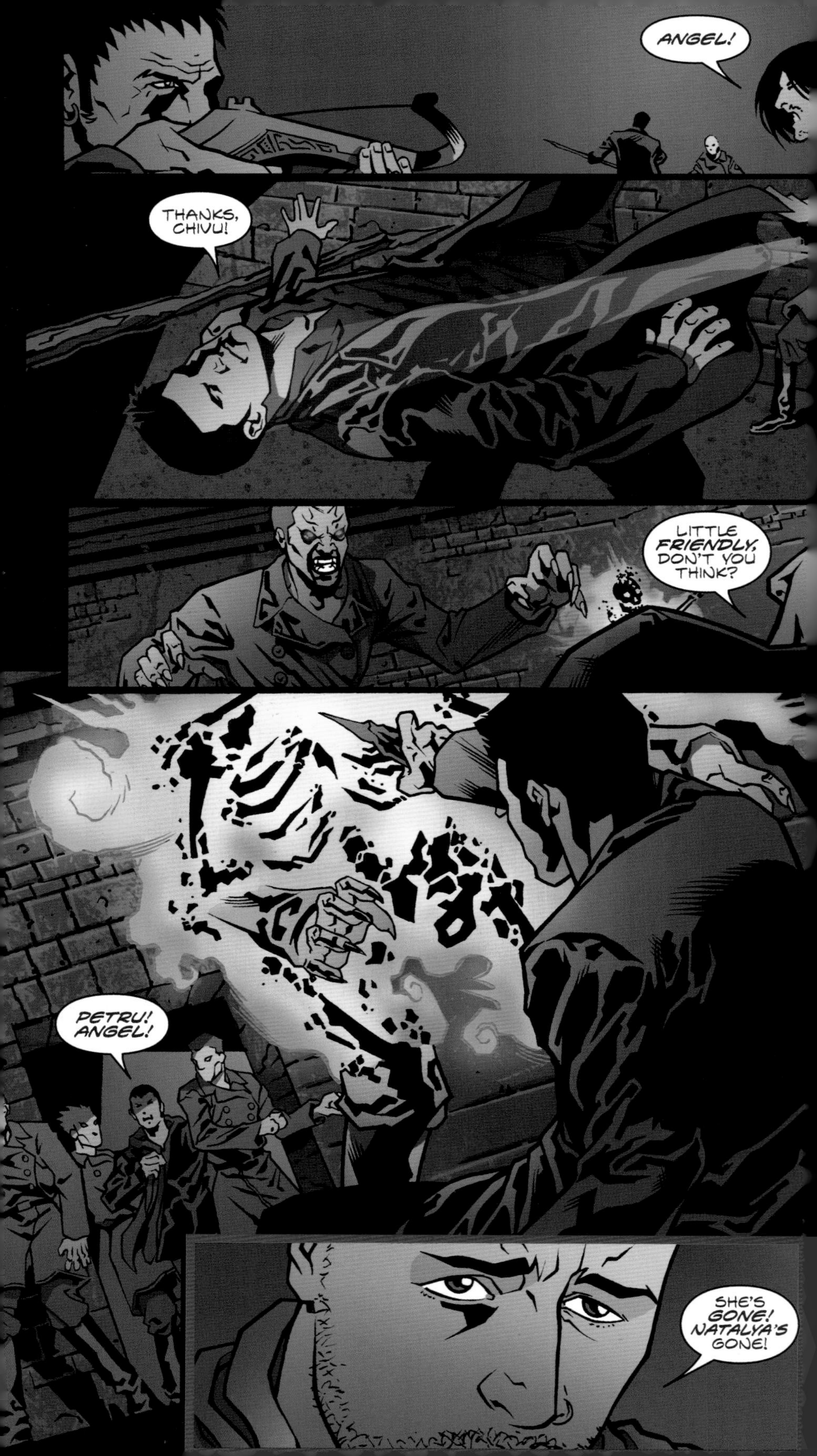
ANGEL!
THANKS, CHIVU!
LITTLE FRIENDLY, DON'T YOU THINK?
PETRU! ANGEL!
SHE'S GONE! NATALYA'S GONE!

chapter five

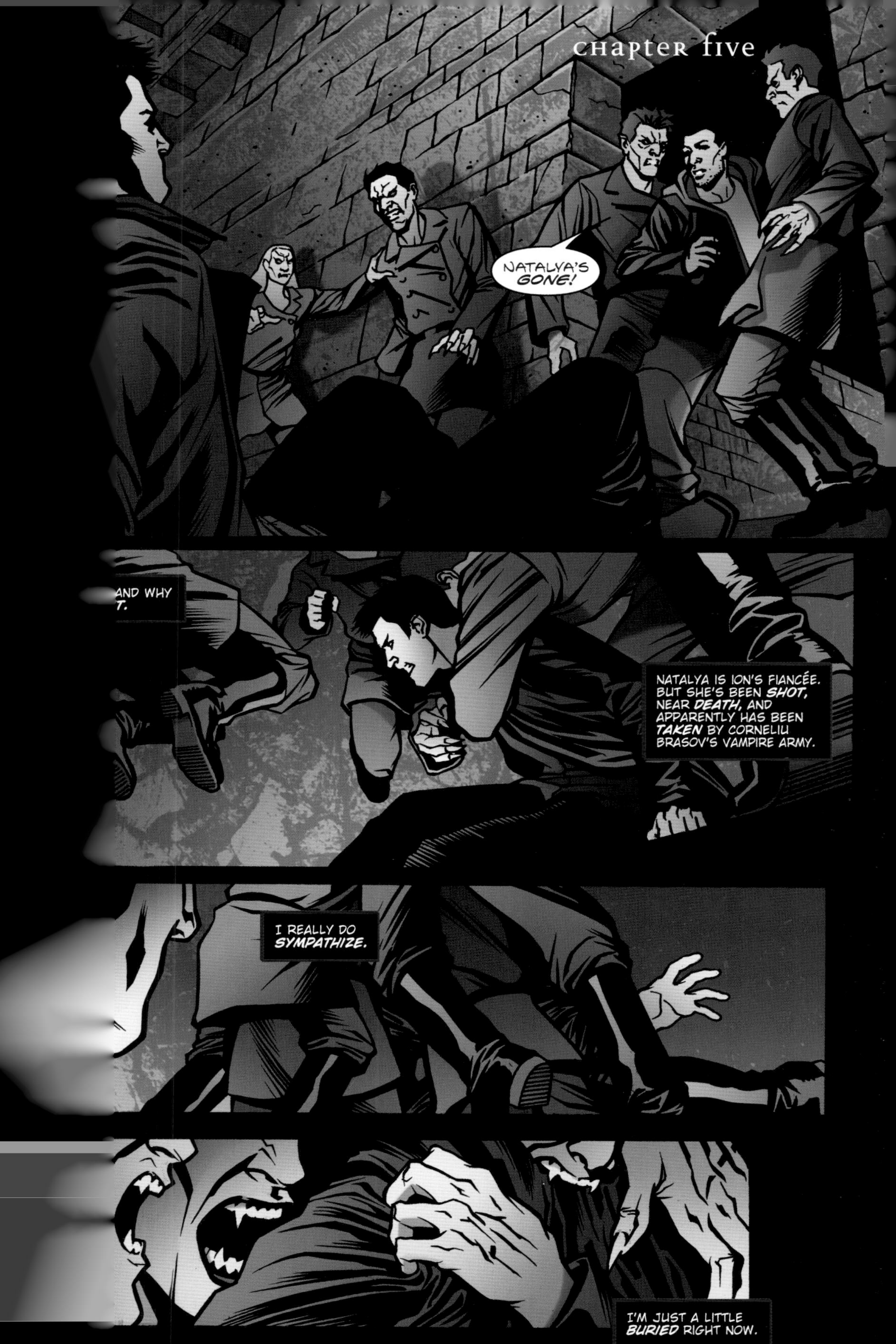
NATALYA'S GONE!
AND WHY
NATALYA IS ION'S FIANCÉE. BUT SHE'S BEEN SHOT, NEAR DEATH, AND APPARENTLY HAS BEEN TAKEN BY CORNELIU BRASOV'S VAMPIRE ARMY.
I REALLY DO SYMPATHIZE.
I'M JUST A LITTLE BURIED RIGHT NOW.

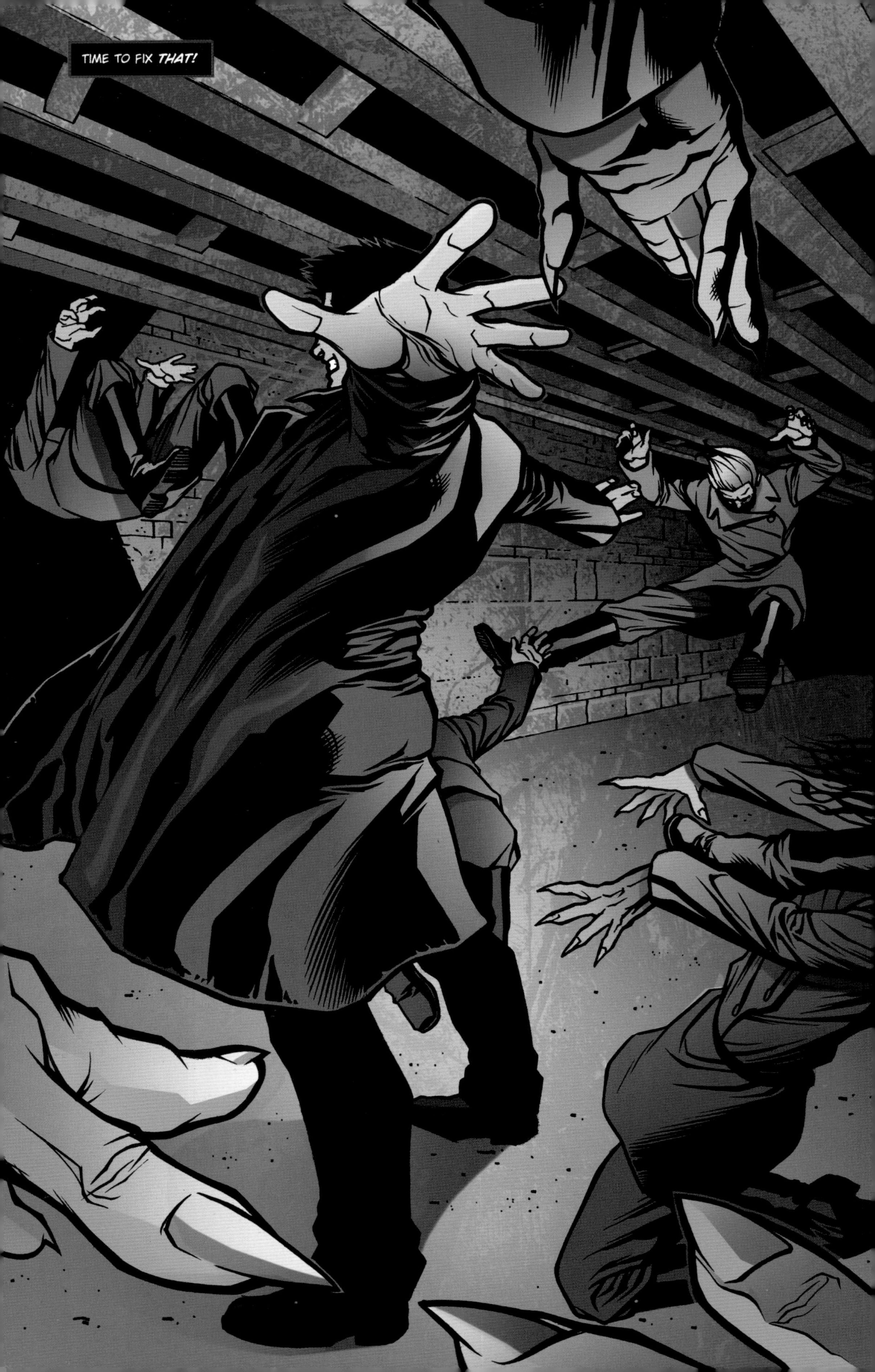
TIME TO FIX THAT!

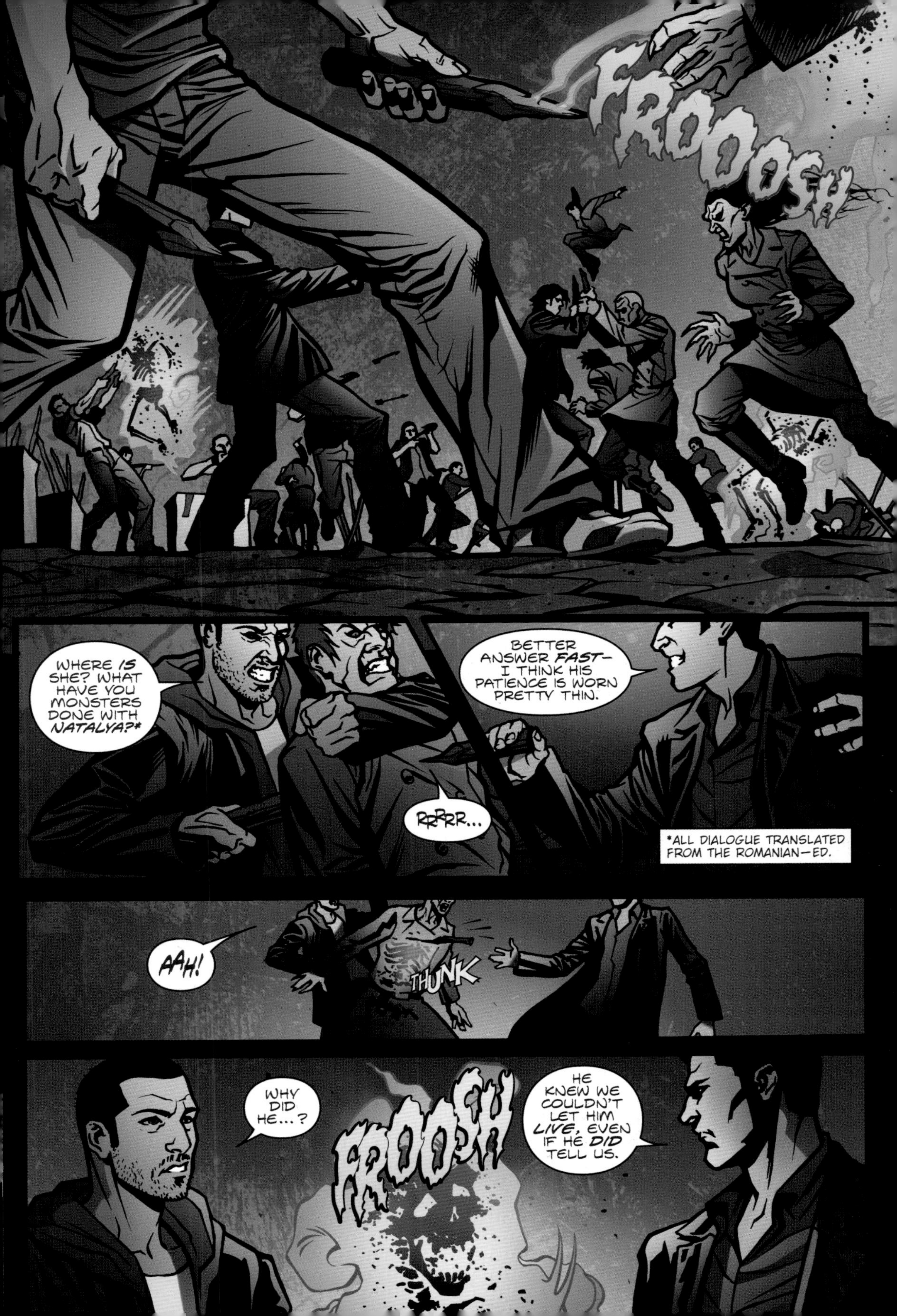
FROOOSH
WHERE IS SHE? WHAT HAVE YOU MONSTERS DONE WITH NATALYA?*
BETTER ANSWER FAST— I THINK HIS PATIENCE IS WORN PRETTY THIN.
RRRRR...
*ALL DIALOGUE TRANSLATED FROM THE ROMANIAN—ED.
AAH!
THUNK
WHY DID HE...?
FROOSH
HE KNEW WE COULDN'T LET HIM LIVE, EVEN IF HE DID TELL US.

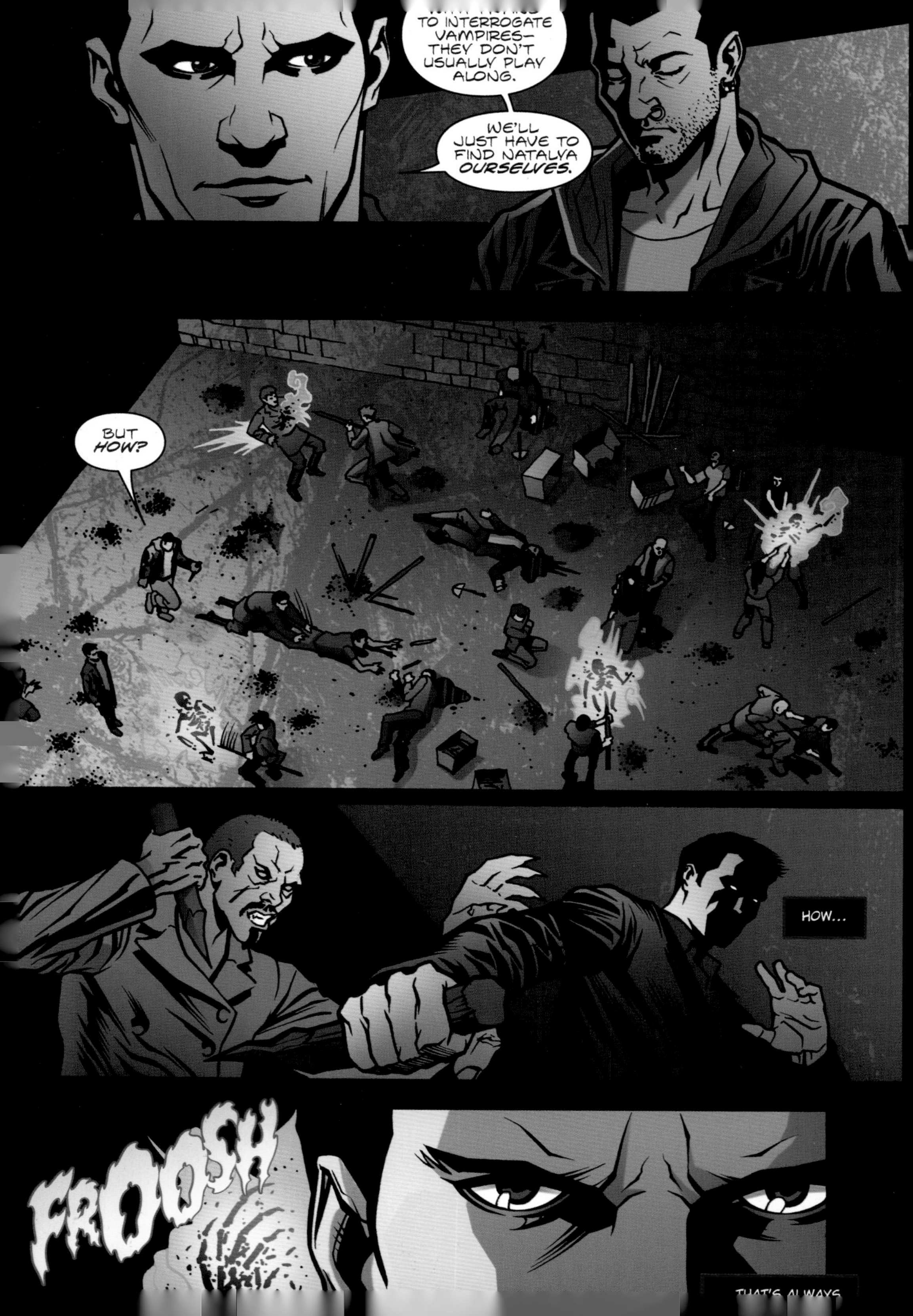
TO INTERROGATE VAMPIRES— THEY DON'T USUALLY PLAY ALONG.
WE'LL JUST HAVE TO FIND NATALYA *OURSELVES*.
BUT *HOW?*
HOW...
FROOSH
THAT'S ALWAYS

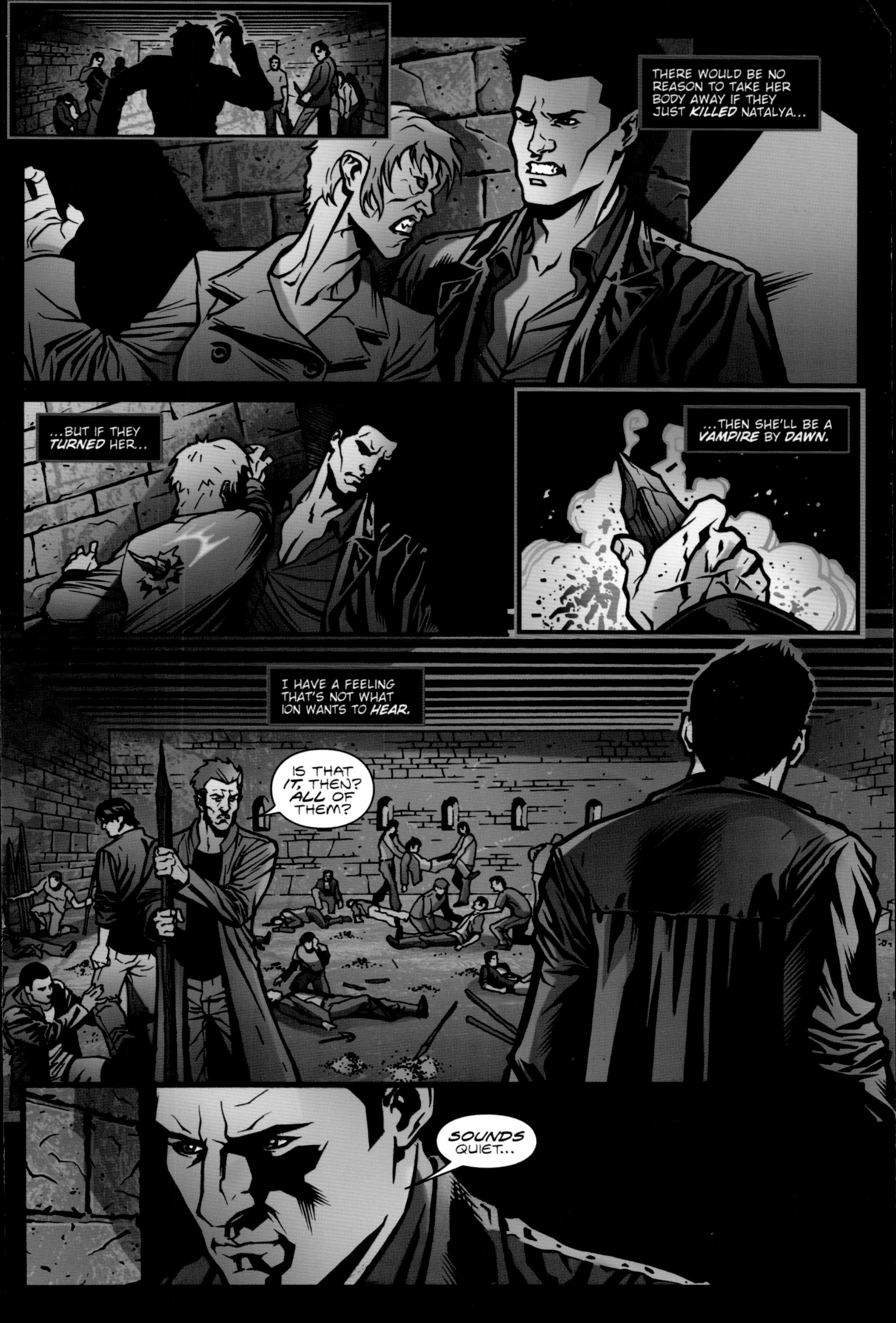
THERE WOULD BE NO REASON TO TAKE HER BODY AWAY IF THEY JUST KILLED NATALYA...
...BUT IF THEY TURNED HER...
...THEN SHE'LL BE A VAMPIRE BY DAWN.
I HAVE A FEELING THAT'S NOT WHAT ION WANTS TO HEAR.
IS THAT IT, THEN? ALL OF THEM?
SOUNDS QUIET...

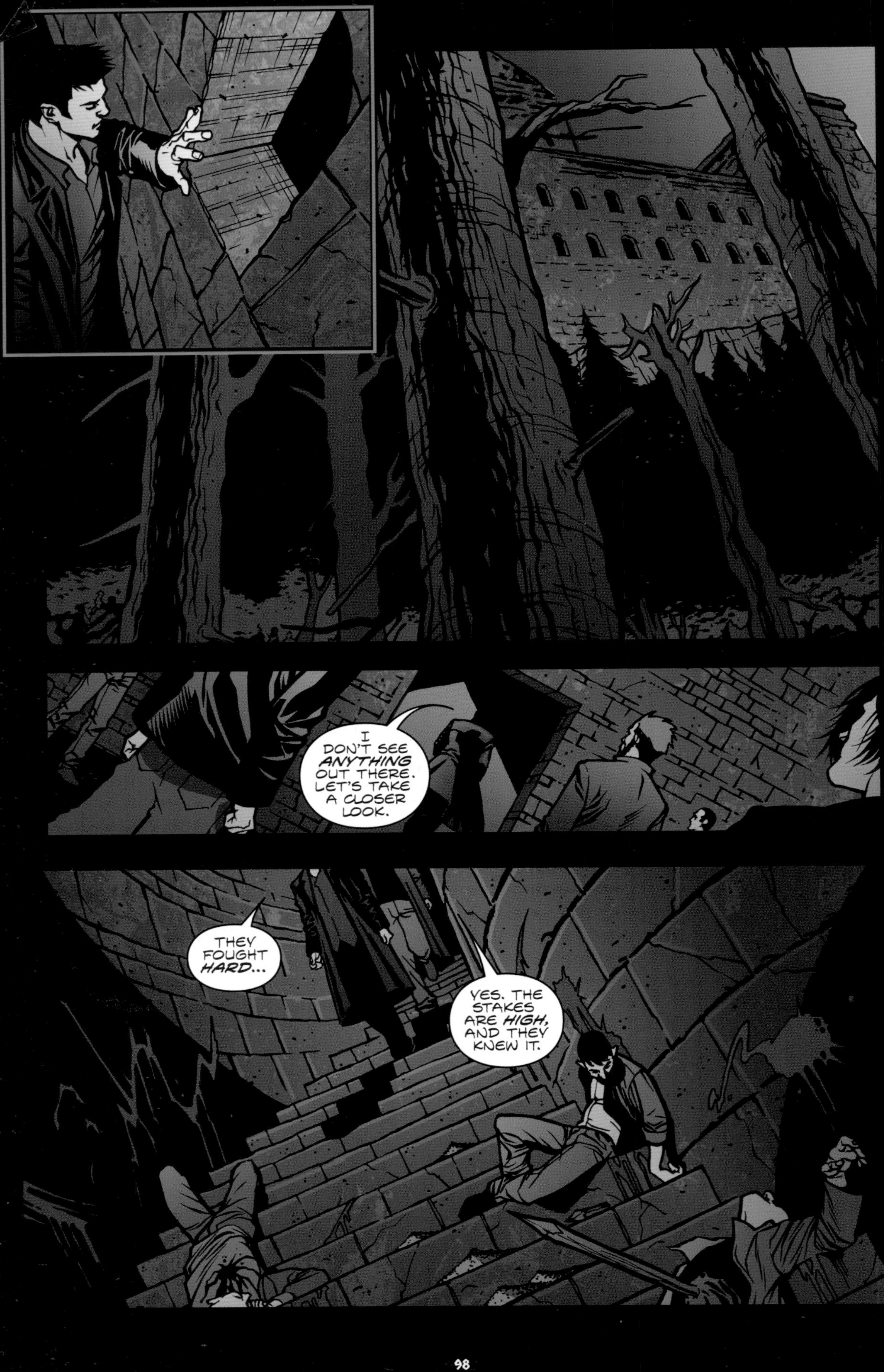
I DON'T SEE ANYTHING OUT THERE. LET'S TAKE A CLOSER LOOK.
THEY FOUGHT HARD...
YES. THE STAKES ARE HIGH, AND THEY KNEW IT.

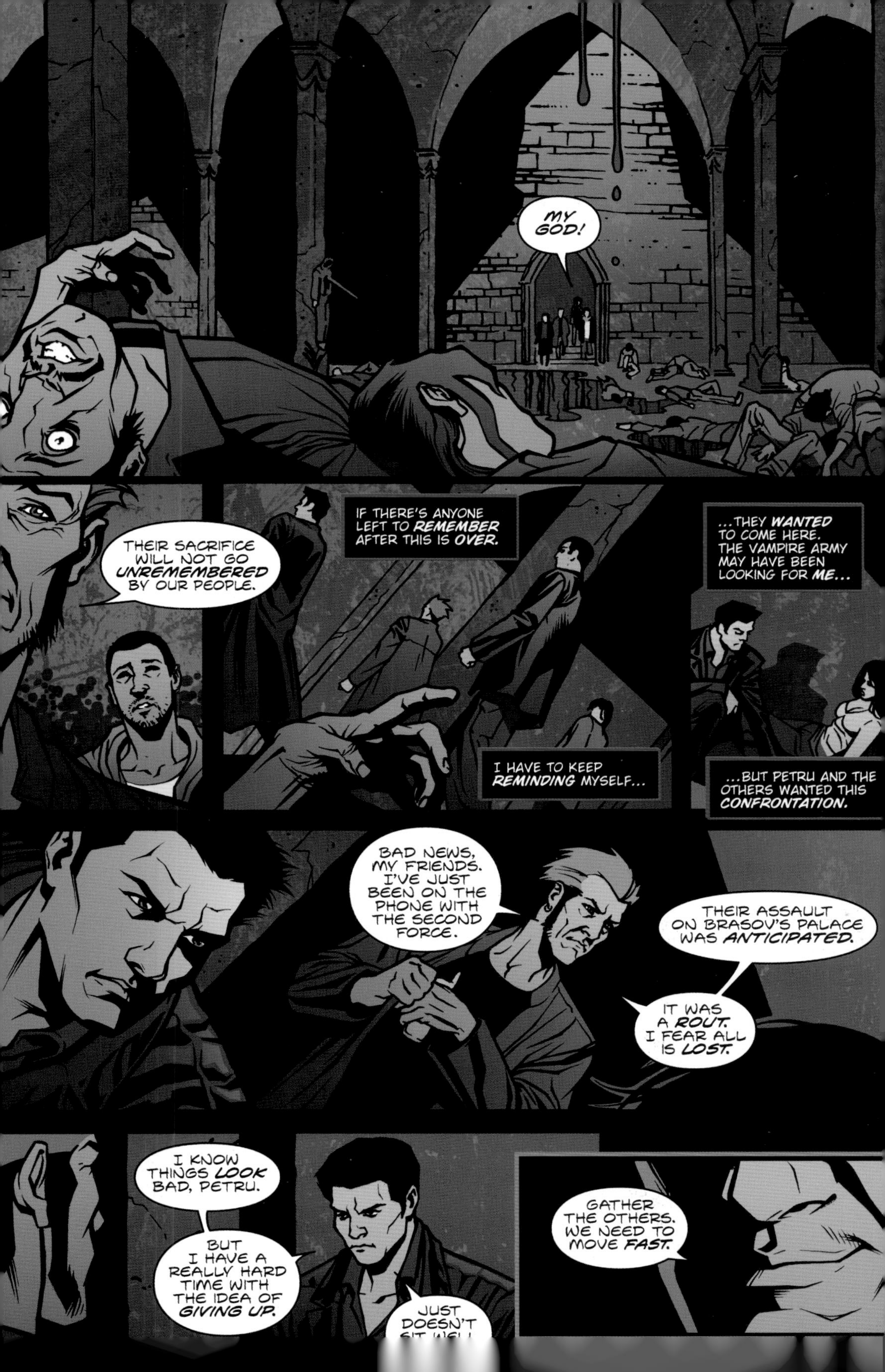
MY GOD!
THEIR SACRIFICE WILL NOT GO UNREMEMBERED BY OUR PEOPLE.
IF THERE'S ANYONE LEFT TO REMEMBER AFTER THIS IS OVER.
I HAVE TO KEEP REMINDING MYSELF...
...THEY WANTED TO COME HERE. THE VAMPIRE ARMY MAY HAVE BEEN LOOKING FOR ME...
...BUT PETRU AND THE OTHERS WANTED THIS CONFRONTATION.
BAD NEWS, MY FRIENDS. I'VE JUST BEEN ON THE PHONE WITH THE SECOND FORCE.
THEIR ASSAULT ON BRASOV'S PALACE WAS ANTICIPATED.
IT WAS A ROUT. I FEAR ALL IS LOST.
I KNOW THINGS LOOK BAD, PETRU.
BUT I HAVE A REALLY HARD TIME WITH THE IDEA OF GIVING UP.
JUST DOESN'T
GATHER THE OTHERS. WE NEED TO MOVE FAST.

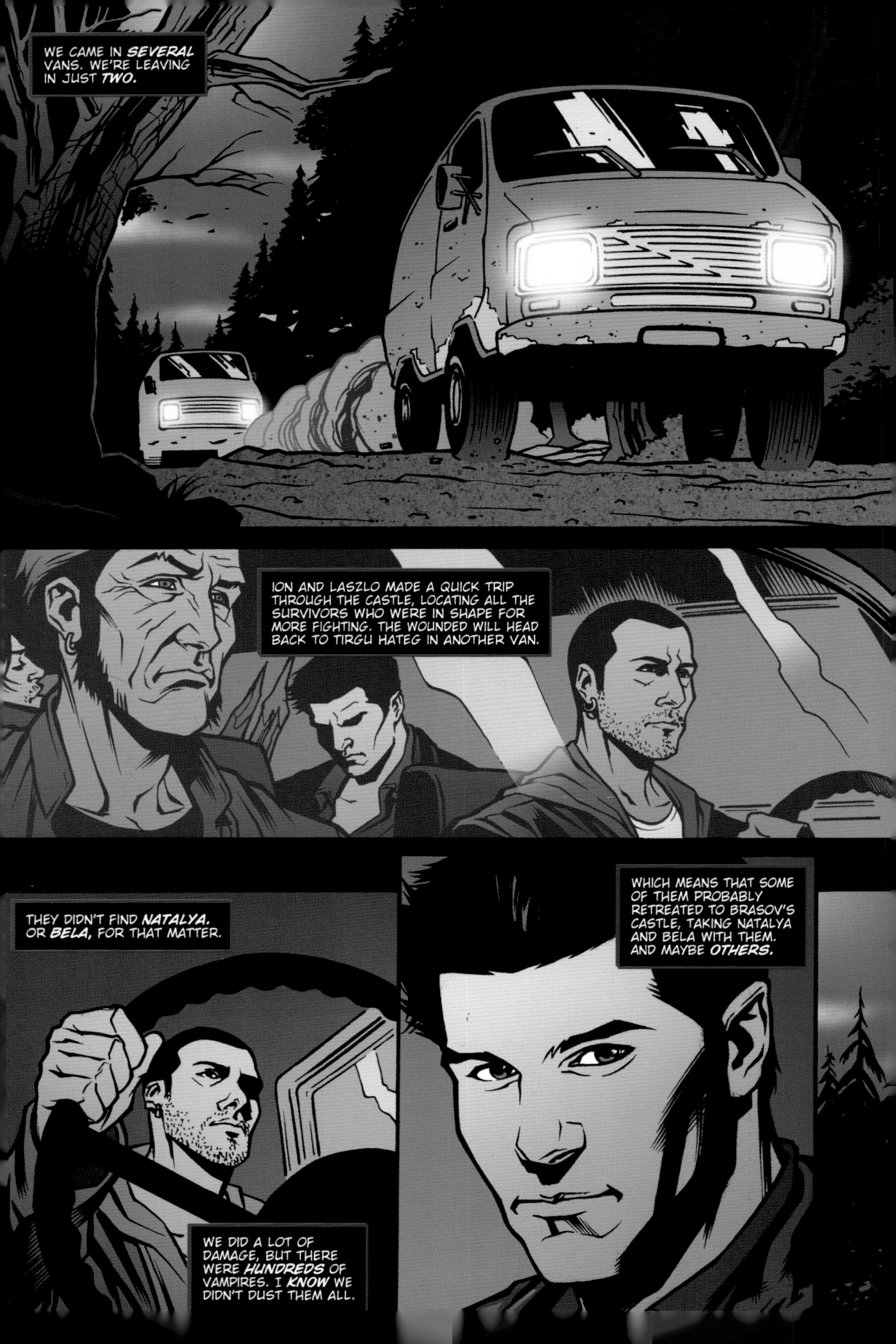

WE CAME IN SEVERAL VANS. WE'RE LEAVING IN JUST TWO.
ION AND LASZLO MADE A QUICK TRIP THROUGH THE CASTLE, LOCATING ALL THE SURVIVORS WHO WERE IN SHAPE FOR MORE FIGHTING. THE WOUNDED WILL HEAD BACK TO TIRGU HATEG IN ANOTHER VAN.
THEY DIDN'T FIND NATALYA. OR BELA, FOR THAT MATTER.
WE DID A LOT OF DAMAGE, BUT THERE WERE HUNDREDS OF VAMPIRES. I KNOW WE DIDN'T DUST THEM ALL.
WHICH MEANS THAT SOME OF THEM PROBABLY RETREATED TO BRASOV'S CASTLE, TAKING NATALYA AND BELA WITH THEM. AND MAYBE OTHERS.

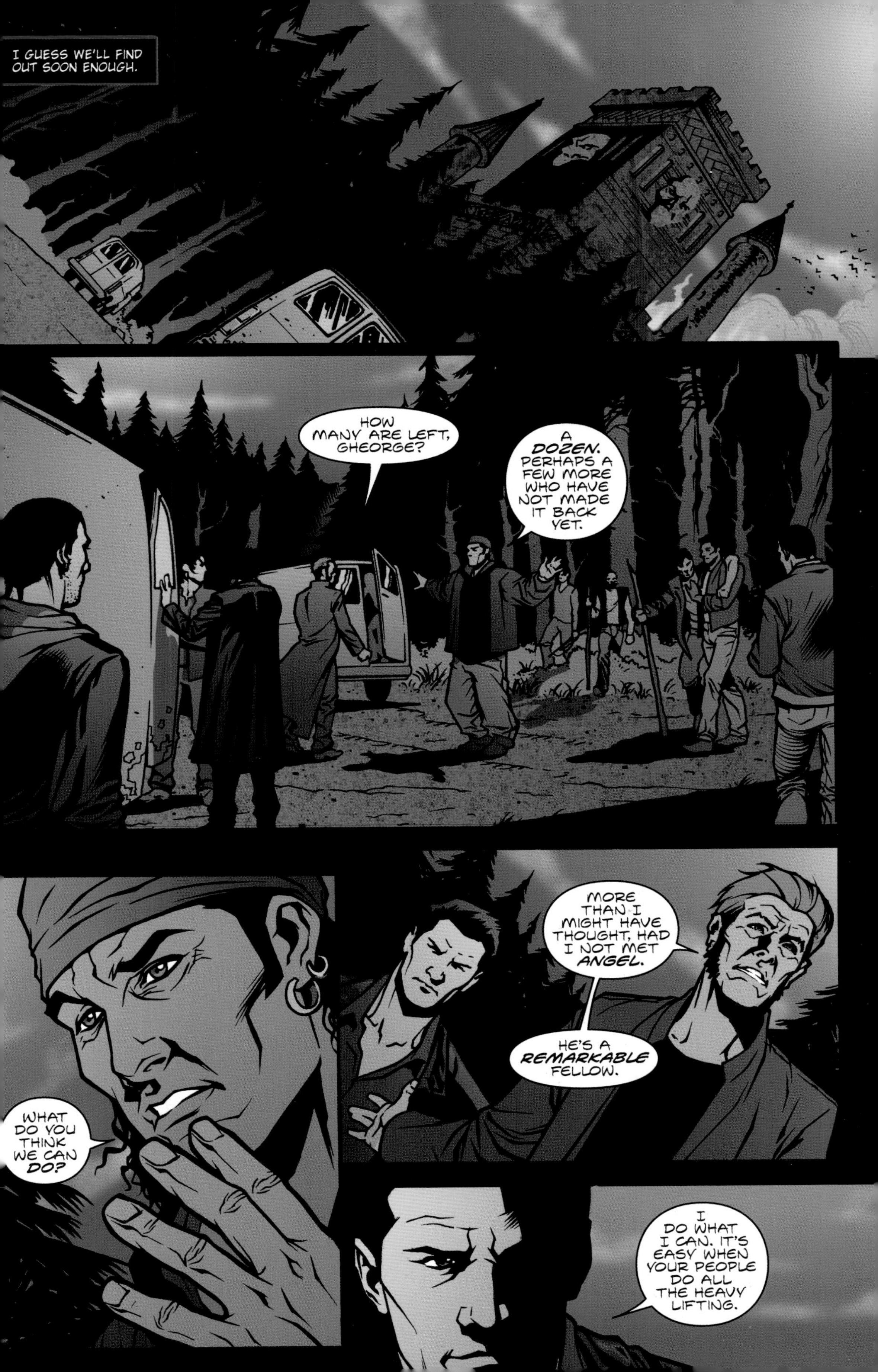
I GUESS WE'LL FIND OUT SOON ENOUGH.
HOW MANY ARE LEFT, GHEORGE?
A DOZEN. PERHAPS A FEW MORE WHO HAVE NOT MADE IT BACK YET.
WHAT DO YOU THINK WE CAN DO?
MORE THAN I MIGHT HAVE THOUGHT, HAD I NOT MET ANGEL.
HE'S A REMARKABLE FELLOW.
I DO WHAT I CAN. IT'S EASY WHEN YOUR PEOPLE DO ALL THE HEAVY LIFTING.

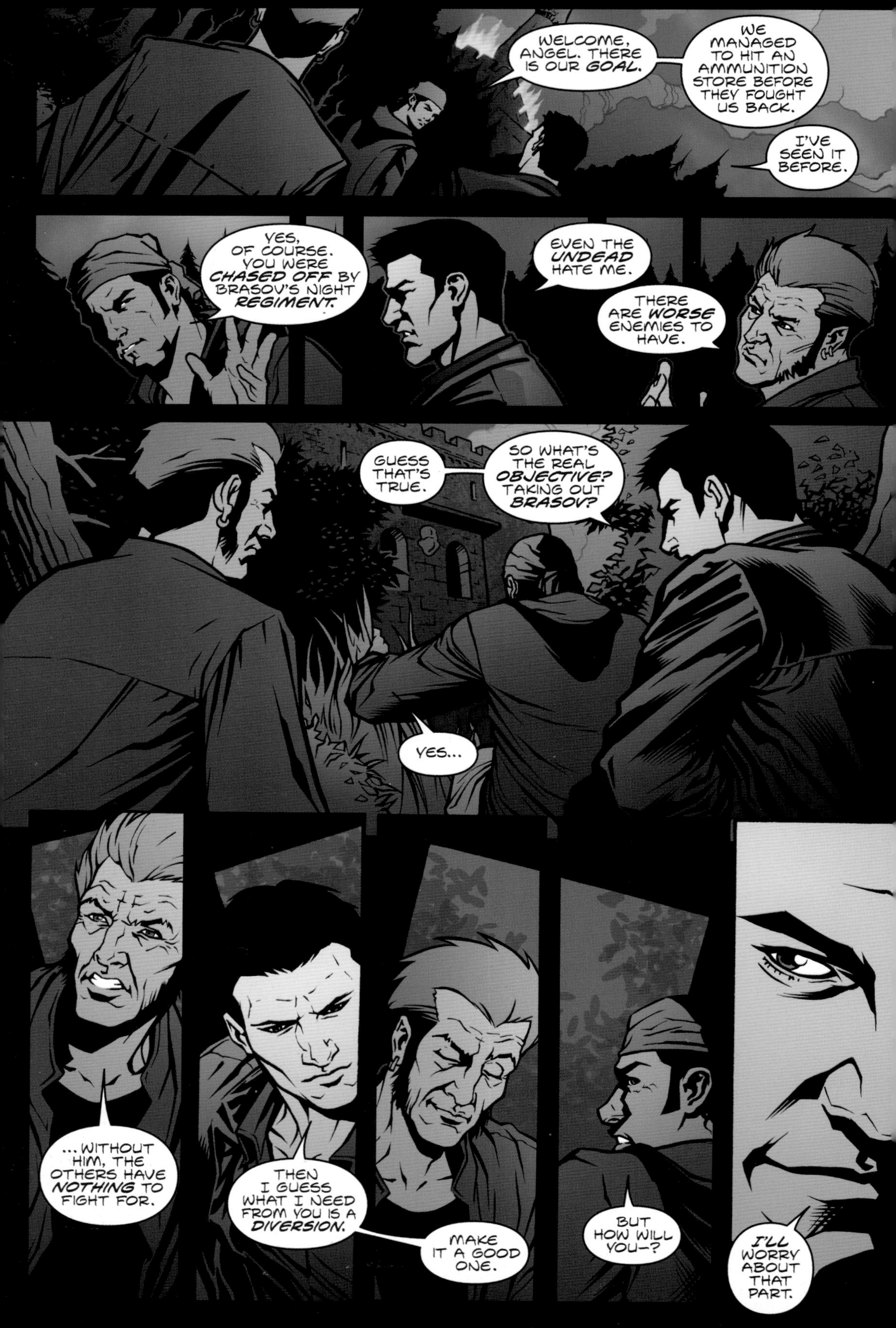
WELCOME, ANGEL. THERE IS OUR GOAL.
WE MANAGED TO HIT AN AMMUNITION STORE BEFORE THEY FOUGHT US BACK.
I'VE SEEN IT BEFORE.
YES, OF COURSE. YOU WERE CHASED OFF BY BRASOV'S NIGHT REGIMENT.
EVEN THE UNDEAD HATE ME.
THERE ARE WORSE ENEMIES TO HAVE.
GUESS THAT'S TRUE.
SO WHAT'S THE REAL OBJECTIVE? TAKING OUT BRASOV?
YES...
...WITHOUT HIM, THE OTHERS HAVE NOTHING TO FIGHT FOR.
THEN I GUESS WHAT I NEED FROM YOU IS A DIVERSION.
MAKE IT A GOOD ONE.
BUT HOW WILL YOU—?
I'LL WORRY ABOUT THAT PART.

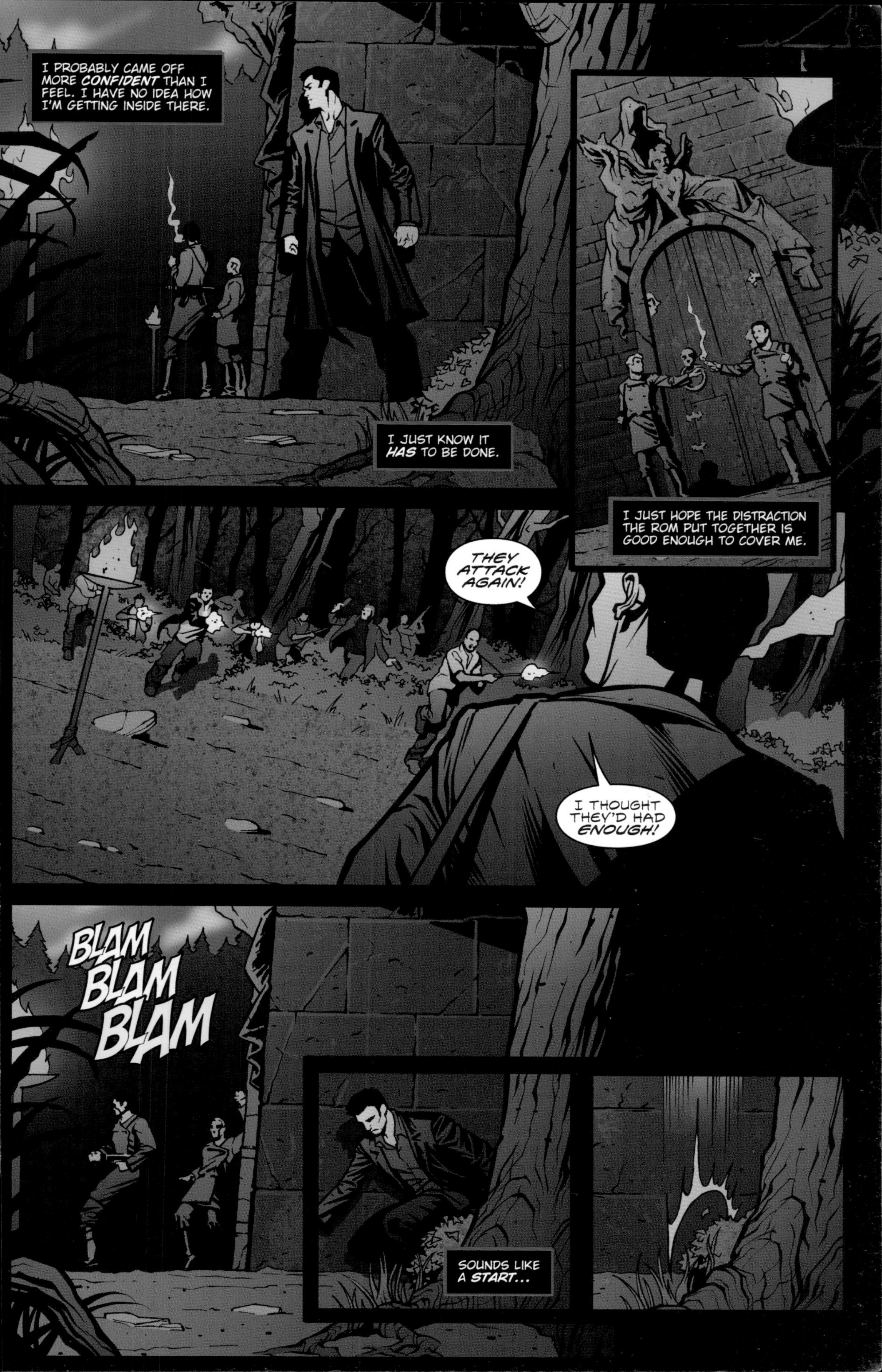

I PROBABLY CAME OFF MORE CONFIDENT THAN I FEEL. I HAVE NO IDEA HOW I'M GETTING INSIDE THERE.
I JUST KNOW IT HAS TO BE DONE.
I JUST HOPE THE DISTRACTION THE ROM PUT TOGETHER IS GOOD ENOUGH TO COVER ME.
THEY ATTACK AGAIN!
I THOUGHT THEY'D HAD ENOUGH!
BLAM BLAM BLAM
SOUNDS LIKE A START...

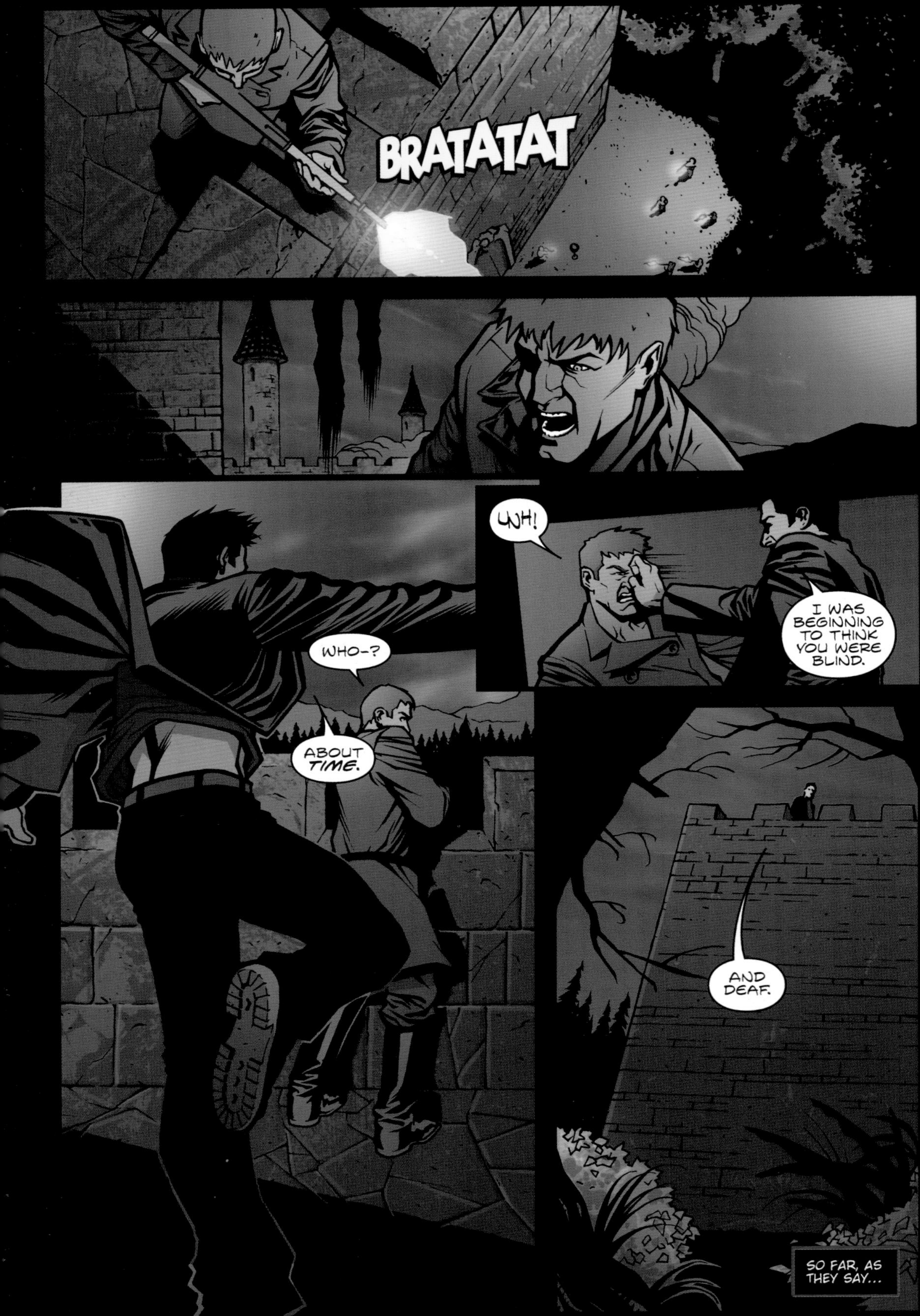
BRATATAT
UNH!
I WAS BEGINNING TO THINK YOU WERE BLIND.
WHO-?
ABOUT *TIME*.
AND DEAF.
SO FAR, AS THEY SAY...

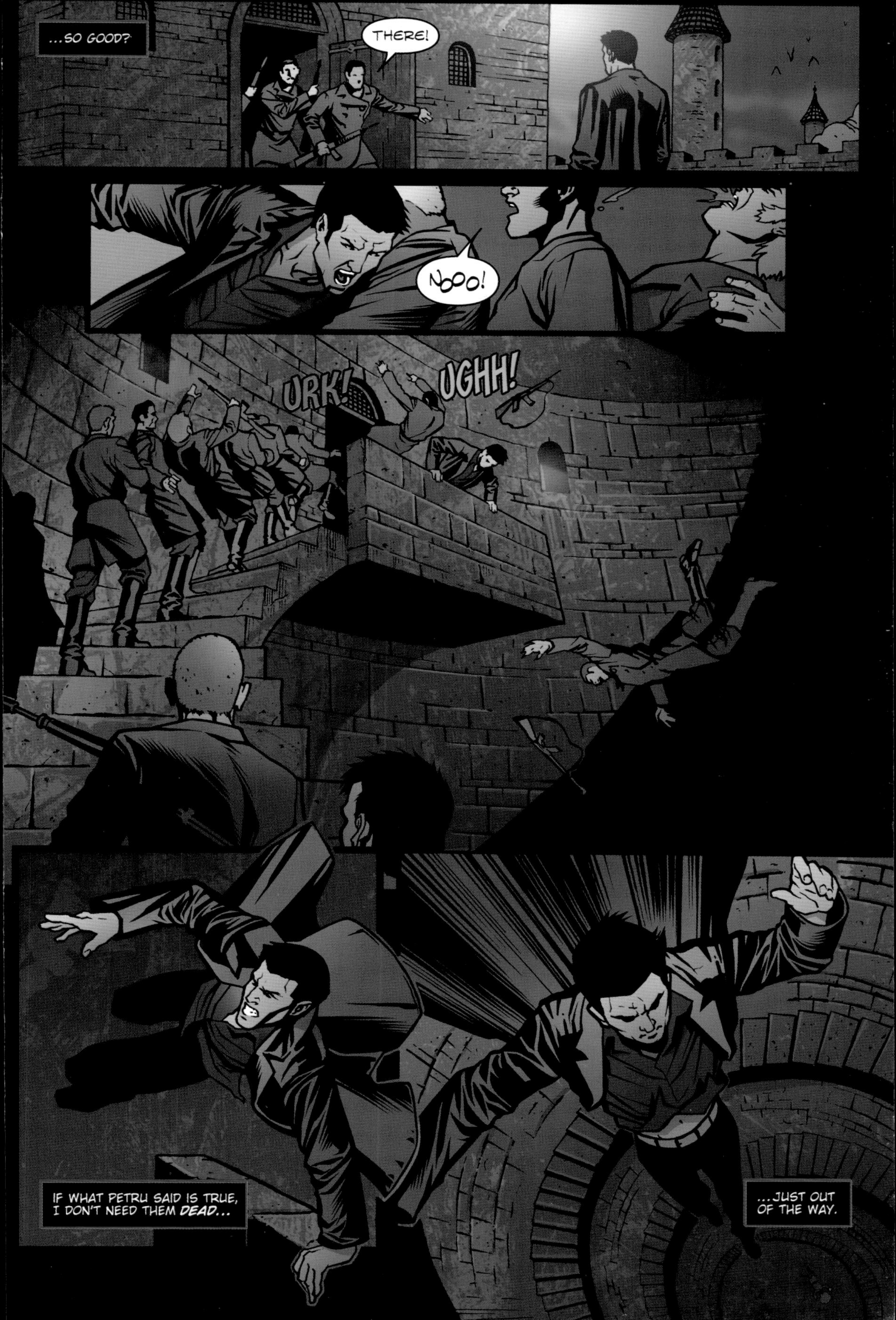

...SO GOOD?
THERE!
NOOO!
URK!
UGHH!
IF WHAT PETRU SAID IS TRUE, I DON'T NEED THEM *DEAD*...
...JUST OUT OF THE WAY.

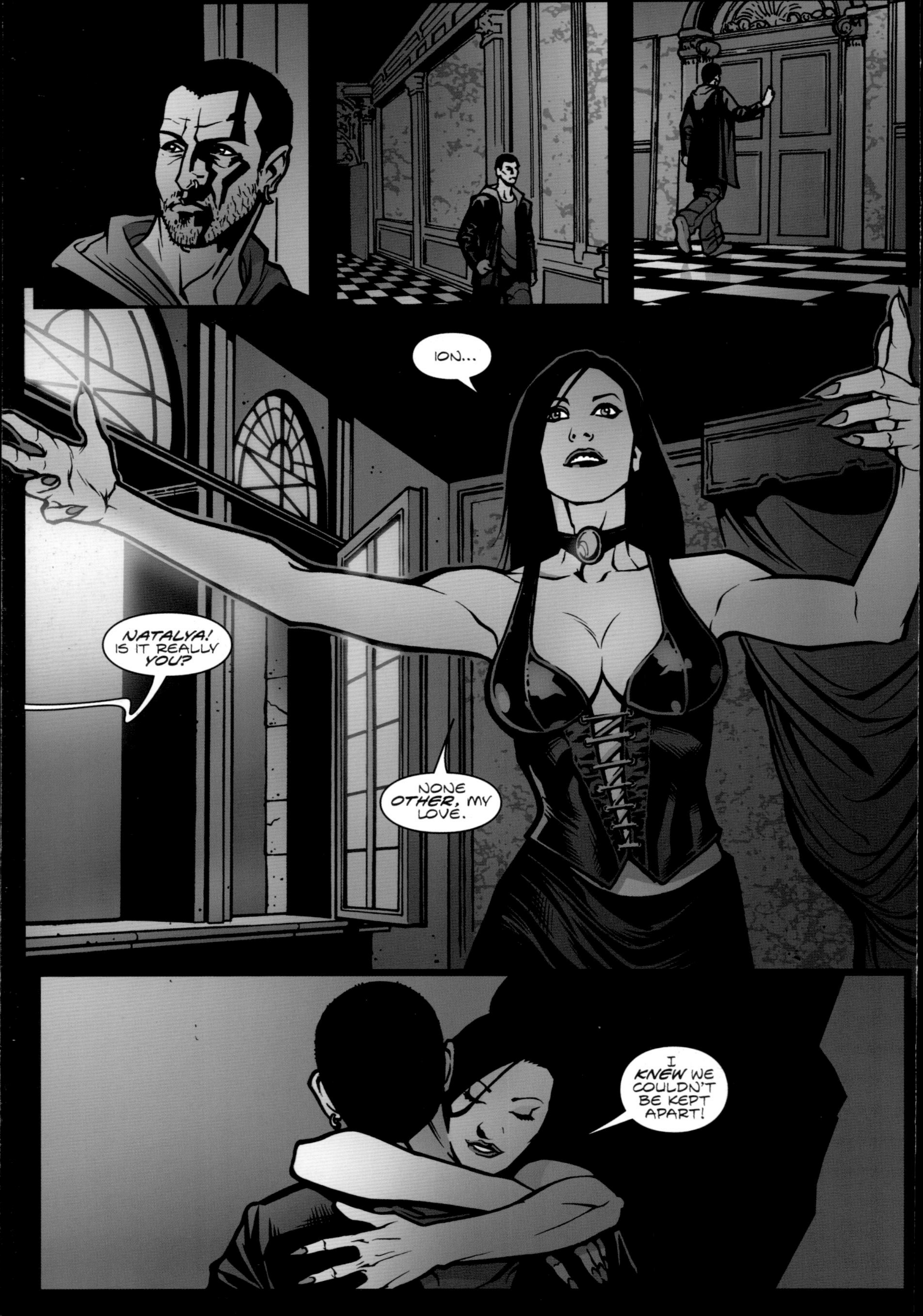
ION...
NATALYA! IS IT REALLY YOU?
NONE OTHER, MY LOVE.
I KNEW WE COULDN'T BE KEPT APART!

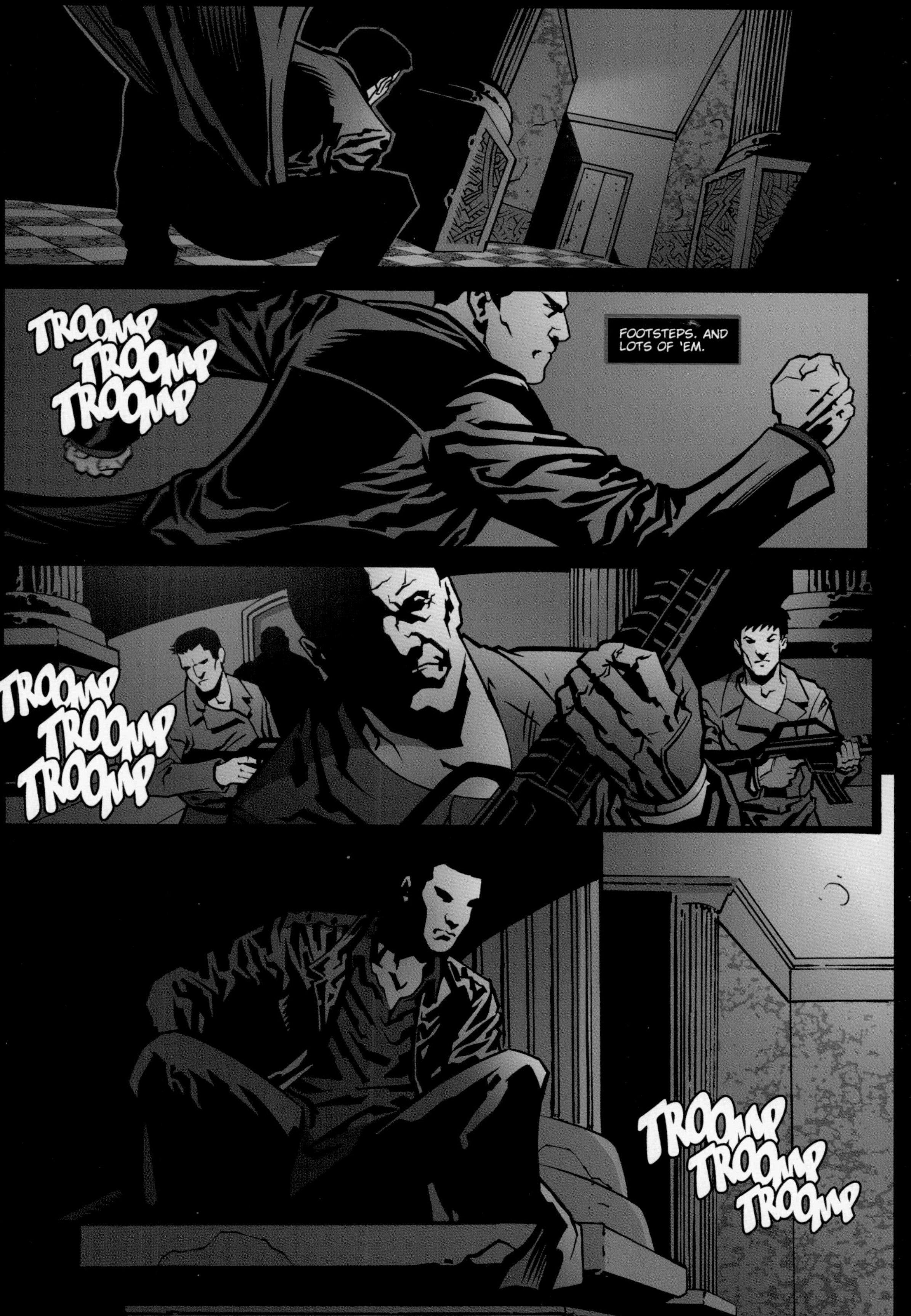

TROOMP TROOMP TROOMP
FOOTSTEPS. AND LOTS OF 'EM.
TROOMP TROOMP TROOMP
TROOMP TROOMP TROOMP

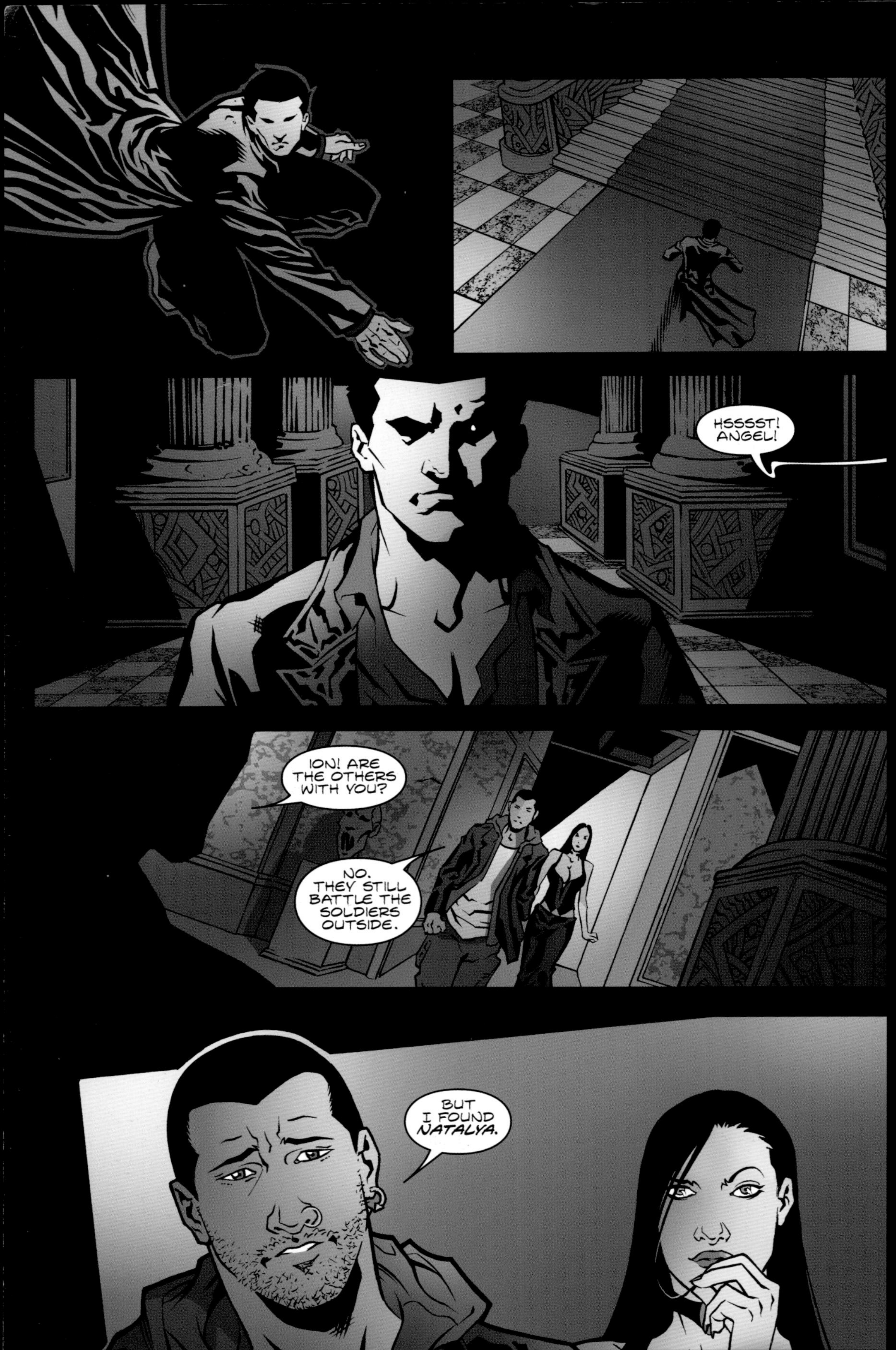
HSSSST! ANGEL!
ION! ARE THE OTHERS WITH YOU?
NO. THEY STILL BATTLE THE SOLDIERS OUTSIDE.
BUT I FOUND NATALYA.

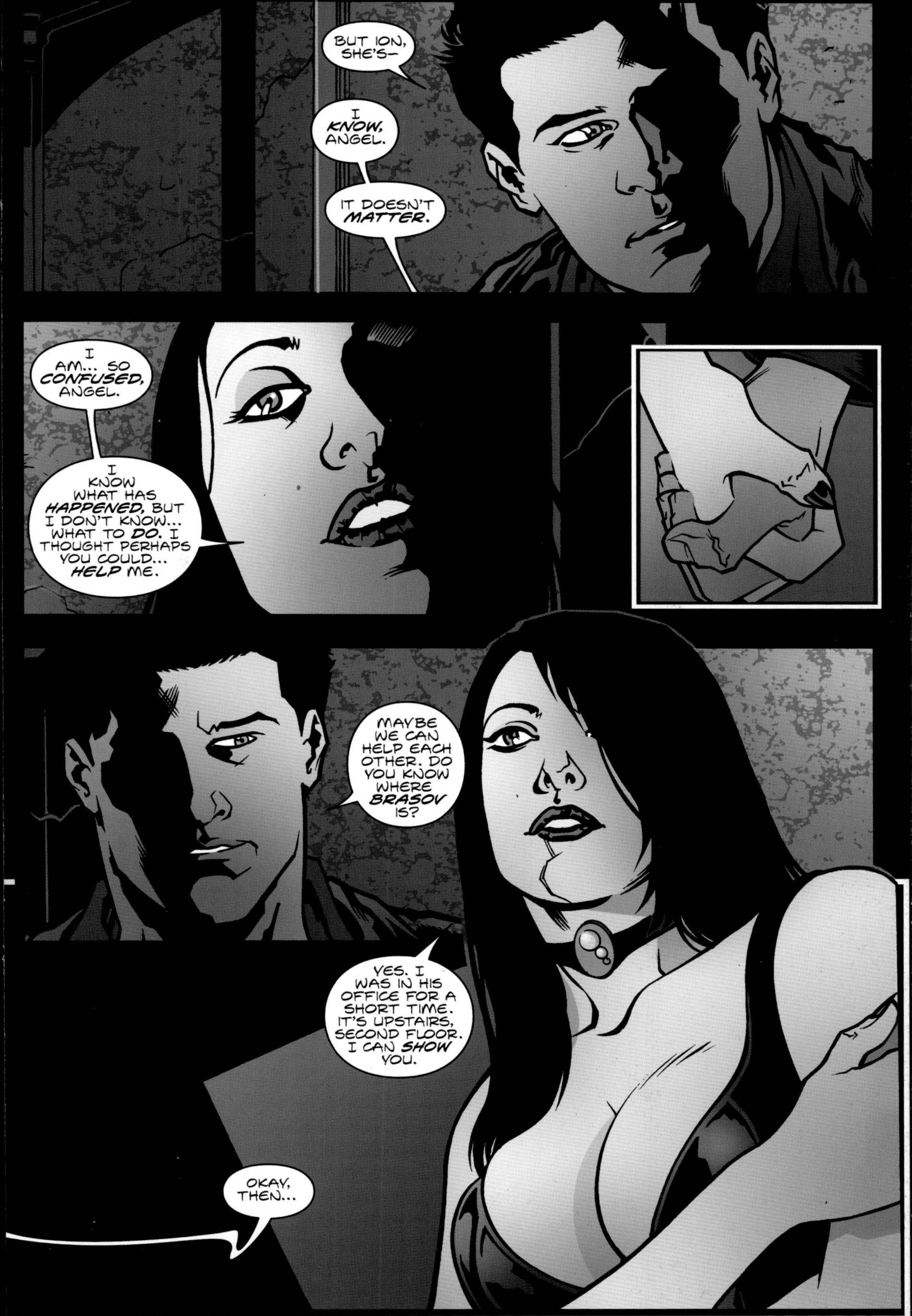
BUT ION, SHE'S—
I KNOW, ANGEL.
IT DOESN'T MATTER.
I AM... SO CONFUSED, ANGEL.
I KNOW WHAT HAS HAPPENED, BUT I DON'T KNOW... WHAT TO DO. I THOUGHT PERHAPS YOU COULD... HELP ME.
MAYBE WE CAN HELP EACH OTHER. DO YOU KNOW WHERE BRASOV IS?
YES. I WAS IN HIS OFFICE FOR A SHORT TIME. IT'S UPSTAIRS, SECOND FLOOR. I CAN SHOW YOU.
OKAY, THEN...

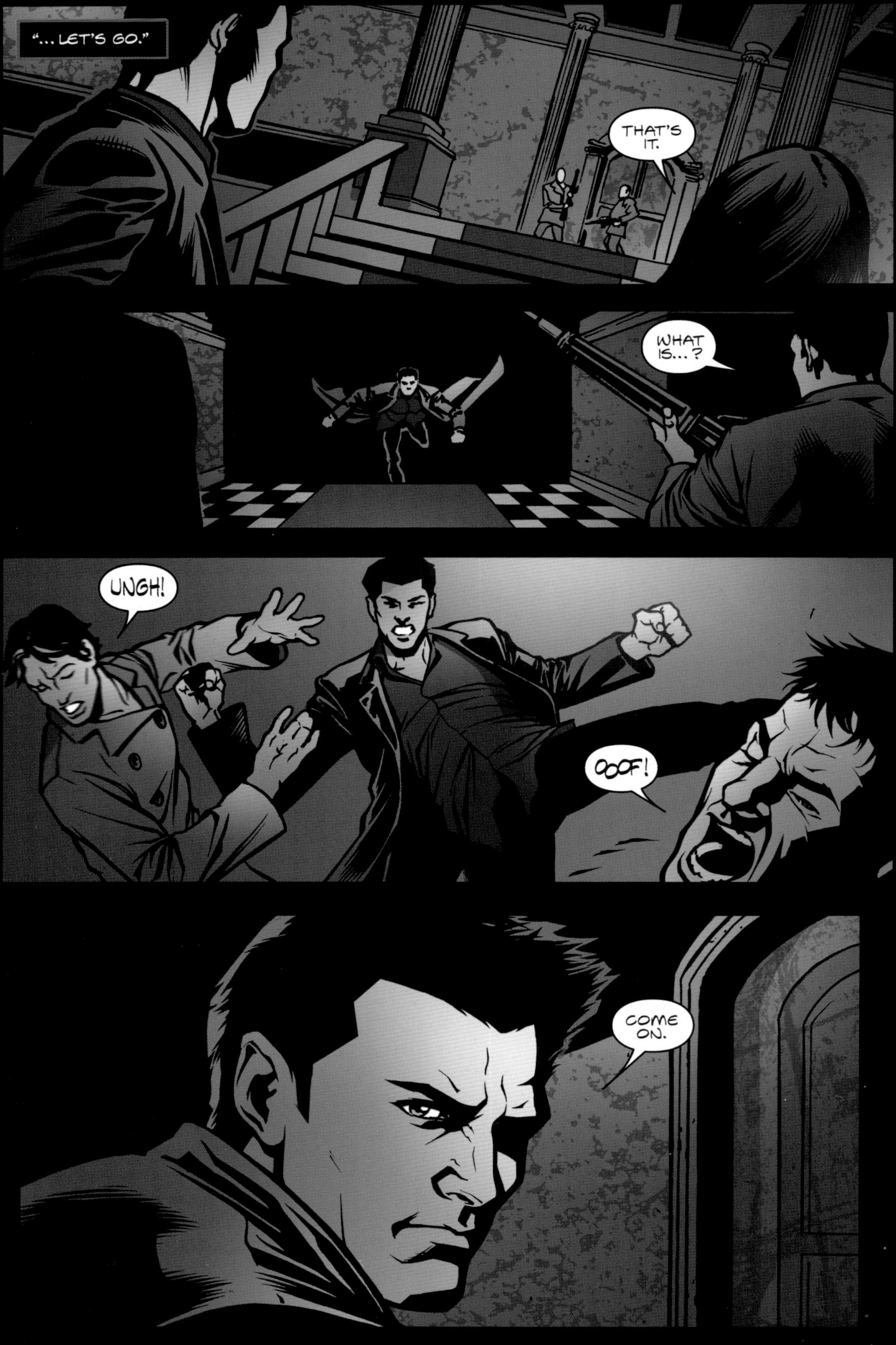
"... LET'S GO."
THAT'S IT.
WHAT IS...?
UNGH!
OOOF!
COME ON.

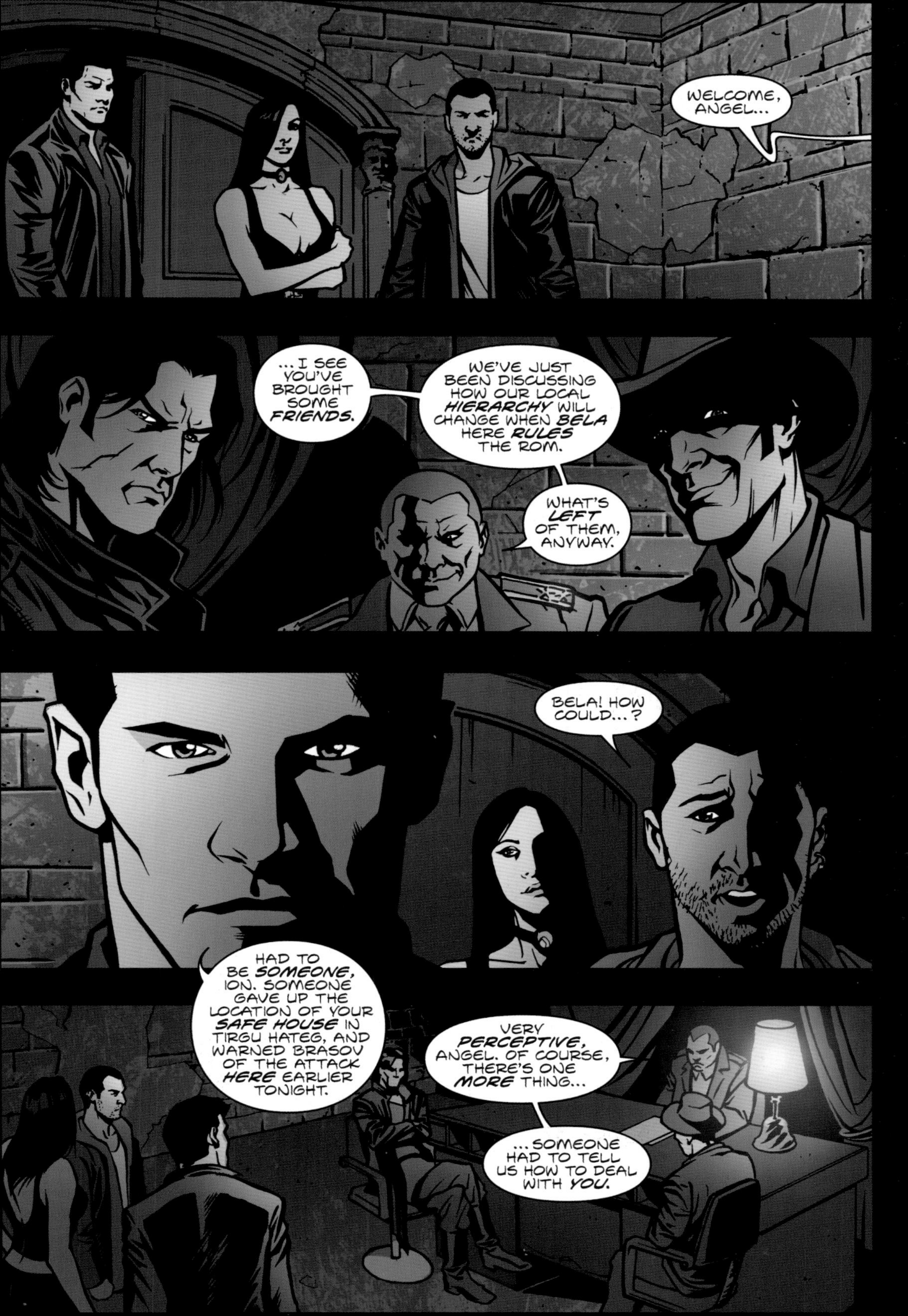
WELCOME, ANGEL...
...I SEE YOU'VE BROUGHT SOME FRIENDS.
WE'VE JUST BEEN DISCUSSING HOW OUR LOCAL HIERARCHY WILL CHANGE WHEN BELA HERE RULES THE ROM.
WHAT'S LEFT OF THEM, ANYWAY.
BELA! HOW COULD...?
HAD TO BE SOMEONE, ION. SOMEONE GAVE UP THE LOCATION OF YOUR SAFE HOUSE IN TIRGU HATEG, AND WARNED BRASOV OF THE ATTACK HERE EARLIER TONIGHT.
VERY PERCEPTIVE, ANGEL. OF COURSE, THERE'S ONE MORE THING...
...SOMEONE HAD TO TELL US HOW TO DEAL WITH YOU.

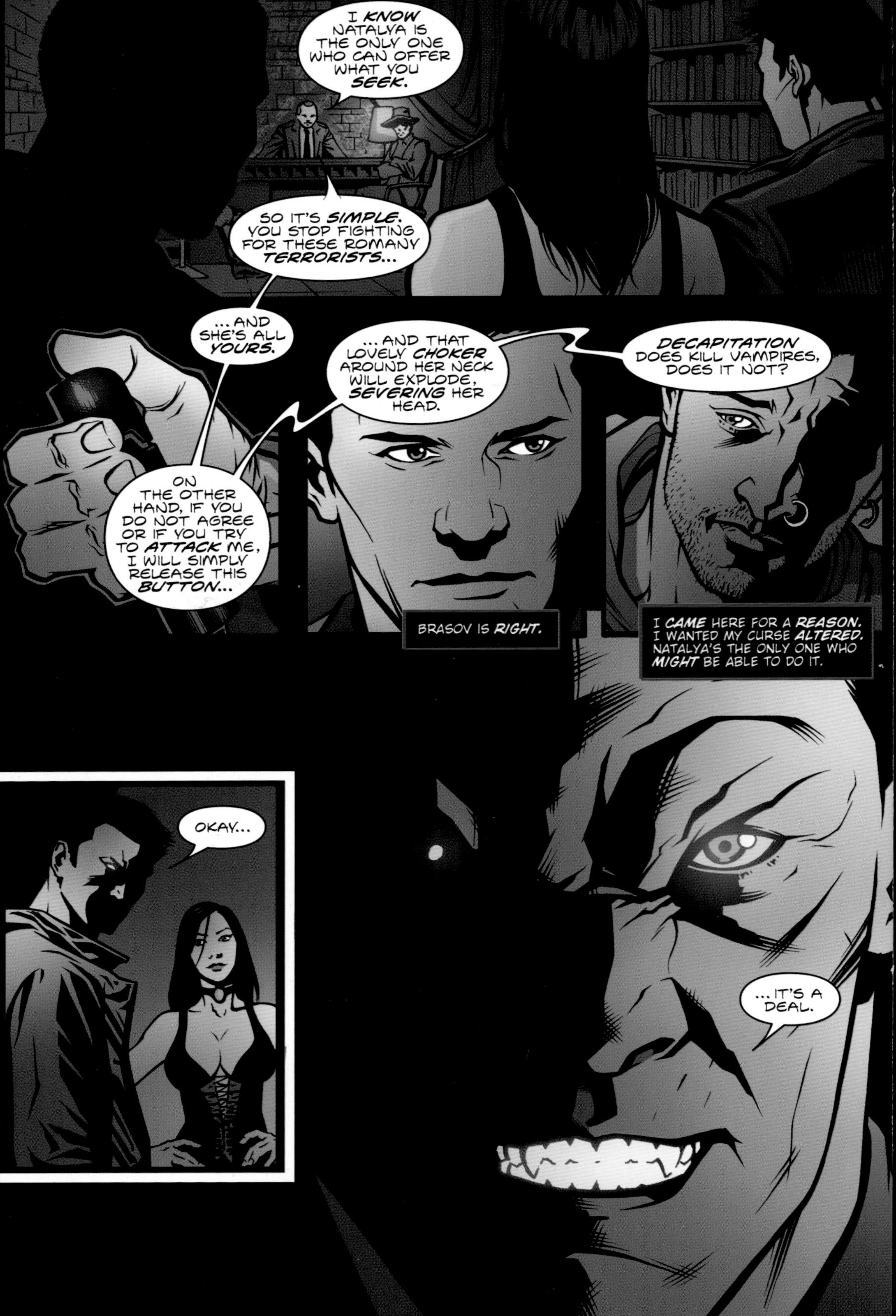
I KNOW NATALYA IS THE ONLY ONE WHO CAN OFFER WHAT YOU SEEK.
SO IT'S SIMPLE. YOU STOP FIGHTING FOR THESE ROMANY TERRORISTS...
...AND SHE'S ALL YOURS.
ON THE OTHER HAND, IF YOU DO NOT AGREE OR IF YOU TRY TO ATTACK ME, I WILL SIMPLY RELEASE THIS BUTTON...
...AND THAT LOVELY CHOKER AROUND HER NECK WILL EXPLODE, SEVERING HER HEAD.
DECAPITATION DOES KILL VAMPIRES, DOES IT NOT?
BRASOV IS RIGHT.
I CAME HERE FOR A REASON. I WANTED MY CURSE ALTERED. NATALYA'S THE ONLY ONE WHO MIGHT BE ABLE TO DO IT.
OKAY...
...IT'S A DEAL.

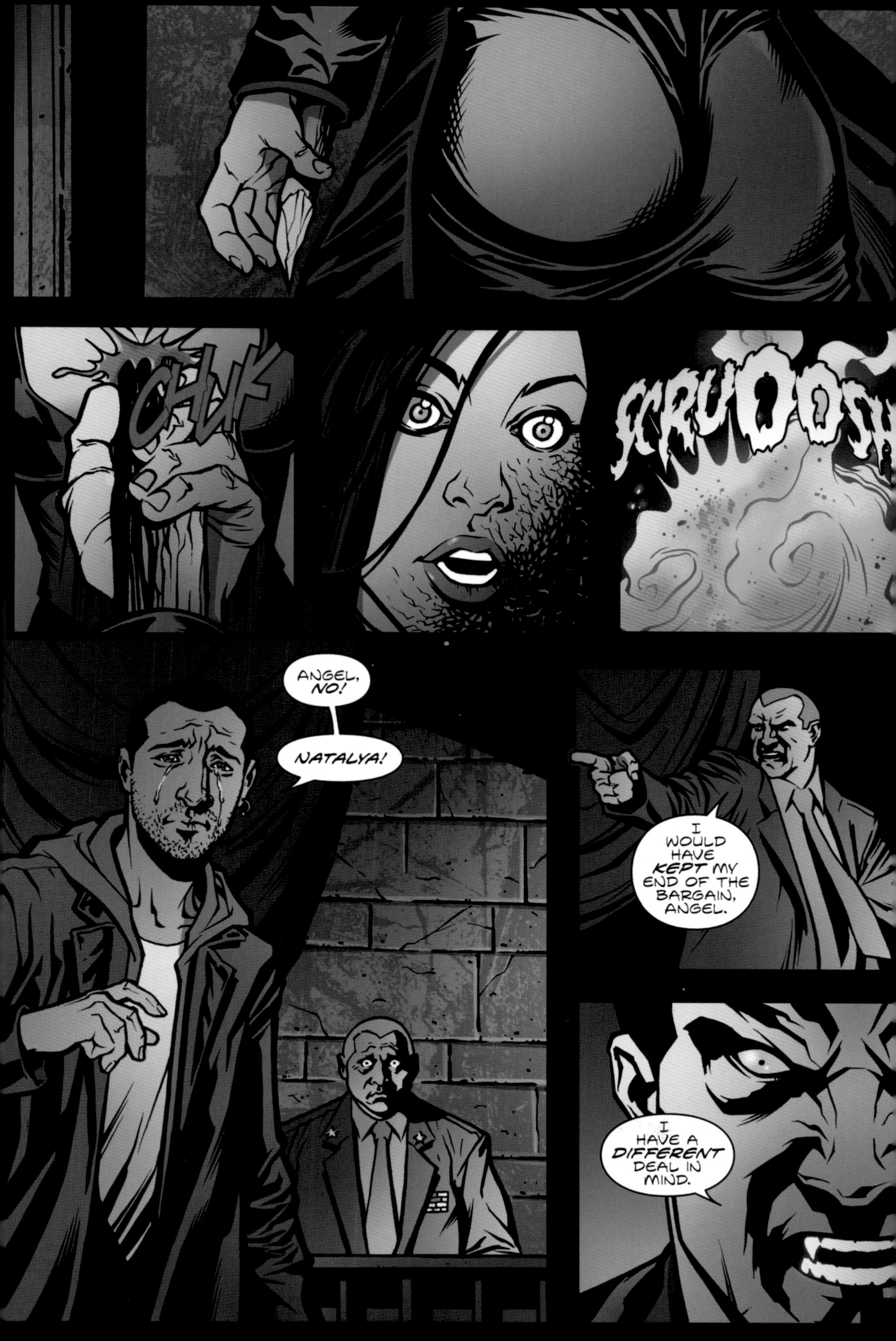
CHUK
SCRUOOSH
ANGEL, NO!
NATALYA!
I WOULD HAVE KEPT MY END OF THE BARGAIN, ANGEL.
I HAVE A DIFFERENT DEAL IN MIND.

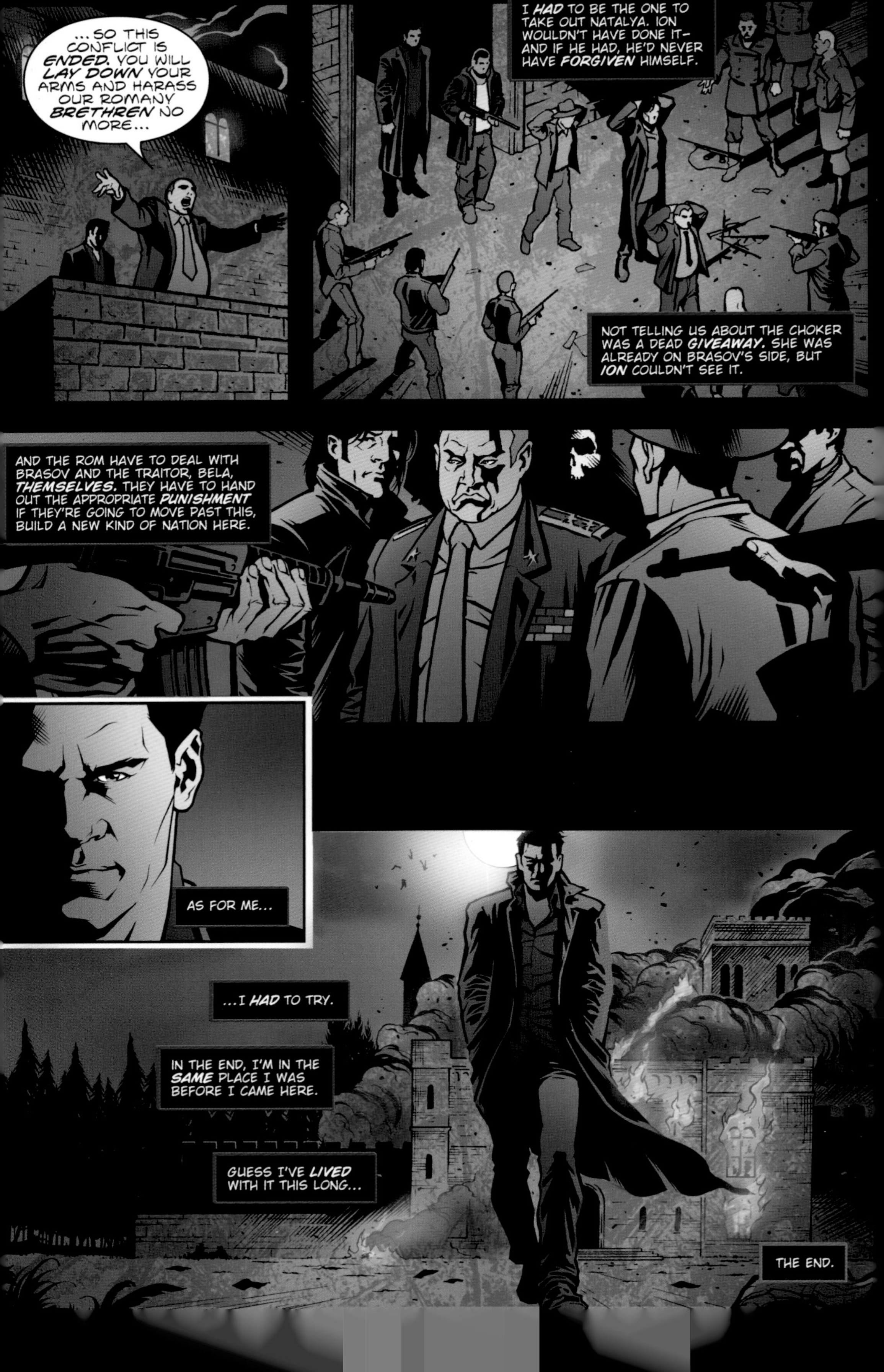
...SO THIS CONFLICT IS ENDED. YOU WILL LAY DOWN YOUR ARMS AND HARASS OUR ROMANY BRETHREN NO MORE...
I HAD TO BE THE ONE TO TAKE OUT NATALYA. ION WOULDN'T HAVE DONE IT-- AND IF HE HAD, HE'D NEVER HAVE FORGIVEN HIMSELF.
NOT TELLING US ABOUT THE CHOKER WAS A DEAD GIVEAWAY. SHE WAS ALREADY ON BRASOV'S SIDE, BUT ION COULDN'T SEE IT.
AND THE ROM HAVE TO DEAL WITH BRASOV AND THE TRAITOR, BELA, THEMSELVES. THEY HAVE TO HAND OUT THE APPROPRIATE PUNISHMENT IF THEY'RE GOING TO MOVE PAST THIS, BUILD A NEW KIND OF NATION HERE.
AS FOR ME...
...I HAD TO TRY.
IN THE END, I'M IN THE SAME PLACE I WAS BEFORE I CAME HERE.
GUESS I'VE LIVED WITH IT THIS LONG...
THE END.

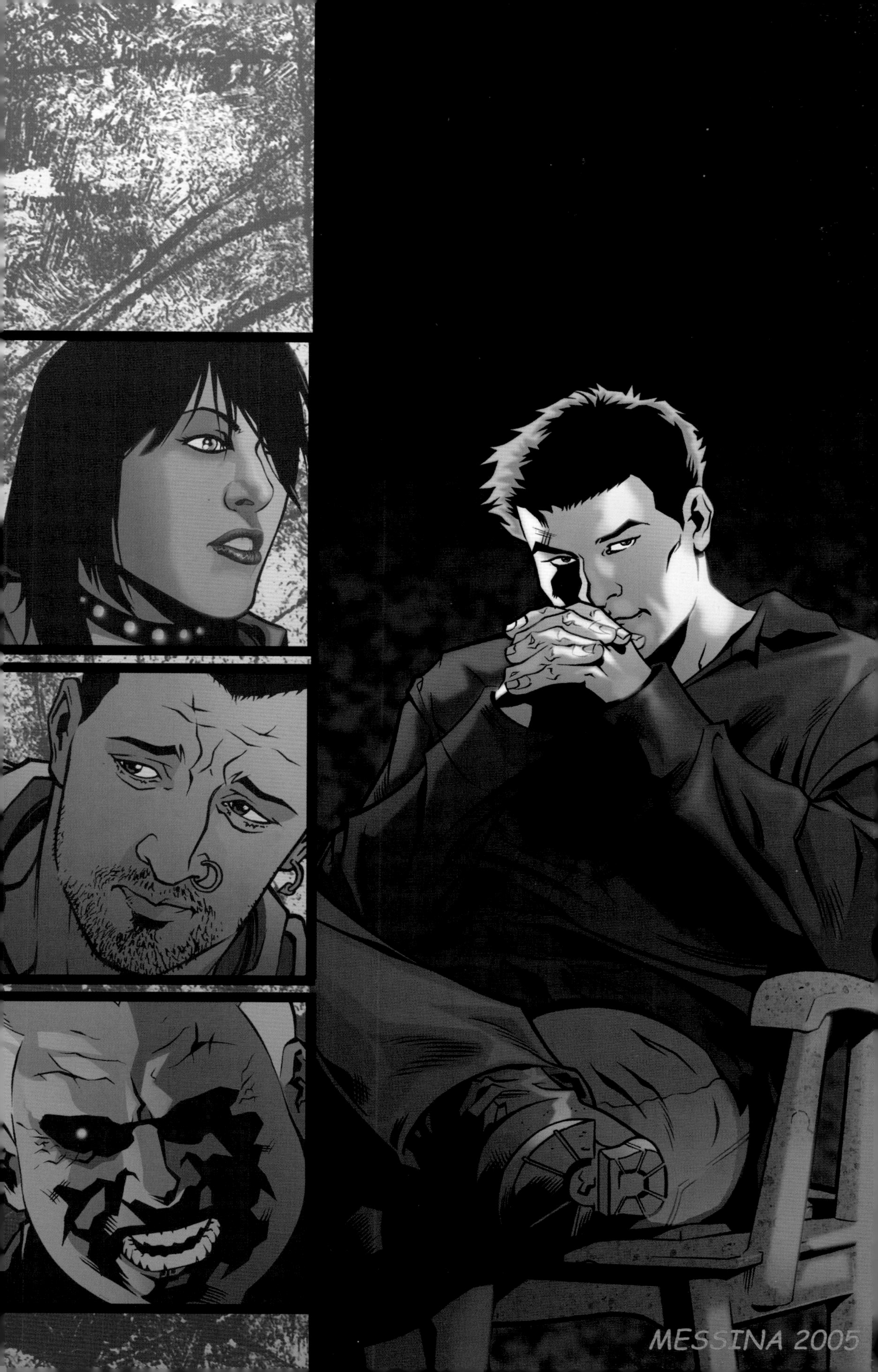
MESSINA 2005

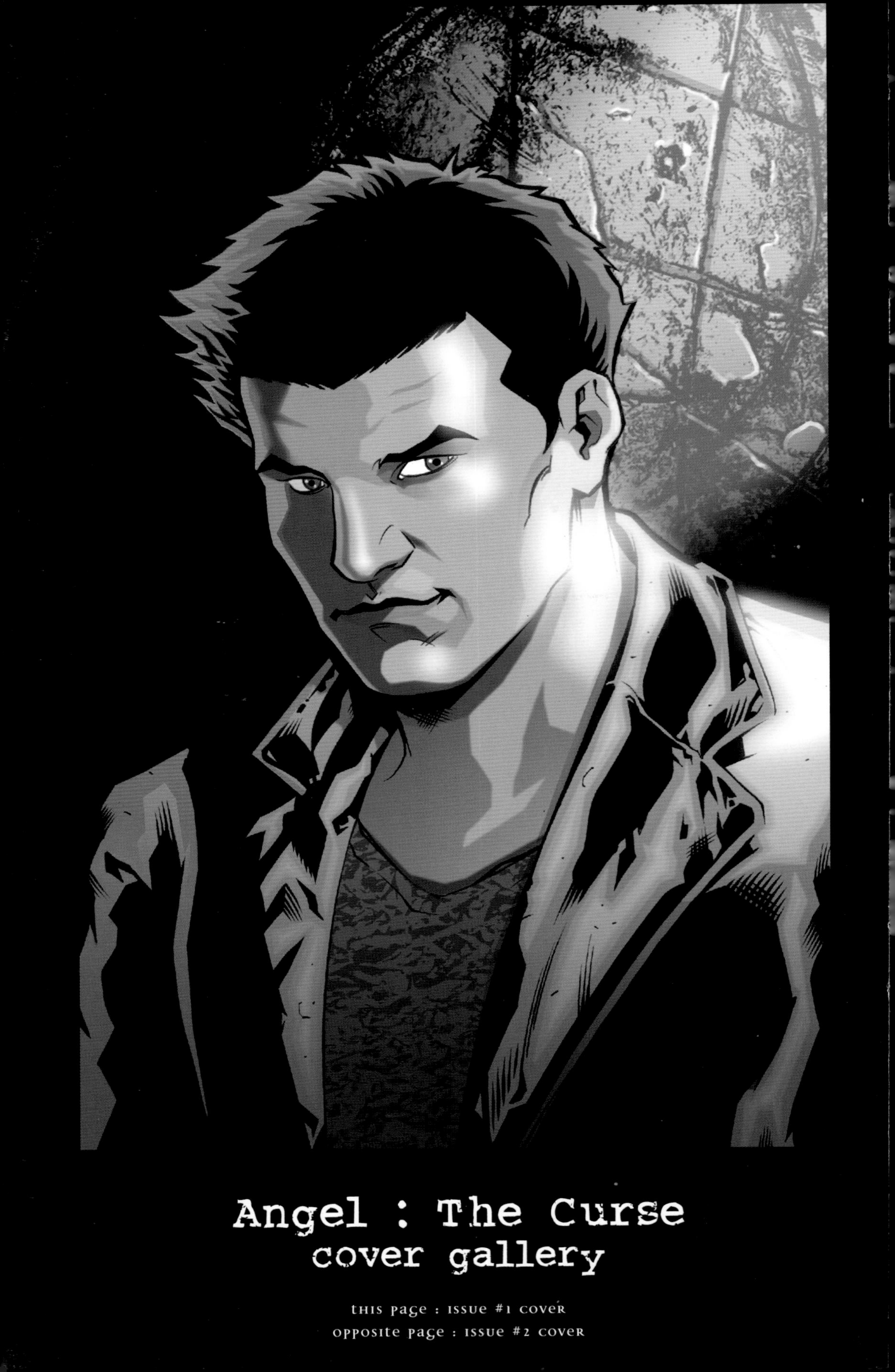

Angel : The Curse
cover gallery

this page : issue #1 cover
opposite page : issue #2 cover

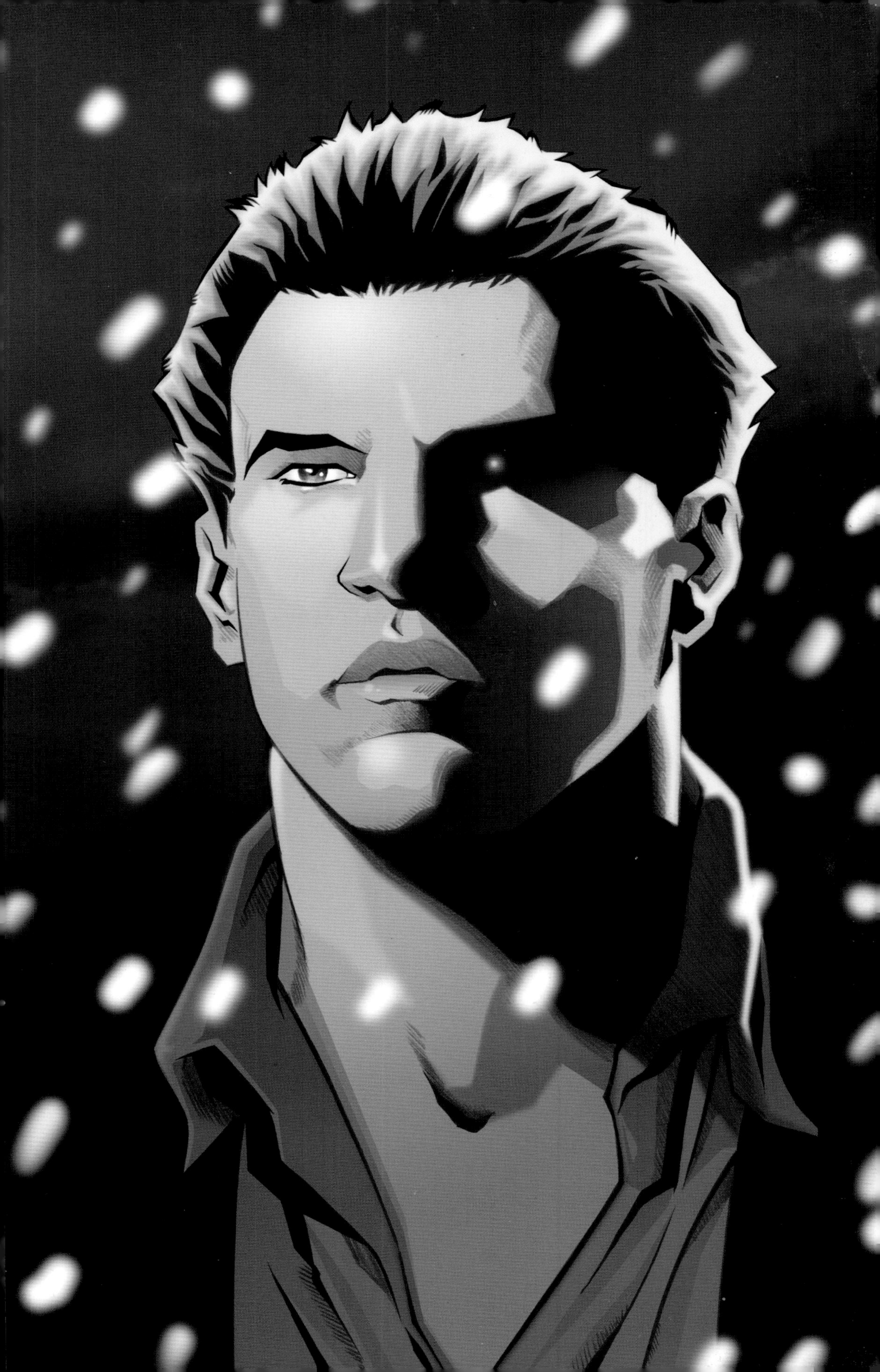

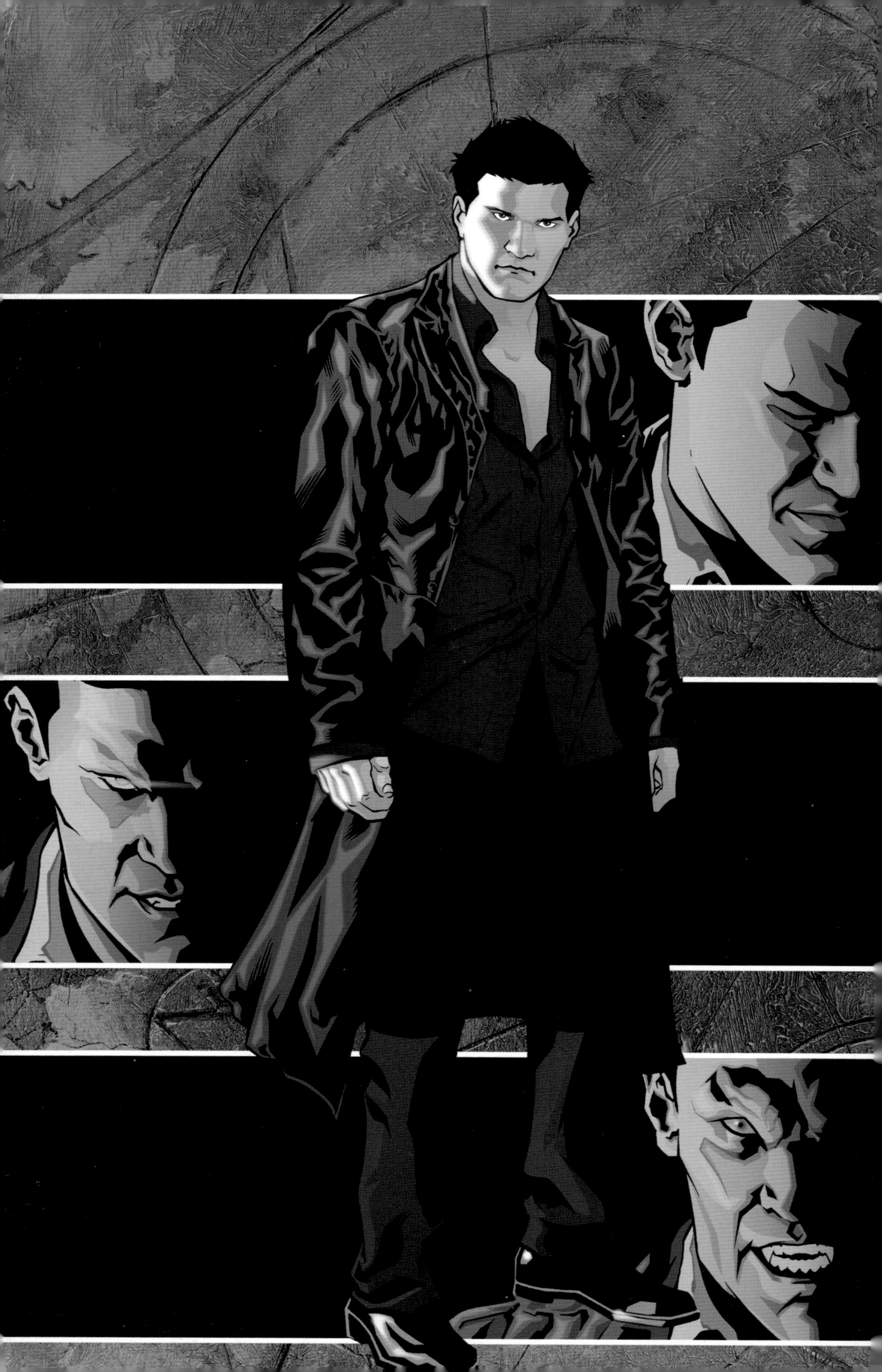

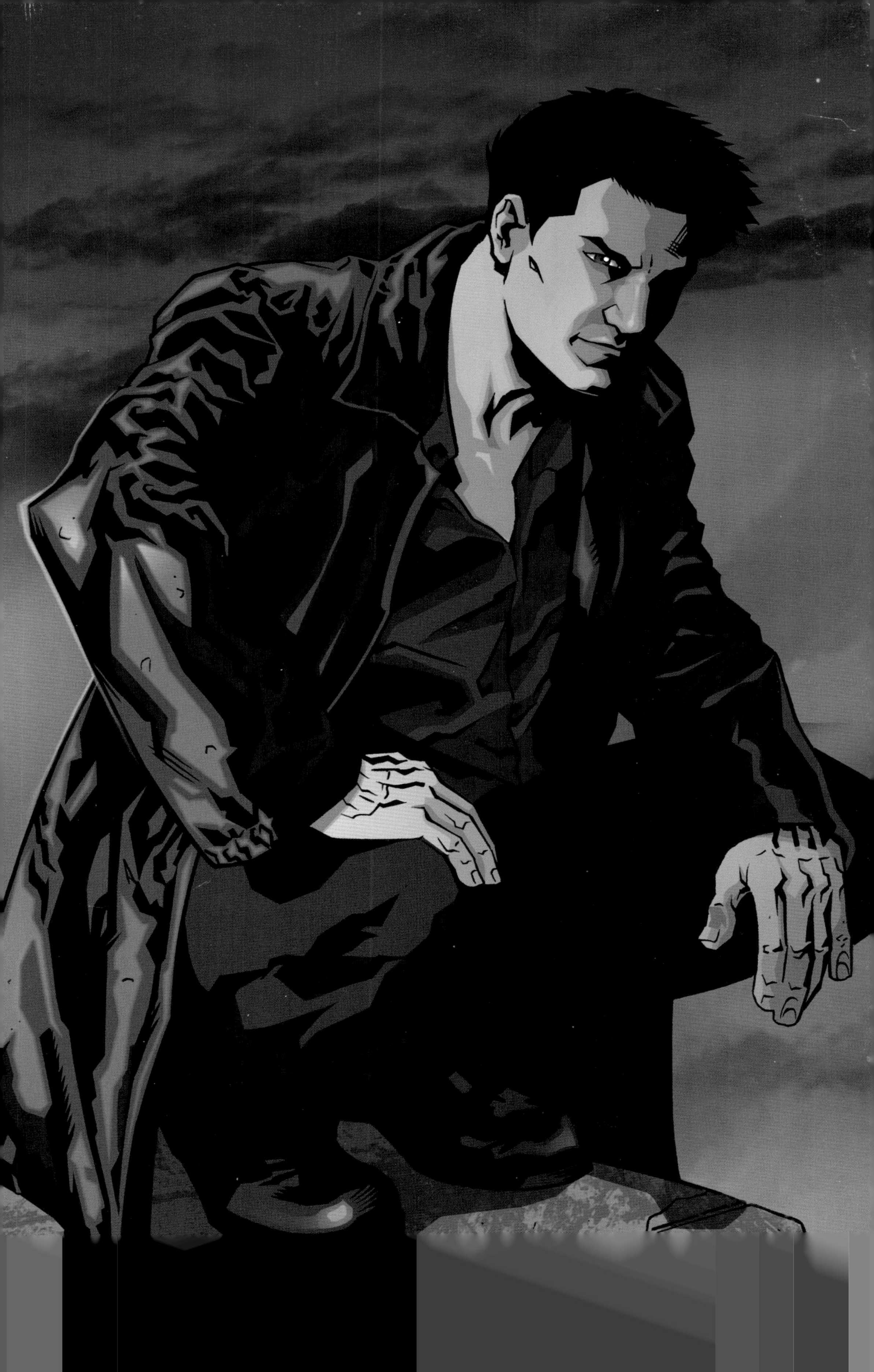

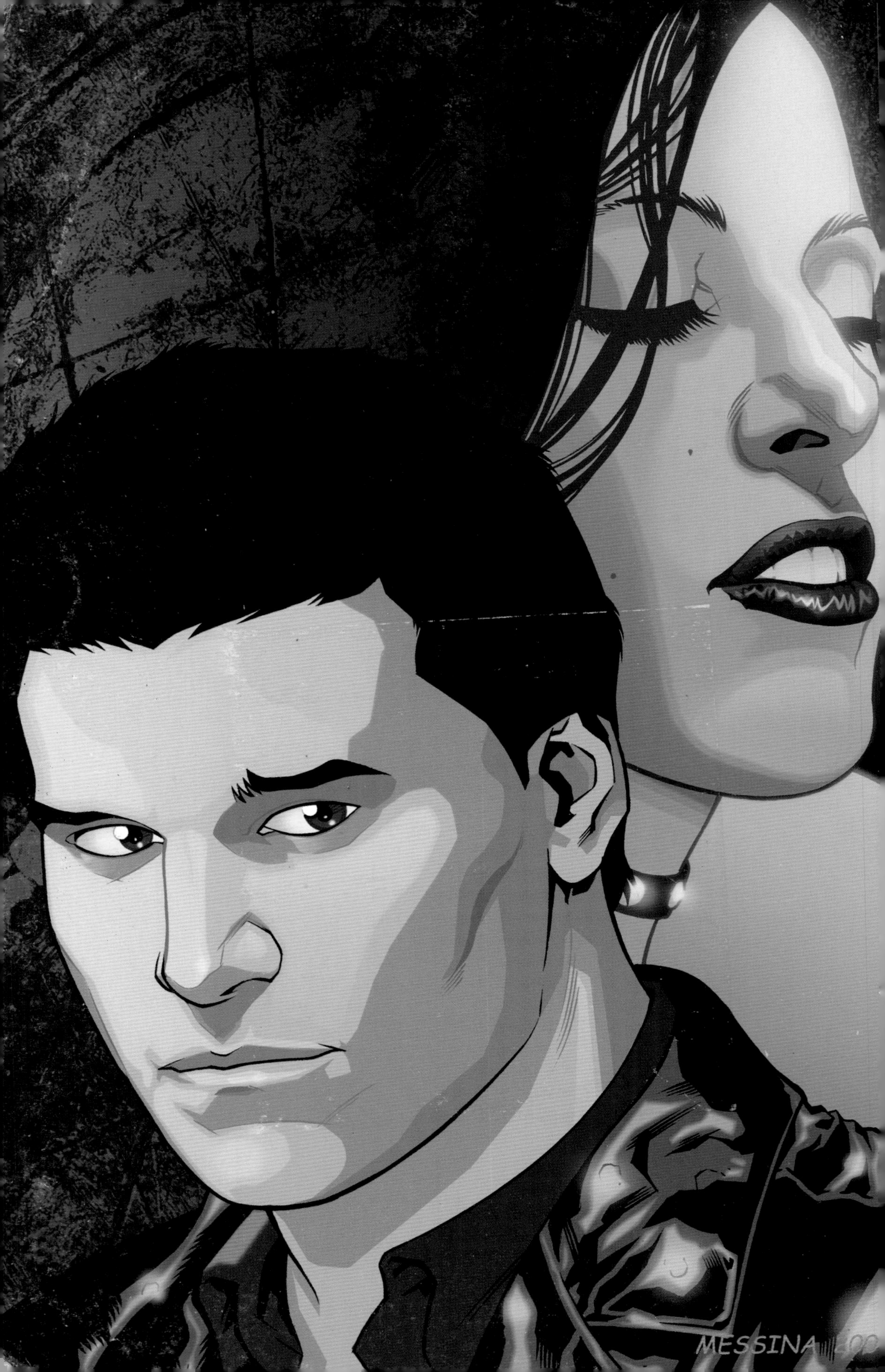
MESSINA